£ 13.50

STUDIES IN

ANCIENT ROME

Edited by Dianne Hennessy

Contributors:
Kate Cameron, Jane and Bruce Dennett, Dianne Hennessy,
Nigel Irvine, Jennifer Lawless, Kathryn Welch

NELSON

First published in Australia in 1990

Reprinted in 1991

THOMAS NELSON AUSTRALIA
102 Dodds Street
South Melbourne 3205

Studies in Ancient Rome.

  Bibliography.
  Includes index.
  ISBN 0 17 007413 7.
  1. Rome - History. 2.
  Rome - Politics
  and government. I.
  Hennessy, Dianne, 1952-

937

Cover illustration:
Leaf of ivory diptych showing priestess sacrificing at an
altar. Victoria & Albert Museum, London

Edited by Sue Harvey
Designed by Sarn Potter Graphics
Maps by Diana Murray
Typeset in 12pt Bembo by Post Typesetters, Brisbane.
Printed in Hong Kong

CONTENTS

PREFACE

Studies in Ancient Rome is aimed at senior secondary students of ancient history. Focusing on the last years of the Roman Republic and the Julio-Claudian Emperors, it examines the concept of power as the ancient Romans perceived it, gained it and used it.

The first two chapters examine the history of Rome up to 78 BC and the ways of obtaining power in the Roman Republic. The rest of the text comprehensively examines the roles of significant people and the events which shaped their lives.

Each chapter includes a range of primary source material which will enhance the student's understanding of the issues and encourage further exploration of the topic. Archaeological evidence is integrated into the text or used as illustrative material. A series of exercises has been provided to promote critical thinking about the major issues.

Studies in Ancient Rome is the first of a series of senior secondary ancient history books. The other books are *Studies in Ancient Greece* and *Studies in the Ancient Near East*.

NOTES TO REFERENCES

The notations to all quoted material in this book list the author and title (sometimes abbreviated), details of which are provided in full in the list of references at the end of each chapter. In addition, each entry includes either a page number (in the case of secondary sources) or the appropriate book, chapter, paragraph or line reference (in the case of ancient sources).

Wherever possible, the traditional referencing systems for the ancient sources have been used. Note that while quotations from Tacitus *The Annals of Imperial Rome* have been taken from the Penguin edition, the notations refer to the traditional divisions of books and chapters. (These can be found at the top of each page in the Penguin edition.) Also note that in quotes from *Cicero's Letters to his Friends* and *Cicero: Selected Letters*, the translator's numbering system has been followed by the more common reference. I have adopted this system so that students undertaking further research will be able to find the appropriate book, chapter and paragraph in an ancient source should they use a different translation from that used in this book.

Dianne Hennessy

CHAPTER ONE

ROMAN HISTORY TO 78 BC

DIANNE HENNESSY

From the time of the legendary founding of Rome by Romulus and Remus in 753 BC until the year 78 BC where this book begins its study, much had occurred to shape the character of Roman history. This chapter is intended to provide only a thumbnail sketch of Rome's history up to 78 BC, a history largely determined by the pursuit of power and domination.

THE GEOGRAPHY OF ITALY

Probably the most significant physical feature of Italy is its mountainous landscape. The Apennines which run down the centre of the country give the appearance of a backbone. At their northern end they join the Alps which run west to east. The land between the Alps and the northern Apennines (known as 'continental Italy') is divided in two by the Po River valley. Mainland Italy or 'peninsular Italy' begins around Genoa and encompasses all the southern land.

The Apennines winding down the centre of the country influenced settlement patterns, with isolated villages developing throughout the plains. The best agricultural land of peninsular Italy was in the areas between the Arno and Tiber Rivers (Etruria); surrounding the city of Rome (Latium); and between the Liris River and the Bay of Naples (Campania). See Figure 1.1.

Continental Italy, on the other hand, was well forested and provided good livestock land, but in ancient times was extremely marshy in the lowland areas of the Po valley. This land only became agriculturally productive after the end of the second century BC, when an effective drainage system was begun.

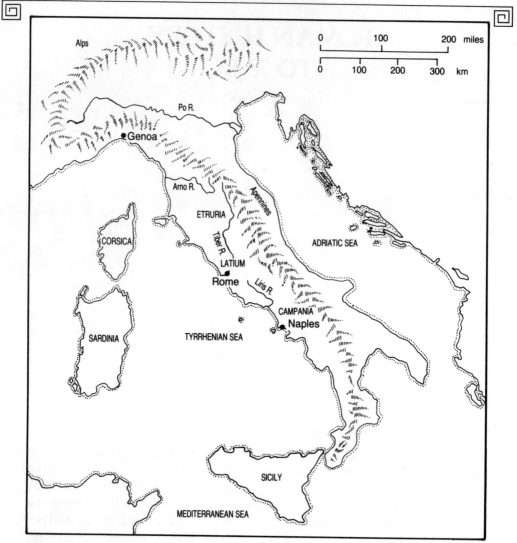

FIGURE 1.1   GEOGRAPHICAL FEATURES OF ITALY

Italy is divided into a number of regions corresponding to the settlement of some of the earliest people. These are seen in Figure 1.2.

EARLY HISTORY

From the time of its foundation, Rome was a monarchy. Legend has it that the last of the Roman Kings, Tarquinius Superbus, was expelled after his son Sextus supposedly raped Lucretia, the wife of a Roman governor, Collatinus. It is more likely, however, that the last monarch was under attack from an invader. Whatever the cause, the end result was the same — the downfall of the monarchy in 509 BC and the birth of the Roman Republic.

FIGURE 1.2   REGIONS OF ITALY

The following is an account of the institution of the Republic.

But when he had done speaking, they all cried out, as from a single mouth, to lead them to arms. Then Brutus, pleased at this, said: "On this condition, that you first hear the resolution of the senate and confirm it. For we have resolved that the Tarquinii and all their posterity shall be banished both from the city of Rome and from all the territory ruled by the Romans; that no one shall be permitted to say or do anything about their restoration; and that if anyone shall be found to be working contrary to these decisions he shall be put to death. If it is your pleasure that this resolution be confirmed, divide yourselves into your *curiae* and give your votes; and let the enjoyment of this right be the beginning of your liberty." This was done; and all the *curiae* having given their votes for the banishment of the tyrants, Brutus again came forward and said: "Now that our first measures have been confirmed in the manner required, hear also what we have further resolved concerning the form of our government. It was our decision, upon considering what magistracy should be in control of affairs, not to establish the kingship again, but to appoint two annual magistrates to hold the royal power, these men to be whomever you yourselves shall choose in the comitia, voting by centuries. If, therefore, this also is your pleasure, give your votes to that effect." The people approved of this resolution likewise, not a single vote being given against it. After that, Brutus, coming forward, appointed Spurius Lucretius as *interrex* to preside over the comitia for the election of magistrates, according to ancestral custom. And he, dismissing the assembly, ordered all the people to go promptly in arms to the field where it was their custom to elect their magistrates. When they were come thither, he chose two men to perform the functions which had belonged to the kings—Brutus and Collatinus; and the people, being called by centuries, confirmed their appointment. Such were the measures taken in the city at that time.

Dionysius, *Roman Antiquities*, 4.84

✦　✦　✦

ROMAN CONFEDERACY

In the first 250 years of the Republic, Rome's sphere of influence grew from a small area south of the River Tiber to encompass all of Italy south of the River Arno. This extension of power happened gradually, often in response to threats to Rome's position. What finally emerged from years of struggle and battle is termed the 'Roman Confederacy', a system of classification of the people of Italy based upon their relationships with Rome. The inhabitants of Italy were divided into 'citizens' or 'allies' with different categories of rights and responsibilities. See Table 1.1.

Rome's consistency and fairness in dealings with each of the groups in the Confederacy resulted in a degree of loyalty which was to be of benefit in later times. Nevertheless, the Romans did adopt a policy of 'divide and rule' (by creating a separate treaty with each ally and forbidding them from forming treaties with each other) to ensure the continuance of Roman supremacy.

PATRICIANS AND PLEBEIANS

Another major issue of the early Republic was the 'struggle between the orders', brought about by the people's desire for equality. The struggle between the orders was a series of political manoeuvres to improve the lot of the plebeians in relation to that of the patricians. There has been some debate over the distinction between patrician and plebeian. Consider these definitions taken from the *Oxford Classical Dictionary*.

Patricians were the privileged class of Roman citizens. Their name is probably connected with *pater*, meaning "member of the Senate" . . . The patricians were the holders of the magistracies and of the most important religious offices. It has been suggested by some modern scholars that they served in the cavalry, and that six centuries were probably reserved to them . . . Only a patrician could become *rex sacrorum* [a priest, holding the religious functions once carried out by the kings], *interrex* [leader of the government appointed on a short term basis whilst awaiting the appointment of the next permanent head of state] and perhaps *princeps senatus* [leader of the Senate].

✦　✦　✦

TABLE 1.1   RIGHTS AND RESPONSIBILITIES OF CITIZENS AND ALLIES

GROUP	CRITERIA	RIGHTS/OBLIGATIONS
Full citizens	• lived in Rome • had been given individual allotments of public land • had been chosen to set up Roman colonies in strategic locations on public land throughout Italy, and to act as a garrison • had been classified as Roman citizens but settled in country areas of Italy • lived in communities which had been brought into the 'Roman state' because of their close proximity to Rome. (Only one of the above criteria had to be met.)	• paid taxes in time of need • undertook compulsory military service • had full civic rights which included judicial, political, economic and religious rights.
Half citizens	• were deemed not to be ready for full citizenship but would be granted full rights as soon as practicable.	• paid taxes in time of need • undertook compulsory military service • had legal rights but only local or regional political rights—no Roman political rights.
Allies of Rome	The highest status of alliance was given to areas known as 'Latin colonies'.	• had fully independent internal government • were bound separately to Rome and not to any other colony • could trade with Rome • had to give compulsory military or naval unit. Individuals from the Latin colonies could marry Roman citizens.
Other allies	This was the remaining category. Each ally in this category had a separate and different treaty with Rome.	The privileges given to each ally depended on their history of loyalty to Rome. They were largely independent locally, but still had to supply a military or naval unit.

Note: Because women had no political rights, only men are considered in these groups. The status of Roman women is discussed in chapter two.

Plebs was the name given to the general body of Roman citizens, as distinct from the privileged *patricii* . . . The contrast between it and the *patricii* no doubt arose through the differentiation of certain wealthier and more influential families into a separate class . . . The plebeians were originally excluded from religious colleges, magistracies and perhaps also from the Senate, and by a law of the XII Tables [the earliest Roman code of laws] they were debarred from intermarriage with patricians. But they were enrolled in the *gentes* [Roman clan—a group of families linked by common beliefs and ancestry], *curiae* [subdivisions within the ten tribes of Rome] and *tribus* [tribes of Rome]; they served at all times in the army and could hold the office of *tribunus militum* [military tribune, senior officer of a legion].

✎**Using the information supplied for you, draw up a table to show the similarities and differences between the patricians and the plebeians of the early Republic.**

In ancient Rome, wealth was not synonymous with class: there were poor patricians and wealthy plebeians. The plebeians won many rights in the 'struggle' which occurred between 494 BC and 287 BC. Some of the more significant victories were:

- plebeians could have their own assembly, *concilium plebis*, and pass plebiscites (which eventually stood as laws binding on all Romans);
- plebeians could elect their own officials, called 'tribunes of the plebs';
- tribunes were sacrosanct—anyone found guilty of harming a tribune could be put to death;
- tribunes had the power of veto over proceedings in both the Senate and the assemblies;
- plebeians could marry patricians;
- plebeians had access to all magistracies (government offices), and laws were passed to ensure that plebeians represented in two of the highest offices of the state, the consulship and the censorship, although this was not always carried out.

FROM CONFEDERACY TO EMPIRE

By 146 BC the Roman world had changed dramatically since its first involvement in a foreign war: it had gone from continental power to empire, as can be seen in Figure 1.3. By this time Rome controlled six provinces: Sicily, Sardinia and Corsica, Nearer Spain, Further Spain, Macedonia and Africa. With the exception of Macedonia, all were gained as a direct result of war with Carthage. See Table 1.2.

ISSUES EMERGING FROM ROME'S EXPANSION

Rome's victories at war, and the provinces acquired as a result, changed Rome considerably. Neither the government nor the society was prepared for the upheaval which occurred, and the failure of the Romans to solve these problems contributed to the eventual downfall of the Republic one hundred years later.

TABLE 1.2   EXPANSION OF THE ROMAN WORLD, 264 – 146 BC

First Punic War	264 – 241 BC	Sicily became Rome's first province.
Between the wars	240 – 219 BC	Rome won Sardinia and Corsica from Carthage.
Second Punic War	218 – 201 BC	Spain became two provinces under Roman control: Nearer and Further Spain.
Macedonian wars	214 – 148 BC	There were four wars between Rome and Macedonia during this period. At the end of the fourth war, Rome declared Macedonia a province.
Third Punic War	150 – 146 BC	This war resulted in the destruction of Carthage. The area once controlled by this great city became the new province of Africa.

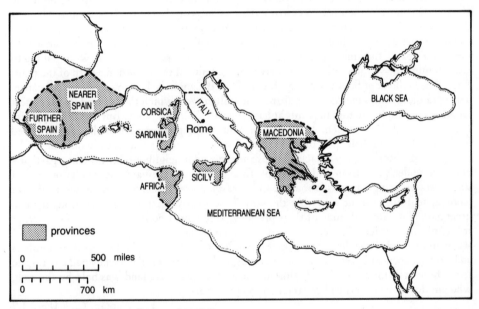

FIGURE 1.3   PROVINCES OF ROME IN 146 BC

THE PEASANTRY

Rome's constant involvement in war since 264 BC had a disastrous effect on the peasantry. Not only had their land been devastated by Hannibal's fifteen years of occupation during the Second Punic War, but their absence on military service had meant financial ruin for many peasants. Many of the wealthy used their war profits for the speculative purchase of small landholdings, eventually amassing huge properties. In addition, the public land, *ager publicus*, which had been taken over by the government from those cities which had succumbed to Hannibal, was now being leased out in large allotments to the wealthy. No longer was Italy to be an agricultural society with peasants owning and working the land.

The influx of slaves acquired as part of war booty further compounded this problem. Depending on their qualifications, these slaves were employed in domestic service, in craft industries, in mines or on the land. Those who worked the land took away the last hopes of the peasants. It was cheaper for the wealthy landowners to employ slaves to cultivate their land than to reinstate the peasants to their traditional work.

> **Read the following extract which examines the long-term trend of displacing the peasants. Is there any suggestion that action could have been taken by the Roman government at a much earlier time to protect the interests of the peasants?**

The Romans, as they subdued the Italian peoples successively in war, used to seize a part of their lands and build towns there, or enrol colonists of their own to occupy those already existing, and their idea was to use these as outposts; but of the land acquired by war they assigned the cultivated part forthwith to the colonists, or sold or leased it. Since they had no leisure as yet to allot the part which then lay desolated by war (this was generally the greater part), they made proclamation that in the meantime those who were willing to work it might do so for a toll of the yearly crops, a tenth of the grain and a fifth of the fruit. From those who kept flocks was required a toll of the animals, both oxen and small cattle. They did these things in order to multiply the Italian race, which they considered the most laborious of peoples, so that they might have plenty of allies at home. But the very opposite thing happened; for the rich, getting possession of the greater part of the undistributed lands, and being emboldened by the lapse of time to believe that they would never be dispossessed, absorbing any adjacent strips and their poor neighbours' allotments, partly by purchase under persuasion and partly by force, came to cultivate vast tracts instead of single estates, using slaves as labourers and herdsmen, lest free labourers should be drawn from agriculture into the army. At the same time the ownership of slaves brought them great gain from the multitude of their progeny, who increased because they were exempt from military service. Thus certain powerful men became extremely rich and the race of slaves multiplied throughout the country, while the Italian people dwindled in numbers and strength, being oppressed by penury, taxes, and military service. If they had any respite from these evils they passed their time in idleness, because the land was held by the rich, who employed slaves instead of freemen as cultivators.

Appian, *Civil Wars*, 1.7

These unemployed, discontented people had few options left. They migrated to the cities in the hope of finding work, but the slave population made that difficult. This created a sub-culture within the cities, a group of people who were apt to follow a political champion of their cause or to sell their votes to the highest bidder.

THE ROLE AND STATUS OF THE SENATE

The wars had brought other more direct political changes to Rome. Since its establishment after the fall of the monarchy, the Roman Senate had only ever been an advisory institution. Constitutionally, it had no governing power, but its advice became law simply because the people accepted it. Over time, the Senate gained great prestige and power.

The supremacy of the Senate was reaffirmed at a crucial point in Rome's history. During the Second Punic War, Fabius Maximus, the dictator appointed from the Senate, implemented 'delaying tactics', recommending that Rome avoid a frontal assault on the Carthagian army which had entered Italy and was achieving success. However, the people, tired of Fabius's tactics, took the matter out of the hands of the Senate and ordered an attack. In the fighting that ensued, thousands of Roman soldiers died at the Battle of Cannae (216 BC) in the worst and most humiliating defeat suffered by Rome during the war. Following this debacle, the Senate resumed control of the war, handling it with competence and ensuring final victory. The Senate's status had been raised and remained unchallenged for most of the second century.

The Emerging Role of 'General'

An important precedent established during the Punic Wars was the appointment of a general to lead the Roman army. Previously, the Roman army had been led by politicians drawn from the ranks of the Senate. Even if these people had military experience, they need not necessarily have demonstrated either competency or flair in this field. Rather, the criterion used was that an army commander had to have been at least praetor and preferably consul. During the Punic Wars, Scipio Africanis, later known as the 'saviour of Rome', was appointed commander with proconsular power and sent to fight in Spain. Although he had been neither consul nor praetor, he was nominated for this position by the people and endorsed by the Senate. As he had only served as an aedile, he was given the power of a consul without having held an elected position. He was the first 'general' as we understand this term. (See chapter two for an explanation of the various offices of Roman government.)

The Equestrians

The acquisition of provinces (areas outside Italy governed by Rome) proved to be something of a problem. Rome's organisation of the Italian Confederacy, based on different levels of citizenship and relying on military contingents from all parts of Italy, would not extend overseas. So the Senate embarked on a separate system for provincial administration, placing a Roman governor, appointed from the ranks of the Senate, at the head of each province. The provincials would not be asked to give military service to Rome; instead they would be taxed.

Rome had no mechanism for carrying out this tax collecting, so it was contracted to the *equestrians*, the capitalist class in Rome. The company that bought the contract had the sole right to collect these taxes, and they made a substantial profit. Tax-collecting added to the already long list of enterprises of the equestrians.

One fundamental problem of the equestrians was that they lacked political power. Under Roman law, senators were not permitted to participate in trade. They were forbidden to own any more ships than necessary to transport agricultural products from their own land. Consequently, the equestrians were not represented in the Senate. As they became increasingly wealthy, they demanded a political voice; the Senate was eventually compelled to address this problem as it was raised and used against them.

ATTEMPTS AT POLITICAL REFORM

THE GRACCHI

Tiberius and Gaius Gracchus were two brothers from the *nobiles* class of Roman society who both became tribunes in Rome. Their father had been consul twice and censor. Tiberius became tribune in 133 BC, while his younger brother Gaius took office ten years later. Both the reform programmes they tried to initiate and the way they died made the Gracchi famous.

TIBERIUS GRACCHUS

In *Tiberius Gracchus*, Plutarch tells that Tiberius was inspired to work towards improving the lot of the landless peasantry after travelling through Etruria and witnessing the displacement of the native inhabitants of the land by slave labour. Tiberius put to the Senate an agrarian reform bill to create allotments out of the large area of public land acquired by the Republic after the Second Punic War. Much of this land was held by a few wealthy owners, many of them senators. Tiberius's law stated that anyone holding more public land than the legal limit of 500 iugera (about 310 acres) should give up the surplus. Furthermore, he proposed that if the landholder had children they could have an additional 250 iugera per child, *but no individual could own more than 1000 iugera*. In return for surrendering the excess land to the state, the landholder would become the legal owner of the remaining land and would not have to pay rent. Thus the state would acquire the land to redistribute to the poorer Roman citizens. These people would each receive an allotment no larger than 30 iugera and the state would assist in establishing and stocking the farm. The peasants in return were to pay a small rent and not sell the farms.

Speaking many years after the event, Cicero, a prominent Roman senator, levelled his opposition to the bill on these grounds:

Tiberius Gracchus proposed an agrarian law. The law was acceptable to the People: the fortunes of the poorer classes seemed likely to be established. The Optimates opposed it, because they saw in it an incentive to dissension, and also thought that the State would be stripped of its champions by the eviction of the rich from their long-established tenancies.

Cicero, *Pro Sestio*, 103

However, the bill had much in its favour. There could be no legal objection to the resumption of the excess land, as those who had taken it over had done so illegally.

And it is thought that a law dealing with injustice and rapacity so great was never drawn up in milder and gentler terms. For men who ought to have been punished for their disobedience and to have surrendered with payment of a fine the land which they were illegally enjoying, these men it merely ordered to abandon their injust acquisitions upon being paid their value, and to admit into ownership of them such citizens as needed assistance.

Plutarch, *Tiberius Gracchus*, 9

Tiberius had good reason to expect opposition to the bill, as those most affected would be the senators. These people had been on the land for some time, had built houses and family tombs, and had made many improvements to the estates. They would not give way easily.

As could be expected, the Senate opposed the bill and successfully urged a fellow tribune, M. Octavius, to veto it. Tiberius then went to the people with another bill, much harsher than the first, which offered no compensation to the 'squatters'. However the bill could not be passed while Octavius remained so staunchly on the side of the Senate.

When, however, Octavius was not to be persuaded, Tiberius introduced a law depriving him of his tribuneship, and summoned the citizens to cast their votes upon it at once... And so the law was passed, and Tiberius ordered one of his freedmen to drag Octavius from the rostra...

Plutarch, *Tiberius Gracchus*, 12

The harsher agrarian bill was then carried. Although the reform became law, another problem arose—that of finance. A three-person commission was appointed to see that the law was enacted. However, the Senate refused any financial assistance to the commission. Tiberius was being frustrated again.

When King Attalus of Pergamum died and left his kingdom to the people of Rome, Tiberius threatened to introduce a bill to authorise the use of some of this wealth for the people newly settled on public land in Italy. Further, he claimed he would bring the question of settling Attalus's kingdom before the people.

Tiberius had by then offended the Senate on three counts:
- he took his agrarian bill to the assembly of the people before having it approved by the Senate;
- he had deposed a fellow tribune for his refusal to withdraw his veto;
- he interfered in the Senate's customary right to handle finance and foreign affairs.

The outcome of this was crucial for the Republic. When Tiberius stood for re-election to the tribunate for 132 BC, the Senate feared an insurrection led by Tiberius and his supporters during voting. Led by the chief pontiff, Scipio Nasica, the Senators took their own action: Tiberius and many of his supporters were killed in an open brawl.

GAIUS GRACCHUS

The death of Tiberius in this way did not end a chapter in Roman history; it opened one. When Tiberius's brother Gaius was elected tribune in 123 BC, the people still remembered the events of ten years earlier. Gaius encouraged people to remember and used to advantage their memories of Tiberius's death in pushing through his extensive reform programme.

The ancient writers concluded that vindictiveness was a strong motive for the laws Gaius put before the assembly during his first and second tribunate. Appian, in his *Civil Wars* (1.21), said of Gaius Gracchus, 'Being elected with flying colours he began to lay plots against the Senate'. Plutarch, in *Gaius Gracchus* (5), said, 'Of the laws which he proposed by way of gratifying the people and overthrowing the senate, one was agrarian, and divided the public land among the poor citizens...'

How did Gaius 'plot' against the Senate?

Some of the laws introduced by Gaius Gracchus included:

- prosecution of any magistrate who had banished a Roman citizen without trial;
- appointments of governors to provinces to take place eighteen months before going to the position;
- outlawing courts empowered to administer capital punishment which had not been set up by the people;
- transferral of the extortion courts (set up to try crooked provincial governors) from the control of the Senate to that of the equestrians;
- the criminalisation of bribery of jurors;
- enactment of an agrarian law in line with his brother's;
- regulation of the supply and price of corn to ensure that the poor could always afford it;
- provision by the state of a soldier's clothing;
- foundation of colonies both in Italy and overseas;
- effectively handing over to the equestrians the very lucrative business of tax-farming in Asia.

Which of the above laws would have
- **benefited the ordinary people?**
- **benefited the equestrian order?**
- **most harmed the power and prestige of the Senate?**

In attempting to extend Roman citizenship to the Latins—a privilege which Romans did not generally wish to share—Gaius demonstrated a broad interpretation of his legislative responsibility. Opposition from the

Senate was mobilised when a tribune was found to act on their behalf. The tribune, M. Livius Drusus, won the title 'the Senate's champion'.

Gaius's days were numbered. While he was absent from Italy for a short period, the Roman people were won over by Drusus. On his return, Gaius failed to be elected for a third term. As an ordinary citizen out of favour with the electors, Gaius's legislation was at risk. With a group of supporters, Gaius went to protect the laws he had put forward as tribune. When a fracas broke out, the Senate decreed that national security was at risk and appointed the consul L. Opimius to defend the state. This was the first occasion of the Senate's use of the *senatus consultum ultimum* (final decree of the Senate). Its use not only indicated the seriousness of the situation in Rome but highlighted clearly the Senate's fear of Gaius Gracchus.

Descriptions of Gaius's death provide evidence of the bitterness the Senate felt towards him.

So then, as Caius [sic] fled, his foes pressed hard upon him and were overtaking him at the wooden bridge over the Tiber, but his two friends bade him go on, while they themselves withstood his pursuers, and, fighting there at the head of the bridge, would suffer no man to pass, until they were killed. Caius had with him in his flight a single servant, by name Philocrates; and though all the spectators, as at a race, urged Caius on to greater speed, not a man came to his aid, or even consented to furnish him with a horse when he asked for one, for his pursuers were pressing close upon him. He barely succeeded in escaping into a sacred grove of the Furies, and there fell by the hand of Philocrates, who then slew himself upon his master. According to some writers, however, both were taken alive by the enemy, and because the servant had thrown his arms about his master, no one was able to strike the master until the slave had first been dispatched by the blows of many ... The bodies of Caius and Fulvius and of the other slain were thrown into the Tiber, and they numbered three thousand; their property was sold and the proceeds paid into the public treasury.

Plutarch, *Gaius Gracchus*, 17

Gaius Gracchus had challenged the powers of the Senate, even though his laws were in response to the needs of the people or an attempt to combat corruption. Gaius had blatantly interfered with the Senate's right to sit in judgement of its peers in the extortion courts; its right to handle provincial administration as precedent had set down; its use of prestige and the offer of 'plum jobs' to influence people; and the Senate's sole right to establish colonies. Further, he had widened the gap between senator and equestrian by allowing the latter to sit in judgement of senatorial provincial governors and increasing their potential to become wealthy. Finally, as his brother had done, Gaius introduced legislation through the assembly and not the Senate first.

MARIUS

The Gracchi had challenged the system, and others continued this trend. In the next forty years the Romans were to suffer immeasurably at the hands of powerful people.

One such man, Marius, gained prominence through military achievements and reached the consulship in 107 BC, as a *novus homo* (a new person in the Senate whose family had never before reached senatorial status). As consul, Marius had the African command against Jugurtha, the Numidian king, transferred from Metellus to himself.

Read the following extract. How did Marius have the command transferred?

After the lapse of many years the consulship was given to a "new man". Afterwards, when the tribune Titus Manlius Mancinus asked the people whom they wished to have as leader of the war with Jugurtha, they chose Marius by a large majority. It is true that the senate had shortly before this voted Numidia to Metellus, but their action was to no purpose.

Sallust, *Jugurtha*, 73.7

To guarantee a victory against Jugurtha, Marius set about raising more troops, but once again he broke the established rules.

He himself in the meantime enrolled soldiers, not according to the classes in the manner of our forefathers, but allowing anyone to volunteer, for the most part the proletariat. Some say that he did this through lack of good men, others because of a desire to curry favour, since that class had given him honour and rank. As a matter of fact, to one who aspires to power the poorest man is the most helpful, since he has no regard for his property, having none, and considers anything honourable for which he receives pay.

ibid., 86

Marius equipped these men and trained them to be a well-disciplined professional fighting force. Their success and their livelihood depended upon the good generalship of Marius, and it was to him, rather than the state, that they owed allegiance. Under Marius's consulship, Rome entered a period where generals with a strong army became the true power base. So long as there was booty to be gathered from victorious battles and land provided for their retirement as 'veterans', the soldiers of the Republic would go anywhere their general took them.

Marius was hailed the victor in Africa, and with the support of the people in Rome he was unconstitutionally elected consul a second time in 104 BC, (there should have been a ten year gap between consulships).

But when it was announced that the war in Numidia was ended and that Jugurtha was being brought a captive to Rome, Marius was made consul in his absence and Gaul was assigned him as his province. On the Kalends of January he entered upon his office and celebrated a triumph of great magnificence. At that time the hopes and welfare of our country were in his hands.

ibid., 114

Marius's success in the next four years brought him four more consulships, but he was not a skilled politician. Using the support of the people to ensure his continuance at the head of his army, he had rescued Italy from the dangers posed by the Germanic tribes to the north. However after his triumphant return to Rome in 100 BC (the year of his sixth consulship), Marius fell from favour. This resulted from his association with the tribune Saturninus who proposed an unpopular agrarian law which included a clause to force senators to abide by it or be removed from the Senate. Later that year the Senate called upon Marius to defend the security of the state against Saturninus and his political ally Glaucia, but the situation got out of hand and the people attacked and killed them. By aligning himself unwisely, Marius lost everything he had gained and had little option but to leave Rome. The established order, however, had been broken.

SULLA

The next ten years were relatively quiet, but in 90 BC a revolt of many of Rome's Italian allies broke out. Eventually, Roman citizenship was granted to those states which were prepared to lay down their arms. Amid the crisis, Marius returned to prominence, and an intense rivalry which had begun many years earlier was renewed between him and Lucius Cornelius Sulla.

The eighties were a decade of power struggle and bloodshed in which many of Rome's finest citizens were killed. During this period, Italy was split between the supporters of Marius and those of Sulla. For the first time in its history, civil war struck Rome. Sulla emerged victorious in 82 BC, but his work was only beginning.

Sulla now busied himself with slaughter, and murders without number or limit filled the city. Many, too, were killed to gratify private hatreds, although they had no relations with Sulla, but he gave his consent in order to gratify his adherents. At last one of the younger men, Caius Metellus, made bold to ask Sulla in the senate what end there was to be of these evils, and how far he would proceed before they might expect such doings to cease. "We do not ask thee," he said, "to free from punishment those whom thou hast determined to slay, but to free from suspense those whom thou hast determined to save." And when Sulla answered that he did not yet know whom he would spare, "Well, then," said Metellus in reply, "let us know whom thou intendest to punish". This Sulla said he would do. Some, however, say that it was not Metellus, but Fufidius, one of Sulla's fawning creatures, who made this last speech to him. Be that as it may, Sulla at once proscribed eighty persons, without communicating with any magistrate, and in spite of the general indignation, after a single day's interval, he proscribed two hundred and twenty others, and then on the third day, as many more. Referring to these measures in a public harangue, he said that he was proscribing as many as he could remember, and those who now escaped his memory, he would proscribe at a future time... Those who fell victims to political resentment and private hatred were as nothing compared with those who were butchered for the sake of their property, nay, even the executioners were prompted to say that his great house killed this man, his garden that man, his warm baths another.

Plutarch, Sulla, 31

Once rid of his political enemies, Sulla entered upon a dictatorship with no time limit. His main aim was to restore the Senate to its traditional position of pre-eminence in Rome.

The reforms Sulla introduced were extensive. As you read through those listed overleaf, consider the following questions.

\Which reforms would be unlikely to last long?

\Which reforms attacked the power of the people?

\Which reforms attacked the power of the equestrians?

\Which reforms were most significant in Sulla's plan to rejuvenate the Senate?

THE REFORM PACKAGE

- Entry into the Senate was restricted to a minimum age.
- Magistrates had to follow the accepted career path (quaestor, praetor, consul).
- There was to be a ten-year gap between holding the same magistracy twice.
- Tribunes could no longer enter *other* offices after their year was over.
- Tribunes could not put forward legislation in the people's assembly.
- Tribunes' right of veto was restricted.
- The extortion courts were handed back to the Senate, thereby removing the influence of the equestrians.
- The number of magistrates in the Senate was increased, including many equestrians among the new people.
- The number of people elected to hold office annually was increased— there were both more quaestors and praetors.
- The Senate was to allocate a special province to each of the praetors and consuls at the end of their year of office.
- Provincial governors were appointed for one year only.
- The extent of power of provincial governors was strictly regulated.
- Permanent courts were set up to try specific crimes, with juries drawn exclusively from the Senate.

When Sulla completed his work in 79 BC, he retired from public office. He died in 78 BC. It remained to be seen whether the impact of the period 133 BC – 80 BC could be overturned by a series of reforms.

LIST OF REFERENCES

ANCIENT SOURCES

Appian, *Appian's Roman History, Vol. 3: The Civil Wars*, Loeb Classical Library, 1972

Cicero, 'Pro Sestio' in *The Speeches*, Loeb Classical Library, 1966

Dionysius, *Roman Antiquities of Dionysius of Halicarnassus*, Loeb Classical Library, 1961

Plutarch, 'Gaius Gracchus' and 'Tiberius Gracchus' in *Plutarch's Lives*, Vol. 10, Loeb Classical Library, 1968

—— 'Sulla' in *Plutarch's Lives*, Vol. 4, Loeb Classical Library, 1968

Sallust, 'The War with Jugurtha' in *Sallust*, Loeb Classical Library, 1977

SECONDARY SOURCES

Hammond, N. G. L. and Scullard, H. H., eds, *The Oxford Classical Dictionary*, Second Edition, Oxford University Press, Oxford, 1979

CHAPTER TWO

ROADS TO POWER IN THE ROMAN REPUBLIC

KATHRYN E. WELCH

In modern society, the most obvious reason for wishing to hold power is to achieve objectives, usually connected with wealth and economic control. While this was certainly true in the Roman Republic, a more important philosophy of the governing elite was the pursuit of power for the sake of glory. The small number who were eligible to participate in republican government spent their own money and other people's in order to maintain or increase individual and family honour.

In the Roman Republic, there was no moral dilemma about whether or not one should be ambitious. A Roman male of the senatorial class was destined for glory and fame, and it was his duty to achieve both to the fullest possible extent. Ambition was a virtue, not a fault. *Ambitio* in Latin means 'a going around' or, in its political sense, campaigning for votes. This process started very early in a young man's life and culminated for the very few in the consulship, the pinnacle of Roman achievement.

The four most important Roman magistracies (government offices) in ascending order were *quaestors* (financial officials); *aediles* (administrators of public works and entertainment); *praetors* (judges and army commanders) and *consuls* (supreme heads of the state). As a man achieved each rung of the *cursus honorum* (the race for honours) he won a lifelong status which could be changed only by progressing higher up the ladder or by suffering public disgrace.

In seeking the consulship, a Roman politician did not have to promise 'programmes' (such as relief for the urban poor or the betterment of conditions for soldiers and miners). If he was able to earn greater glory by performing services for others, so much the better, but it would be hard to find a Roman who entered political life solely for this reason. The pursuit of fame and glory for himself and his family was a respectable activity.

The unwritten law for a Roman male was to equal or better the status of his father (or highest ranking ancestor). Some went much further than any previous relative, thereby earning great fame in the family annals. Others were only excused by illness from carrying on a tradition. If one generation fell below standard, the next was expected to raise the family back to its former position. This placed a great burden on families with a long history of providing consuls. Whether or not he had the talent or the inclination, a man from such a background had to attempt the consulship by any means available. While the nature of Roman society gave him a greater chance of success than the *novus homo* (a man who had no consular ancestors), it also imposed greater obligation.

THE *NOBILES*: CONSULAR FAMILIES IN ROME

The consulship conferred status not only on the man who won it, but upon his family. The descendant of a consul belonged to a specific group in Roman society. He was called a *nobilis* (*nobiles* in the plural), a possessor of *nobilitas*. The families of *nobiles* could be either plebeian or patrician, for both orders were eligible to provide consuls from at least 342 BC.

The Latin *nobilis* resembles our English word 'noble' but the two do not mean the same thing. *Nobilitas* was not a virtue; rather, it meant that a member of one's family had been consul. In a sense, the *nobilis* inherited all the *dignitas* (worth) of his ancestors, and was therefore immediately more 'worthy' than the *novus*, who had to emphasise his superior personal talents and worth. Of course, some *nobiles* had far more *nobilitas* than others: a consulship held by a distant ancestor and not followed up in the recent past was of limited value, while a family with many and recent consulships outdid another with only one or two. (This topic can be followed up in Earl, *The Moral and Political Tradition of Rome*, chapters 1–2).

Thus, the political advantages of *nobilitas* were tangible. Because of their respect for tradition, the voters of Rome preferred the *nobiles*; generals liked to have well-known names among their officers; foreign kings often felt safer with a man who had the same name as a previous ambassador.

The members of a consul's immediate family shared in the glory of this position and their status reflected his. Because of this, the wives of consuls were of higher social rank than other women. Cicero refers to Clodia, one of the famous women of the late Republic, as a *consularis* because she was married to a consul. (Cicero, *Atticus*, 2.1) The fact that he thought she was unworthy and enjoyed insulting her whenever he had the opportunity did not diminish her rank. Clodia was also distinguished because her own family, the Claudii Pulchri, was among the most noble in Rome, as well as belonging to the patrician order.

In 56 BC, Clodia had accused her former lover, M. Caelius Rufus, of trying to rob and murder her. Cicero defends Caelius by maintaining that Clodia was of unsavory reputation

Bust of Cicero (Louvre, Paris. Photo K. Welch)

and unworthy of her great family, the patrician Claudii. Caelius was acquitted, because Clodia was discredited. As a 'loose' woman, she was seen as a disgrace to the family. In the election campaign of a Claudian, the names of famous ancestors were used to prove the greatness of the candidate.

And indeed I never imagined I should have to engage in quarrels with women, much less with a woman who has always been widely regarded as having no enemies since she so readily offers intimacy in all directions.

However, there it is; and I shall begin by asking her a question. Does she prefer me to deal with her according to the stern, severe tradition of ancient times, or in a light-hearted, mild and civilized fashion instead?

If in the bleak old manner and style, then I must call up from the dead one of those personages with heavy beards—not the modern sort of neat little beard which she is so keen on, but the bristling kind that we see on antique statues and busts—to reprimand the woman and speak to her in my place (which has the advantage of directing her fury away from myself). So let me conjure up, then, some member of her own family. And why not the venerable Appius Claudius, the Blind—who will suffer less than anybody else because he will not be able to see her?

If he returned to the scene, I imagine this is how he would treat her and what he would say. "Woman, what business have you with Caelius, who is little more than a boy, and is none of yours? Why have you formed such a close friendship with him that you lend him gold, or such a deep enmity that you are afraid of poison? Did you not know, from what you have seen, that your father, and from what you have heard that your uncle, your grandfather, your great-grandfather, your great-great-grandfather, and your great-great-great-grandfather were all consuls? And did you not recall that you had lately been married to Quintus Metellus, a notable, courageous and patriotic man who only had to set foot out of doors to outshine almost all his fellow-citizens in merit, glory and rank? When your marriage had transferred you from one illustrious house to another, what induced you to form so intimate a link with Caelius? Was he, by any chance, a blood-relative, or a marriage connexion, or a close friend of your husband? He was none of these things. What other reason, then, could there be except sheer uncontrollable lust?

"If the statues of the menfolk of our house did not stir your better feelings, were you not aware of promptings from my female descendant, the celebrated Quinta Claudia, to rival her glorious achievement which added to the renown of our house? Did you derive no inspiration from the noble Vestal Virgin Claudia, who during her father's Triumph gripped him tight and did not suffer him to be dragged down out of his chariot by a hostile tribune of the people? Why did you let the vices of your brother influence you more than the virtues of your father and your ancestors—virtues that have reappeared again and again ever since my own time, not only among the men of our family but among the women as well? Did I tear up that bargain with Pyrrhus merely in order that you should drive some disgusting sexual bargain every day? Did I bring water to Rome only that you should have something to wash yourself with after your impure copulations? Was the sole purpose of my Road that you should parade up and down it escorted by a crowd of other women's husbands?"

Cicero, *Pro Caelio*, 12.29

❖   ❖   ❖

SOURCES OF CONSULAR POWER AND STATUS

To understand the power structure of the Roman Republic, it is necessary to understand the status of the consuls and ex-consuls (consulars). Two consuls were elected for each year. During his year, a consul held the chief magisterial authority, which meant he could direct policy and, along with the praetors, could propose laws. Afterwards, he shared in the lifelong status and authority granted to the consulars. This status was an acknowledgement that when they elected him, the Roman people as a body judged him as deserving of honour, that is, it conferred *dignitas* upon him. Bribery, persuasion or underhand ways of raising the money for one's election campaigns could not, unless a man was actually convicted, lessen this *dignitas* or worth. Public disgrace could, and so a Roman politician tried to have his opponents convicted on a capital charge (such as electoral bribery or extortion) or marked as disgraced by the censor. However, until a man was proved guilty, he retained this all important status, even if his innocence was at best official.

Cicero outlines the functions of the various Roman magistrates in his work *The Laws*. Here he discusses the duties of the consul.

There shall be two magistrates with royal powers. Since they lead, judge, and confer, from these functions they shall be called praetors, judges and consuls. In the field they shall hold the supreme military power; they shall be subject to no one; the safety of the people shall be their highest law.

Cicero, *Laws*, 3.3.8

Figure 2.1 shows the various offices of the Roman Senate.

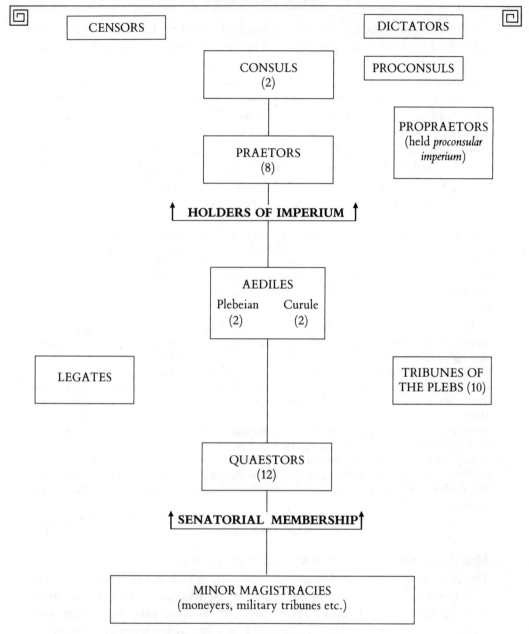

FIGURE 2.1   THE ROMAN SENATE 79 – 49 BC

AUCTORITAS: THE INFLUENCE OF THE CONSULARS

The consulship, and therefore the men who had held it, had a strong, even religious, pre-eminence in republican society. The consulship was one of the main factors which contributed to a man's *auctoritas* (personal authority). Others included family background, personality and wealth. The *auctoritas* of a consul remained with him even after his year of office was over.

When the consulars in the Senate worked together, the *auctoritas* of each individual made the group stronger. The Senate could be dominated by the ex-consuls because they carried a decisive voice in the Senate and within the paternalistic society which it led. This was the basis of *senatorial auctoritas*. Decisions on foreign policy, finance, and domestic concerns were made by these leading senators by means of this unofficial authority. The more the consulars worked together, which was certainly not always the case, the more influence they held. During the last years of the Republic, the consulars failed to maintain a cohesive unit and *consular auctoritas* was split up among various factions. However, the number of consulars in each faction contributed directly to its power and effectiveness.

In 63 BC, as outgoing consul, Cicero defended L. Licinius Murena. Murena had been elected consul for 62, but before he could take up office was prosecuted for electoral bribery (a capital charge) by Servius Sulpicius Rufus, another friend of Cicero's, who was a loser in the same election. If Servius Sulpicius had won the case, he stood a second chance of winning, but Cicero successfully defended Murena, although there was good evidence of actual guilt.

In your canvass, Servius Sulpicius, I admit that I owed to you all my energy and my support in view of our intimacy and I think that I put them at your disposal. When you were canvassing for the consulship, I failed you in nothing which could be asked either of a friend or of an obliging acquaintance or of a consul. That time is past. The case has been altered . . . But my friendship for Murena, gentlemen, is both great and of long standing. This friendship will not therefore be overwhelmed by Servius Sulpicius in a suit involving Murena's civil existence, simply because it was so in a contest with this same man for advancement in office. And if this were not the case, still either the [*dignitas*] of the man or the exalted office which he has attained would have branded me with the crowning infamy of pride and cruelty, if I had refused to defend the case of a man most distinguished by his own honours and those conferred by the Roman people . . . But I, gentlemen, would think myself abominable if I failed a friend, cruel if I failed a man in distress, arrogant if I failed a consul.

Cicero, *Pro Murena*, 7–10

❦ ❦ ❦

MOS MAIORUM: TRADITION AS A KEY TO POWER
The deep respect for tradition (*mos maiorum*) which pervaded Roman life gave great informal power to the consulars. So too did the lack of a written and conclusive constitution. These two factors were interdependent. For many important duties, the Romans had only broad guidelines for deciding who was to carry out government procedures. 'What had been done in the past' was the guiding principle unless there was a direct law concerning a particular practice, in which case the law was followed exactly. Consequently, there were areas which custom had placed in the hands of the consulars since the early days of the Republic.

Until their traditional position was challenged (and even afterwards, especially after 133 BC) the consulars continued to make very important decisions without explicit legal powers to do so. For example, the recorded 'advice of the senate' (*senatus consultum*), although not a law, was virtually binding on both those who put forward laws (the consuls, praetors and tribunes) and the assemblies which voted to pass them. The consulars had by far the greatest influence when the *senatus consulta* were drawn up.

A third factor which vested informal power in the consulars was the military nature of Roman society, with its emphasis on rank. It was normal for the consulars to be chosen as commanders-in-chief and to perform those duties which were not deliberately and legally assigned to others. If no consulars were available, praetorians (ex-praetors) were expected to fulfil these duties, and from there the chain of command continued down to the quaestors (in a manner similar to a modern army). In the event of a military or civil disaster, prefects, centurions and others of minor rank were called upon to take charge, on the grounds that any formal status was better than none. The highest ranking magistrate available was the proper person to take over command if the regularly appointed commander was unable to do so, whether he was the best man for the job or not. This rule could be broken by specially passed laws but these laws aroused controversy and opposition, especially from the conservative consulars who saw their 'rights' being taken away.

The procedures of the Senate also helped the consulars to maintain their dominance. The order of speaking during a senatorial debate was decided at the beginning of the year and usually followed a customary order of precedence. The two consuls would take turns each month to preside over the debate, but the presiding consul did not speak. The debate was led by the *princeps senatus*, the senator chosen by the consuls as the most worthy. The consulars followed, then the praetors and ex-praetors, aediles and ex-aediles took their turn. Finally, the tribunes could speak, and with their power of veto, could overturn a decision. Quaestors, the most junior magistrates in the Senate, did not have the right to speak. Thus, senators lower down the ladder would all know the views of the *principes* (the leading men) before they themselves had their turn. Only a brave and well-supported junior senator would put his future consulship at risk by speaking against his superiors.

GRATIA: THE BASIS OF INFLUENCE

Another source of a consular's power was the ability to assist others to reach their goals. The most common goals were to achieve honours and wealth. When a Roman politician employed his military position, financial resources, influence in the law courts or any other means to find positions for his friends, his status and power grew because he was seen to be effective. This ability to influence was called *gratia*.

All successful politicians possessed some *gratia*, but that of the very powerful men of the late Republic was massive. For example, when Pompey was commander in the East, and later in Spain, he found lucrative posts for any number of broke and ambitious men, who should have then supported him. Once Caesar became proconsul of Gaul in 58 BC, his *gratia* grew because the conquest of Gaul was a huge military undertaking requiring as many legates and officers as he chose to use. A place on Caesar's staff was highly desirable, for Gaul had not previously been plundered by the Romans. This contributed directly to Caesar's power, for in the granting of favours, he also attempted to build up a political party. This is one reason why his opposition tried so fiercely to prevent his appointment.

Cicero, as proconsul of Cilicia, was adamant about not wanting a second year so far away from Rome. To make sure he was 'rescued', he wrote to all his friends in the hope that their influence in the Senate would release him as soon as possible. On this occasion, he used a note of congratulation to M. Marcellus, the consul of 51, whose cousin had recently been elected consul for 50, to appeal for help. Marcellus, because he was the current consul, had immense power in the Senate.

From M. Cicero, Proconsul, to M. Marcellus, Consul, greetings.
I am thoroughly delighted that with C. Marcellus' election to the Consulship you have reaped the reward of your family affection, patriotism, and your own most distinguished and meritorious record in that office. Of sentiment in Rome I have no doubt; as for me, far away as I am, dispatched by none other than yourself to the ends of the earth, I assure you I exalt it to the skies in praises most sincere and well grounded. I have had a very particular regard for you from your childhood. On your side, you have ever desired and believed me to stand high in all respects. And what has now happened, whether we call it your achievement or an expression of the sentiments of the Roman people concerning you, very sensibly augments and enhances my affection for you, and it gives me the keenest pleasure when I hear from persons of the highest perspicacity and [honesty] that in all our words, acts, pursuits, and habits I resemble you—or you resemble me. If only you add one more thing to the splendid achievements of your Consulship, I shall feel that you have left me nothing further to wish for—I mean the early appointment of a successor to my post, or at any rate no extension of the term which you fixed for me by decree of the Senate and by law.

Cicero, *Letters to His Friends*, 101 (15.9)

✳ ✳ ✳

JOBS FOR CONSULARS

After a man had held the consulship, he became eligible to perform several offices at the top of the Roman system. He might become a *censor*, who updated the records of Roman citizens and confirmed or changed their rank, or a *dictator*, whose duties were originally to guide the state through a crisis. There are only two examples of dictators in the late Republic, Lucius Cornelius Sulla and Gaius Julius Caesar. Neither was typical of a dictator of the early period.

Cicero outlines the duties of the censors and dictators.
Censors shall make a list of the citizens, recording their ages, families, and slaves and other property. They shall have charge of the temples, streets, and aqueducts within the city, and of the public treasury and the revenues. They shall make a division of the citizens into tribes, and other divisions according to wealth, age, and rank. They shall enrol the

recruits for the cavalry and infantry; they shall prohibit celibacy; they shall regulate the morals of the people; they shall allow no one guilty of dishonourable conduct to remain in the Senate. They shall be two in number, and shall hold office every five years. The other magistrates shall hold office for one year.

Cicero, Laws, 3.3.7

✼ ✼ ✼

But when a serious war or civil dissensions arise, one man shall hold, for not longer than six months, the power which ordinarily belongs to the two consuls, if the Senate shall so decree. And after being appointed under favourable auspices, he shall be master of the people. He shall have an assistant to command the cavalry [*magister equitum*], whose rank shall be equal to that of the administrator of justice [praetor].

ibid., 3.3.9

A consular usually obtained the office of *proconsul*—one who stood in for a consul in the provinces. Similarly, a praetor could become a *propraetor*. Proconsuls and propraetors held the same rank as the consuls and praetors, but only in their assigned areas. They undertook the same duties: passing legislation, officiating in the law courts and, most importantly, acting as commander-in-chief. Like consuls and praetors in the city, *promagistrates* in the provinces were granted *imperium*, the right to command an army. Governing the provinces provided these promagistrates with opportunities for achieving military glory, increasing their wealth and building up their clientele. For the propraetor, this helped his chances of achieving the consulship; for the proconsul, it contributed to the maintenance of his authoritative position, and often paid his debts.

THE TRIUMPH

An honour reserved for the holder of *imperium* was the right to a *triumph*. This was a victory procession through the streets of Rome when 5 000 or more of a foreign enemy had been slain. The conquering general, riding in a triumphal chariot and wearing a purple robe and laurel wreath, led his troops, treasure, captives and any special exhibits along the Via Sacra to the Temple of Jupiter Optimus Maximus, where he made sacrifice, slaughtered the captives and stored the treasure. Afterwards, a feast was held for the city population.

The honour of a triumph in such a militaristic society cannot be over-estimated. Sometimes wars were begun or peace negotiations delayed because a particular general wanted to guarantee his triumph. It had a deeply religious significance: the *triumphator* painted his face red with *minium*, a custom which is thought to have linked him in some way with Jupiter Optimus Maximus for that day. A man rode behind the general, reminding him that he was still mortal in case all that grandeur attracted the jealousy of the gods.

The triumph was not just a boost to the ego. Practical advantages came the way of the successful general: some of the foreign treasure remained in his possession; he gained popularity and publicity, which added to his *auctoritas*; and his likelihood of receiving future lucrative commands increased, which extended his *gratia*. Very few *triumphatores* were below consular rank. Those who were could usually expect to become consuls in the near future.

Pompey's third triumph in 61 BC on his return from the East was thought to be *the* triumph of republican Rome.

His triumph was on such a scale that, although two separate days were devoted to it, the time was still not long enough, and much of what had been got ready for it—in fact enough to equip another triumphal procession altogether—was not included in the actual spectacle. In front of the procession were carried placards with the names of the countries over which he was triumphing. These were: Pontus, Armenia, Cappadocia, Paphlagonia, Media, Colchis, Iberia, Albania, Syria, Cilicia, Mesopotamia, Phoenicia, Palestine, Judaea and Arabia; there was also the power of the pirates, overthrown both by sea and on land. In the course of these campaigns it was shown that he had captured no less than 1,000 fortified places, nearly 900 cities, and 800 pirate ships; he had founded thirty-nine cities . . . The prisoners led in the procession were, apart from the pirate chiefs, the son of Tigranes of Armenia with his wife and daughter, Zosime, a wife of King Tigranes himself, Aristobulus, King of the Jews, a sister and five children of Mithridates, some Scythian women, and hostages given by the Iberians, by the Albanians, and by the King of Commagene; there were also great numbers of trophies, one for every battle in which he had been victorious, either in person or in the persons of his lieutenants. But what seemed to be the greatest glory of all and one quite unprecedented in Roman history was that this third triumph of his was over the third continent. Others before him had celebrated three triumphs; but his first had been over Libya, his second over Europe, and now this last one was over Asia, so that in his three triumphs he seemed in a sense to have led the whole world captive.

Plutarch, *Pompey*, 45

❋   ❋   ❋

OVATIO: THE SECONDARY TRIUMPH

If a general was victorious but did not defeat a foreign enemy, he could be awarded an *ovatio*, a lesser honour. Instead of a procession in a chariot through the city, the general led a procession on foot up the Alban Mount to the Temple of Jupiter Latiar. Crassus was awarded only an *ovatio* when he defeated Spartacus because the threat was internal rather than external. The honour was still great, but in this particular case, Crassus had reason to be jealous of Pompey, whose second triumph took place at the same time. Adding salt to the wounds was the fact that Pompey's triumph was over 'rebellious' Romans who were operating in Spain, while Crassus had defeated foreign slaves who had overrun Italy.

THE ELECTORAL PROCESS

AMICITIA: THE IMPORTANCE OF FRIENDS

In order to stand for even the lowest magistracies, a Roman had to have access to capital or credit. The chances of success became more difficult as one moved up the ladder, and the expenses also increased. Those who were ambitious but not of the privileged group of *nobiles* had to combine wealth, outstanding talent and patronage with imagination and calculated daring in order to have any chance of success.

Once a source of wealth was established, both *nobiles* and *novi* required friends (*amici*). In Roman politics, friendship was a formal institution and not always a matter of personal choice. One looked for friends from among those who could be most useful, and tried not to disturb friendships until a consulship was safely won. Even then, a politician had to be very sure of his ground before he would offend a former supporter.

Friends were called on in order to help with a political campaign. A famous man would walk in the Forum with the candidate he favoured, or be among those who called at the candidate's house for the customary morning visit; two friends might decide to pool their resources by campaigning together; friends could be brought in from country areas for the vote.

Men claimed friendship for a multitude of reasons: one might have spoken for a friend in the law courts, lent him money, served in his army, known his father, gone to school with him or cultivated him successfully for long enough. Friends who helped a man to be elected could look forward to his support in the coming year. The expectation of a future return was the fundamental issue in assisting a man to any rank within the Roman Senate, but never more so than with the consulship.

THE PATRON-CLIENT SYSTEM

Powerful men (patrons) knew they could count upon certain voters (clients) who were bound to them by *fides*, the bond of trust between patron and client. This system began in the early Republic, when the patricians were the only members of the community who could become magistrates or speak in the law courts. At that time, a patron guarded the interests of a plebeian, who would vote for him in return.

Over the years, some plebeians became powerful and wealthy and became members of the 'patron' group. The underlying principle of voting according to the wishes of one's patron survived even after the secret ballot became customary. Patronage ran in a pyramid fashion throughout society, leading down from the great houses of the *nobiles*. In the early period, the relationship was hereditary. Even in the late Republic, when one could change patrons easily, an influential man still 'inherited' the support of large numbers of clients.

The noble families thus built their support on the basis of patronage. Traditional clients included freed slaves, employees, small-scale farmers who lived in an area where an important family had influence, and soldiers who served under a particular commander. As Roman influence grew and the franchise (right to vote) was extended, communities which had been favoured by various governors showed their gratitude in the appropriate manner. Eventually foreign kings and whole nations came to be clients of individual Romans. See Figure 2.2.

In return for their votes, clients received the benefit of social security from their patron. One important favour was the distribution of grain to one's clients in times of shortage. For this reason, the *nobiles* had the most to lose from the state-based projects of the *populares* (politicians who based their power on popularity). These projects represented a direct method of stealing clients.

Cicero intends to run for the consulship of 63 BC. He sums up his chances in a letter to Atticus, written 17 July 65, a year before the election date of July 64.

The position as regards my candidature, in which I know you are deeply interested, is as follows, so far as can be foreseen up to date: Only P. Galba is canvassing, and he is getting for answer a good old Roman "No", plain and unvarnished. It's generally thought that this premature canvass of his has rather helped my prospects, for people are commonly refusing him on the ground that they are obligated to me. So I hope to draw some advantage when the word goes round that a great many friends of mine are coming to light. I was thinking of starting my canvass just when Cincius says your boy will leave with this letter, i.e. 17 July, at the tribunician elections in the Campus. As apparently certain rivals I have Galba, Antonius, and Q. Cornificius. When you read this last I fancy you will either laugh or cry. Now get ready to slap your forehead: some folk think Caesonius may stand too! As for Aquilius, I don't expect he will. He has both said he won't and entered a plea of ill health and alleged his monarchy over the law courts in excuse. If Catiline's jury finds that the sun doesn't shine at midday, he will certainly be a candidate. I don't think you will be waiting for me to write about Aufidius and Palicanus... For my part I shall spare no pains in faithfully fulfilling the whole duty of a candidate, and perhaps, as Gaul looks like counting heavily in the voting, I shall run down to join Piso's staff in September, in the dead period after the courts have closed, returning in January. When I have made out the attitudes of the nobles I shall write to you. I hope the rest is plain sailing, at any rate as far as these local competitors are concerned. *You* must answer for the other phalanx, since you are not so far away, I mean our friend Pompey's. Tell him I shall not be offended if he doesn't turn up for my election!...

Well, that's how it all stands. But I have something to tell you for which I very much hope you will forgive me. Your uncle Caecilius, having been defrauded by P. Varius of a large sum of money, has taken proceedings against Varius' cousin, Caninius Satyrus, for articles alleged to have been fraudulently conveyed to him by Varius. The other creditors are joined with him, including Lucullus, P. Scipio, and L. Pontius, who they expect will be receiver if it comes to a distraint. But this talk of a receiver is ridiculous. Now for the point. Caecilius asked me to appear against Satyrus. Well, hardly a day passes without this Satyrus calling on me. L. Domitius comes first in his attentions, I next. He made himself most useful both to me and to my brother Quintus when we were candidates. I was naturally most embarrassed in view of my friendship not only with Satyrus but with Domitius, on whom my hopes of success depend beyond any other man. I explained all this to Caecilius, making it clear at the same time that had the dispute been solely between himself and Satyrus I should have met his wishes. As it was, seeing that the whole group of creditors was involved, men moreover of the highest station who would easily maintain their common cause without help from anyone Caecilius might bring in on his own account, I suggested that it would be reasonable for him to make allowance for my obligations and my present position. I had the impression that he took this less kindly than I should have wished or than is usual among gentlemen, and from that time on he entirely dropped our friendly contacts which had begun only a few days previously.

May I ask you to forgive me over this, and to believe that it was good feeling that prevented me from appearing against a friend in great trouble, who had given me every support and service in his power, in a matter most gravely affecting his good name? If however, you like to take a harsher view, you may assume that the exigencies of my candidature made the stumbling-block. *I* consider that even if it were so I might be pardoned . . . You know the game I am playing and how vital I think it not only to keep old friends but to gain new ones. I hope you now see my point of view in the matter—I am certainly anxious that you should.

Cicero, *Atticus*, 3 (1.1)

❋ ❋ ❋

VOTING ASSEMBLIES IN ROME

The Roman method of elections helped the great patrons of Roman society to maintain their power. The Romans voted in groups, with only one vote per group. The population was divided into *centuries* for the election of the two consuls, six praetors and two curule aediles, and into *tribes* for the

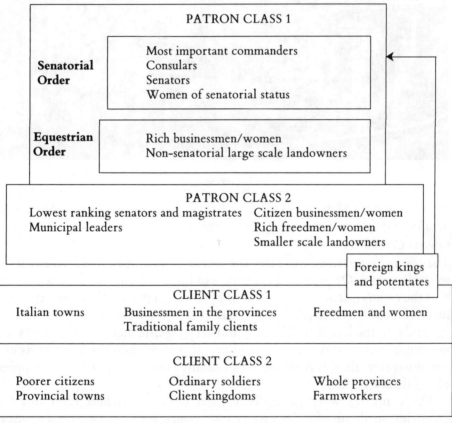

Notes
- The first patron class often had clients among the second patron class. They might also have clients among their own class.
- Both classes of patron could have clients among both classes of client. Clients in Class 1 could have clients from Class 2.
- The situation was fluid—people could move between groups.
- Social relationships are subtle and hard to simplify. While the implications of their relationships were well understood by the Romans and even sometimes by the subject nations, they cannot all be explained by means of a diagram. There are always some who do not fit easily into a pattern. Observe how the system actually *works* as you read about Roman society.

FIGURE 2.2   THE PATRON–CLIENT SYSTEM

The Roman Forum (Mansell Collection)

election of two plebeian aediles and twelve quaestors. See Table 2.1 for details of major and minor voting assemblies.

COMITIA CENTURIATA

The *comitia centuriata* met to elect the senior magistrates, to declare war and to settle peace. Originally a century had been a division of the army, and thus the *comitia centuriata* was a military parade. In this early period, the army met to elect the consuls and praetors because they were at that time also the generals. In the late Republic, the military significance of the century was not important, and the consuls and praetors were more important as civil administrators than as commanders, but this assembly still had the trappings of a military parade.

The centuries were carefully ranked with the richest (and smallest) centuries, made up of those citizens who once formed the cavalry, voting first. Members of the lowest property classes (and therefore of least importance to the army) were in the centuries which voted last. They often found that a majority was reached before their votes were called for. On the rare occasions that the consuls or praetors passed legislation through the *comitia centuriata*, they also knew in advance that the rich would vote first.

COMITIA TRIBUTA

All Roman citizens were assigned to a tribe as well as a century. Membership of one of the thirty-five tribes was proof of citizenship. The tribes met

ASSEMBLY	HISTORY	COMPOSITION	LEGISLATIVE DUTIES	ELECTIVE DUTIES	HOW TO CONTROL IT	MEETING PLACE
Comitia Curiata (of minimal importance during this period)	Original voting wards from the earliest period of Roman history.	Whole people divided into wards or *curia*. Often one man represented the *curia*.	Awarded grants of *imperium*; confirmed elections; organised adoptions.	None.	Know (or be) the *pontifex maximus*; influence the consuls.	Forum; Campus Martius.
Comitia Centuriata	The army assembly, supposedly formed by King Servius Tullus in the sixth century BC.	Whole people divided into property classes and subdivided into *centuries*, (groups for army levies, not necessarily one hundred).	Passed legislation proposed by the consuls and praetors (but legislation was more commonly passed through the *comitia tributa* or the *concilium plebis*).	Elected magistrates with *imperium* (i.e. consuls, praetors, and curule aediles).	The rich voted first so it was necessary to secure their vote. Also, the leading men in each century were essential as they could influence the group vote. Once a clear majority was reached, no further votes counted.	Campus Martius.
Comitia Tributa	Formed in the period when most of the population lived in outlying rural areas and not in the city.	Whole people divided into thirty-five tribes, but all the urban population and ex-slaves were in only four urban tribes.	More common way for the consuls and praetors to pass legislation.	Elected plebeian aediles, quaestors and minor magistrates.	Make sure one's supporters were spread throughout the tribes, especially in the rural tribes (censors could do this); influence leading men of each tribe; spread bribery evenly through the tribes; be popular.	Forum; Campus Martius.
Concilium Plebis	Formed when the plebs gained the right to elect tribunes of the plebs in the fourth century BC.	Only plebeians were members. Patricians were excluded. Plebs were divided into their tribal units. Same structure as the *comitia tributa*.	Passed *plebiscita* (laws for the plebs) which, after 387 BC, were binding on the whole population; laws were proposed by the tribunes; most common form of passing legislation.	Elected tribunes of the plebs.	Be or have influence over a tribune. All rules for the *comitia tributa* applied but popularity was even more important. Influence of the tribunes essential.	Forum.

in the *comitia tributa*. The rural tribes had far fewer members than others, so their votes counted for more within their own tribe than the votes of others. The four urban tribes contained not only the poor and uninfluential city population but freed slaves and some new citizens. The *comitia tributa* was not as easily controlled by the rich as the *comitia centuriata*, as the rich were distributed a little more evenly throughout the thirty-five groups, but because of the patron and client system, men with clients in their own or other tribes were eagerly sought by ambitious candidates and those wanting to pass legislation through the tribal assembly.

Q. Cicero advises his brother Marcus on the necessity of having friends among the 'right' (useful) people during a campaign for the consulship. (The authorship of this letter is contested.)

A campaign for election to a magistracy can be divided into two kinds of activity: firstly to gain the support of one's *amici*, secondly to win the goodwill of the people. The support of one's *amici* should be secured by kindnesses done and repaid, by longstanding acquaintance and by a charming and affable nature. But the word "*amicus*" has a wider application in an election campaign than in the rest of life. Anyone who shows any sympathy towards you, who pays attention to you, who frequents your house should be reckoned among your "*amici*". On the other hand, it is most important to be kind and warm-hearted to those who really are your *amici* through relationship of marriage or blood, through a *collegium* or some other connexion...

It is necessary to have *amici* of every kind: for the sake of appearance, make friends with men who are distinguished in rank and title (these, though they may not actively support the campaign, nonetheless confer some prestige upon the candidate); in order to make good the justice of your claim, make friends with the magistrates—in particular the *consules* [sic], and secondly the *tribuni plebis*; in order to get the votes of the *centuriae*, make friends with men who have exceptional influence. Make special efforts to win over and keep loyal to yourself such men as (because of your influence) have or hope to have the votes of a tribe or a *centuria*, or who can help you in some other way. For in recent years, men of ambition have worked hard with zeal and effort to be able to obtain what they wanted from the members of their tribe. You should endeavour by whatever means you can to see that these men show their support for you with a genuine sincerity...

Although you ought to be able to rely on and be provided with *amicitiae* that have been gained and confirmed already, yet even during the campaign a great number can be gained which are very useful. For, despite the various inconveniences, to stand in an election has this advantage at least: it is perfectly respectable to do things which would be impossible in ordinary life. You can attach to yourself in *amicitia* those whom at any other time you could not allow to be associated with you in such a way without your appearing absurd; but in an election unless you act in this way (quite deliberately, and with many people) you will give the impression of being no kind of candidate.

Q. Cicero, *Guide to Electioneering*, 16, 18, 25

❋   ❋   ❋

CONCILIUM PLEBIS
The *concilium plebis* had exactly the same structure as the *comitia tributa*, but it met under the presidency of a tribune instead of a consul or praetor.

TRIBUNATE OF THE PLEBS: THE 'ALTERNATIVE MAGISTRACY'
In the very early Republic, the oppressed plebeians demanded their own representatives who could protect them from the power of the then

exclusively patrician consuls. For this reason, the *tribunes of the plebs* were introduced. They were not magistrates, as consuls, praetors, aediles and quaestors were. Even when the office of tribune became an accepted part of the system it retained vestiges of its original separateness. Patricians continued to be excluded from the tribunate and the plebeian assembly, though plebeians could hold any of the formerly patrician magistracies. Technically, tribunes were not members of the Senate, though they could convene and attend its meetings and veto its proceedings. The ten tribunes, elected annually, took office on 10 December, while the 'regular' magistrates began their year on 1 January.

The tribunes could call public meetings and could propose laws. They presided over the *concilium plebis*. Their right of veto (*intercessio*) could be used both to stop the actions of the Senate or the passing of legislation in the assemblies. If one tribune of a particular year stood out above the others and combined his tribunate with immense popularity, he could be the most outstanding politician of his year.

Tribunes such as the Gracchi, L. Appuleius Saturninus and M. Livius Drusus challenged the power of the consulship in the period 133 – 91 BC. Without underestimating them, it is important to remember that they were the minority and they were all killed in office or soon after. The consulars of each period retaliated against the challenges to their power and upheld their position by violent methods. Eventually Sulla attempted to destroy the power of the tribunate. After its restoration in 70 BC, it was more often a useful institution to other politicians, rather than a base for independent operations.

If one man could have assumed the power of all ten tribunes, he would have been more than a match for the two consuls. Tribunician power, however, was curtailed by several factors. Firstly, because they aspired to the consulship and were members of the same privileged class which provided the regular magistrates, tribunes had to make and keep friends and allies. This often meant that their tribunician functions were placed at the disposal of more powerful individuals. Secondly, the tribunate was more effective as a method of opposition than attack: in each year the power of the tribunate belonged equally to ten men, so while a tribune could veto a decision of the Senate, he himself could be vetoed by another tribune.

A few noteworthy tribunes had both immense popularity and a large number of personal clients. This was the case with P. Clodius Pulcher (the brother of Clodia, mentioned early in this chapter). He was born a patrician, but had himself adopted into a plebeian family in order to become a tribune for 58 BC. Clodius was a clever politician who capitalised on powerful backing from several sources. At one stage, he made himself indispensible to Pompey, Caesar and Crassus, the three outstanding men of the period, but at the same time managed to harness the men opposed to them. He became a frighteningly powerful tribune. However, the tribunate was only part of Clodius's power base. His family background and the enormous clientele of the Claudii Pulchri continued to help him even after he had been adopted.

The tribunate did not confer on its holder either the social status of the consulship or those positions which were reserved for ex-consuls. Until the civil wars, when the *nobiles* set about slaughtering each other, the consulship was impossible for one who did not come from a senatorial family or the top echelons of the equestrian order. Even the *novi homines* came from wealthy upper class families. Rome was not, and did not pretend or want to be, a democracy; it was an oligarchy. Power derived from the influence (*auctoritas, gratia, nobilitas*) which a man had within this class; if one was not accepted by this class, the consulship was out of reach.

POLITICAL INVOLVEMENT IN THE STATE RELIGION

It was customary for the same men who became magistrates to be appointed or elected as priests (*pontifices*) of the official state cults. There was no 'professional' priesthood, but rather a group who combined their ordinary political activity with religious affairs. The *augur*, another religious official, had to interpret the signs and omens which were thought to be sent by the gods. The consuls themselves sometimes acted as augurs. They 'took the auspices', that is, sacrificed animals and 'read the omens' contained in them. Their readings directly affected the actions of the Roman state. Other *pontifices* were assigned to supervise foreign cults followed in Rome, or organised public banquets in honour of the gods. Declarations of war were made by special priests, the *fetiales*.

The augurs and *pontifices* were all distinguished politicians, or young men of the class who were expected to become so. Being a *pontifex* or augur added enormously to one's political and social standing. Julius Caesar used a vast fortune to secure his election as *pontifex maximus* (chief priest of Jupiter and overseer of all other *pontifices*) over his conservative rivals. Augustus belonged to all the major priestly colleges.

No public business could take place on a day of bad omen: the law courts were shut, meetings of the people or the Senate were illegal and laws passed were technically invalid. Elections had to be rescheduled. Religious obstruction in the hands of unscrupulous politicians could cripple state business. That it did not do so continuously was due to a 'gentlemen's agreement' in politics to be fair. Gentlemen were rarer in the last years of the Republic, and legislation regulating religious interference became necessary.

While the elections are being held for the praetors of 55, Pompey and Crassus, who had already been elected as consuls for 55, are determined to prevent the election of their opponent Cato by any means available. (Note that Plutarch has not properly understood the complicated system used by the Romans. He mentions the 'first tribe', but the praetors were elected in the *comitia centuriata*. He should have said the first century.)

Cato, however, would not give up the fight, but came forward himself as candidate for a praetorship, wishing to have a vantage-point for his struggles against the men, and not to be a private citizen when he was opposing magistrates. But Pompey and Crassus feared this also, feeling that Cato would make the praetorship a match for the consulship. In the first place, therefore, they suddenly, and without the knowledge of the majority, got the senate together, and had a vote passed that the praetors elect should enter upon their office at once, without waiting for the time prescribed by law to elapse, during which time those who had bribed the people were liable to prosecution. In the next place, now that by this vote they had freed bribery from responsibility, they brought forward henchmen and friends of their own as candidates for the praetorship, themselves offering money for votes, and themselves standing by when the votes were cast. But even to these measures the virtue and fame of Cato were superior, since shame made most of the people think it a terrible thing to sell Cato by their votes, when the city might well buy him into the praetorship; and therefore the first tribe called upon voted for him. Then on a sudden Pompey lyingly declared that he heard thunder, since it was customary to regard such things as inauspicious, and not to ratify anything after a sign from heaven had been given. Then they resorted again to extensive bribery, ejected the "best citizens" from the Campus Martius, and so by force got Vatinius elected praetor instead of Cato.

Plutarch, *Cato the Younger*, 42

❋ ❋ ❋

ALTERNATIVE METHODS OF HOLDING POWER

Two groups excluded from magisterial power, one by law, the other by custom, who sometimes managed to find other methods of wielding power, were women and newly-made provincial-born citizens.

WOMEN AND POWER

Roman women had very few legal rights. They could not be named as the principal heir of a rich man, although they could share in the estate of a man who died intestate and could inherit wealth from their fathers by other means. They could not represent themselves in court, and could not vote (which meant they were not eligible to stand for office). However, they *were* citizens and those of the governing class had important social status. They could be very wealthy, and had jurisdiction over that wealth. Some major priestesses, especially the chief Vestal Virgin, were women of considerable influence.

As well as having independent resources, women shared in the rank and fame of the families of both their fathers and husbands. Roman married women were traditionally forthright: stories in ancient sources show that a strong woman who put her country first was much admired. However, a woman's political power was circumscribed. It depended completely on the status (especially consular) of her husband(s), sons, sons-in-law, brothers and friends.

SERVILIA: ROMAN *MATRONA* PAR EXCELLENCE

Servilia, an outstanding figure of the late Republic, foreshadowed the women who were to dominate the Julio-Claudian household in the early Empire. She was married to a consul (D. Iunius Silanus, consul in 62 BC), but was also reputedly the mistress of Caesar during the late sixties. This gave her notoriety and extensive power. However, she still had to bow to the will of her brother, Cato, when he refused to allow her daughters to marry Pompey and his son. After Cato's death, she attempted to direct the careers of her son Marcus Brutus and her son-in-law C. Cassius. She had a senatorial decree changed for the benefit of her sons. Her friendship with Caesar survived Cato's opposition before and during the civil war. It is not surprising that Brutus and Cassius were the two supporters of Pompey who advanced most quickly after Caesar came to sole power. Two other sons-in-law were consuls, P. Servilius Isauricus in 48 and M. Aemilius Lepidus in 46 BC.

Servilia had to work through her men. She could do nothing about Cato's opposition to Caesar or Pompey, and could not prevent her son Marcus Brutus from either joining his uncle in Pompey's camp in 49 or conspiring to assassinate Caesar in 44. The best she could do was pick up the pieces after these events and hope that her power could be renewed through other allies. Lepidus and Servilius Isauricus were on the other side of the political fence, but once they lost power to Octavian, Servilia's own influence disappeared. If she continued to work through her other sons, we do not hear of it.

One of the best pictures of a family council is to be found in another of Cicero's letters to Atticus dated 7 June 44. Caesar had been assassinated three months before and the conspirators had lost the political initiative to Antony and Octavian. Note Servilia's treatment of Cicero and the presence of wives at a council about to decide their husband's actions and safety. (Tertulla is Servilia's daughter and wife of Cassius. Porcia is the daughter of Cato and wife of Brutus.)

I arrived at Antium before midday. Brutus was glad to see me. Then before a large company, including Servilia, Tertulla, and Porcia, he asked me what I thought he ought to do. Favonius too was present. I gave the advice I had prepared on the way, to accept the Asiatic corn commission. I said his safety was all that concerned us now; it was the bulwark of the Republic itself. I was fairly launched on this theme when Cassius walked in. I repeated what I had already said, whereupon Cassius, looking most valorous I assure you, the picture of a warrior, announced that he had no intention of going to Sicily. "Should I have taken an insult as though it had been a favour?" "What do you mean to do then?" I inquired. He replied that he would go to Greece. "How about you, Brutus?" said I. "To Rome," he answered, "if you agree." "But I don't agree at all. You won't be safe there." "Well, supposing I could be safe, would you approve?" "Of course, and what is more I should be against your leaving for a province either now or after your Praetorship. But I cannot advise you to risk your life in Rome." I went on to state reasons, which no doubt occur to you, why he would not be safe.

A deal of talk followed, in which they complained, Cassius especially, about the opportunities that had been let slip, and Decimus came in for severe criticism. To that I said it was no use crying over split milk, but I agreed all the same. And when I began to give my views on what should have been done (nothing original, only what everyone is saying all the time), not however touching on the point that someone else ought to have been dealt with, only that they should have summoned the Senate, urged the popular enthusiasm to action with greater vigour, assumed leadership of the whole commonwealth, your lady friend exclaimed "Well, upon my word! I never heard the like!" I held my tongue.

Anyway it looked to me as though Cassius would go (Servilia undertook to get the corn commission removed from the decree), and our friend Brutus was soon persuaded to drop his empty talk about wanting to be in Rome.

Cicero, *Atticus*, 118 (15.11)

※ ※ ※

MEN BEHIND THE SCENES: THE ADVISERS

In 90 BC the Romans went to war with their Italian allies rather than grant them citizenship. This was known as the Social War. After winning the war, Rome gave the Italians the vote. Despite this enfranchisement, however, Rome would not have considered the Italians as suitable candidates for the consulship (except favoured men from *municipia* which had held the franchise for many generations). Still less could the governing class think that those men from outside Italy who were later awarded citizenship would ever become Roman magistrates.

The Romans were unashamedly racist. Cicero, for example, won an extortion case by appealing to the anti-Greek prejudice prevalent in Rome. Because of the prevailing attitude against provincials, men from this background who sought power had to do so through a powerful patron. They also had to be rich (of course). Two men from the late Republic managed to build up great power bases.

The first, Theophanes of Mytilene, was made a citizen by Pompey in 61 when he was returning from the East. The two became close friends and Theophanes accompanied Pompey back to Rome. By the late fifties, Cicero referred to him as the man who had most *auctoritas* with Pompey, and used him to find out what the great man was thinking.

The second, Lucius Cornelius Balbus, was a Spaniard from Gades (Cadiz). Although Pompey was also responsible for his citizenship, Balbus eventually attached himself to Caesar and survived the latter's death to become the first provincial-born consul, in 40 BC. A Gaditane aristocrat, he combined financial wizardry with dexterous political ability. Balbus became Caesar's news service, propaganda manager and financial adviser. During the years of Caesar's dictatorship, he and his partner, Gaius Oppius, virtually ran Rome in Caesar's absence.

Balbus demonstrated an understanding of Roman politics: he set up his own network of friends and increased his own wealth. When Caesar died, Balbus was able to rely on his friendship with Cicero and men like the consul designate for 43, Aulus Hirtius, to maintain his position. He placed his wealth at the disposal of Octavian, who used both the money and the advice of a man who had spent twenty years in the thick of Roman intrigue.

CONCLUSION

The rules of power changed gradually under the Emperors and this allowed men like Theophanes and Balbus to achieve power more easily. Once the Emperor took over its functions, the consulship conferred great prestige, but less actual power. However, in the first stages of his career, Augustus himself relied on holding the consulship. This changed with the settlement of 23 BC (see chapter seven). Until this time the consulship was the pinnacle of Roman power and honour. After the death of Julius Caesar, the 'republicans' spent their personal fortunes, drained the provinces, and fought virtually to the last *nobilis* for the position the consulship represented.

LIST OF REFERENCES
ANCIENT SOURCES

Cicero, 'Cicero to M. Marcellus' in *Cicero's Letters to his Friends*, Vol. 1, Penguin, 1978

—— *Laws (De re Publica de Legibus)*, Loeb Classical Library, 1951

——'Cicero to Atticus' in *Selected Letters*, Penguin, New York, 1982

—— 'Pro Caelio' (In Defence of Marcus Caelius Rufus) in *Selected Political Speeches of Cicero*, Penguin, 1979

—— 'Pro Murena' in *The Speeches*, Loeb Classical Library, 1946

Q. Cicero, *A Short Guide to Electioneering*, London Association of Classical Teachers, 1979

Plutarch, 'Cato the Younger' in *Plutarch's Lives*, Vol. 8, Loeb Classical Library, 1919

—— 'Pompey' in *Fall of the Roman Republic*, Penguin, Middlesex, 1974

BIBLIOGRAPHY
SECONDARY SOURCES

Earl, D.C., *The Moral and Political Tradition of Rome*, Thames and Hudson, London, 1967

POMPEY
SOURCES OF POWER

KATE CAMERON

He was powerful without destroying freedom
—Lucan

106 BC	Pompey born to an equestrian family in a time of political upheaval
85	When only twenty-three, Pompey raises three legions to fight for Sulla against the Marians
82	Senate gives Pompey *propraetorian imperium* to fight the Marians in Sicily and Africa
	Pompey victorious, gains control of Africa
80	Celebrates his first triumph—the first equestrian to do so
77	Senate gives Pompey *propraetorian imperium* to defend Rome against Lepidus; Pompey victorious
71	Pompey defeats fugitives from Spartacus's revolt; regarded as hero
70	At thirty-six, and having held no public office, Pompey is made consul
	As consuls, Pompey and Crassus reduce powers of senators in law courts
67	Pompey given extraordinary powers to defeat pirates
66	Pompey given eastern command against Mithridates
62	After victories and judicious settlements, Pompey returns from the East the most wealthy and powerful man in Rome; Senate refuses to ratify his settlements and give land for his veterans
60	Enters into political pact with Caesar and Crassus—the 'First Triumvirate'; he gains what the Senate has denied him
57	Pompey given *proconsular imperium* for five years as controller of the grain supply
56	Conference at Luca reconfirms the triumvirate
55	Pompey and Crassus are consuls

54	Death of Crassus; Pompey breaks with Caesar
53	Gang warfare in Rome—Senate declares state of emergency, gives Pompey proconsular command to control the situation
52	Pompey is made sole consul, an unprecedented office
49	Senate fears attack from Caesar, gives Pompey proconsular power and command of all forces in Italy—his last command

Pompey had a most extraordinary political career, in which he was able to gain power both within and outside traditional channels. At the age of twenty-three he raised an army to fight for Sulla in the civil war against Marius. Three years later, while still a private citizen, he was given *propraetorian imperium* (the right to command an army) to fight against the Marians in Sicily and Africa. His success resulted in a triumph—the first celebrated by a non-senator. After further successful campaigns, one in which he was given proconsular command, Pompey returned to Italy with his army. At thirty-six years of age, and having held none of the prerequisite offices, he was elected consul.

In 67 BC, after his term as consul, Pompey was given extraordinary powers over the Mediterranean region for three years to defeat pirates, a task he accomplished in three months. Following this he commanded the war against Mithridates. He successfully concluded this campaign and brought great riches and territorial gains to Rome and immense wealth and great glory to himself. It is not surprising he was known in his own lifetime as *Pompeius Magnus*—'Pompey the Great'.

In 55 BC Pompey was elected consul for the second time. As the political situation in Rome deteriorated and civil strife seemed imminent, the Senate looked to Pompey for protection. In 52 BC he was made sole consul, an indication of the abnormal circumstances of the times. In 49 BC, when the Senate seemed in danger from Caesar, Pompey was given proconsular command of all forces in Italy. This was to be his last command.

Pompey achieved all this without having followed the traditional road to power. In order to appreciate how unusual his career was, it is necessary to look at the pattern of an 'ordinary' political career.

The *Cursus Honorum*: a Traditional Political Career

A law enacted in 180 BC, the *Lex Villia*, defined the course of a public career, whereby political and military offices were set out in the order in which they were to be attained. The law also defined the length of time to be allowed between each office. This progression of offices was known as the *cursus honorum*.

A normal career would begin with ten years military service, including terms as a minor magistrate or military tribune. Then, by following the steps of the *cursus honorum* as quaestor, aedile and so on, a man would hope to enter the Senate at about thirty years of age and be eligible for the consulship at thirty-three. Sulla modified the *cursus honorum*, increasing the age at which a man was able to enter particular offices. By Pompey's time it was customary that no man could become quaestor till he was thirty, praetor till he was thirty-nine and consul till he was at least forty-two. Sulla believed that greater age would bring wisdom, and that the eight years spent in public affairs before reaching the praetorship would provide valuable experience.

SOURCES OF POMPEY'S POWER

The glory of men's ancestors is ... like a light shining on their descendants which allows neither their virtues nor their vices to be hidden ...

Sallust

❋ ❋ ❋

POMPEY'S INHERITANCE

The Romans valued the achievements of their ancestors and strove to equal or better them, so it is worth considering how Pompey's father, Strabo, may have inspired him and what, if anything, he bequeathed to his son.

Pompey's family owned large estates in north-eastern Italy. They were not part of the established nobility, but *novi homines*, or those recently ennobled. In the Social War (between Rome and her allies) Strabo was given the task of suppressing a revolt in the area. He quickly raised an army and ruthlessly put down the revolt. A successful general who pacified many hostile tribes, Strabo was awarded a triumph and was made consul in 89 BC.

In *Pompey* (1) Plutarch suggests that Strabo was not the most popular military commander, claiming that the Romans never hated any of their generals so much and so bitterly as they hated Pompey's father, Strabo. Some modern historians have a similar opinion, describing him as brutal, corrupt and a sinister and disruptive force in politics.

What did Strabo do to deserve such a reputation? To begin with, when he was quaestor, he tried to prosecute his own commanding officer. Such unorthodox conduct set a lot of people against him. Then during the Social War, his savage capture of Asculum (in which there were executions, violent destruction and looting) generated more hostility. The Roman government was particularly upset because Strabo did not give his booty to the treasury, which was seriously depleted. When it was time to hand over his army to the new consul in 88 BC, the consul was murdered and Strabo was given back his command. For the remainder of the war Strabo seemed to switch sides as it suited him:

... he maintained a doubtful and neutral attitude between the two parties, so that he seemed to be acting entirely in his own interest and to be watching his chance, turning with his army now to one side now to the other, according as each offered a greater promise for power for himself.

Velleius Paterculus, Roman History, 2.21

Bust of Pompey
(Gliptoteca, Copenhagen. Courtesy Mansell Collection)

When Strabo died in 87 BC the Romans tore his body to pieces. So much for the glory of Pompey's ancestors!

On the credit side, however, Strabo had been a successful general and he had reached the consulship. He was an astute politician who took every available opportunity to extend his clients and supporters. He gave his soldiers generous rewards in money, decorations and citizenship.

Pompey benefited from the power bases established by his father. While he was consul, Strabo passed a law which gave Latin status to the towns of the Transalpine region, which meant that citizens of those towns were able to achieve Roman citizenship by holding municipal office. He gave full citizenship rights to people south of the Po River in Cisalpine Gaul. The Transalpine, Picenum and parts of Spain were to provide Pompey with vast sources of manpower and support throughout his career, both in war and in peace.

From the day on which he had assumed the toga [Pompey] had been trained to military service on the staff of that sagacious general, his father, and by a singular insight into military tactics . . . developed his excellent native talent.

ibid., 2.29

There was one reason and one only for the hatred felt against Strabo, namely his insatiable love of money.

Plutarch, Pompey, 1

＊ ＊ ＊

Strabo was a sinister character, "hated by heaven and by the nobility", for good reasons. There were no words to describe Cn. Pompeius the son.

Syme, The Roman Revolution, 28

＊ ＊ ＊

At the time that Pompey's father died, Pompey had little experience other than of the camp. Moreover, as he seems to have remained under his father's command, he had spent the impressionable years from the age of sixteen or seventeen to nineteen owing the twofold duty of a son and a military cadet to a general whose career was marked by disloyalty, brutality, self-interest and apparently a lack of any firm political convictions.

Rawson, The Politics of Friendship, 23

＊ ＊ ＊

From his father ... Pompey had inherited a large band of loyal veterans who had been richly rewarded by the elder Pompey; he had also inherited masses of clients in Picenum, where his father had vast estates ... The elder Pompey had also won a large following both in the Gallic cities south of the Po and in the teeming and vigorous population north of the Po, where he had, under a consular law, bestowed Latin rights on the towns. He also had numerous clients in Spain, to many of whom he gave citizenship.

Taylor, Party Politics in the Age of Caesar, 45

＊ ＊ ＊

What did Pompey inherit from his father? Consider both positive and negative aspects.

What might Pompey have learnt from his father's mistakes?

POMPEY'S PERSONAL ACHIEVEMENTS

Strabo's legacy to Pompey in the form of land and patronage was valuable, but it did not include the network of friendships and connections within the nobility necessary for a successful political career. The nobility despised Strabo and did not look with favour on his son. How did it come about, then, that the Senate gave Pompey such extraordinary powers throughout his career and ultimately chose him to defend them and the Republic against the threat of Caesar? How did he use his military successes to gain political advancement? Keep these questions in mind while reading about Pompey's career.

FIGHTING FOR SULLA

Pompey was only twenty-three years old when he raised three legions to fight for Sulla in the civil war against Marius. In *Pompey* (6) Plutarch tells us that Pompey provided his legions with food, transport, animals, wagons and all other necessary equipment. The troops and the wealth were part of his inheritance from his father, but Pompey must be given the credit for his victories and the uses he made of them.

If Plutarch's account is reliable, Pompey's first military conquests were not spectacular. While he showed considerable bravery and tactical skill, confusion among the enemy and the defection of enemy troops contributed in a large way to Pompey's victories. Nevertheless, they impressed Sulla, who hailed the young self-appointed general as *imperator* (victor).

Sulla demonstrated his gratitude by making Pompey his legate in Sicily to pursue Marian forces based there. Once in Sicily, Pompey quickly defeated the enemy and executed prominent leaders. While Plutarch condemns the inhumane manner of this particular trial and execution, both Plutarch and Cicero give examples of other ways in which Pompey showed himself to be a wise and humane victor. He showed humanity to the cities which had been badly treated, and leniency in bestowing pardons to others. When his soldiers acted in a disorderly way he had their swords sealed up in their scabbards and punished any who broke the seal.

AFRICAN CAMPAIGNS

During this campaign in Sicily, Pompey received his next command, to fight Domitius in Libya. The extraordinary thing about the command was that Pompey was invested with *propraetorian imperium* by a decree of the Senate, even though he was clearly not eligible for such a position. In 81 BC he set off for Africa with 120 warships, 800 transports and six legions. On his arrival in Carthage, 7 000 of the enemy immediately defected to Pompey. Plutarch gives the details of the battle against Domitius, after which the soldiers saluted Pompey as *imperator*. (*Pompey*, 12) He continued into Numidia, where he restored the authority of Roman government. According to Plutarch, it took him only forty days to annihilate the enemy army, gain control of Libya and settle relations with and between its kings.

To someone like Pompey, the settlements made after victories were just as important as the battles, as they provided the opportunity to extend influence and support. Cicero indicates that it was customary for generals who accepted the surrender of a defeated enemy to subsequently become their patrons. Pompey most certainly followed this custom throughout his career. The settlements he made with the kings of Numidia and Mauretania established a relationship for Pompey which lasted well after his death and made Africa a strong centre of resistance to Caesar.

RETURN TO ROME

After this campaign in Africa, Pompey received orders from Sulla to discharge five of his six legions. For the first time Pompey disobeyed orders and returned to Rome with his full army, where he was greeted by Sulla as '*Pompeius Magnus*'. Despite the warmth of his welcome, Sulla refused Pompey's request for a triumph. Sulla rightly argued that Pompey was not eligible because he was neither a consul nor a praetor and was far too young to be a senator.

But Pompey was an extremely popular young general and his recent victories were greatly appreciated. Sicily and Africa were important grain producers; had the Marians established control they could have threatened Rome's food supply. Pompey's tactic of returning to Rome with his army paid off. He did not have to threaten to use violence—the presence of so many of his loyal soldiers was enough to make Sulla reconsider. He relented and allowed Pompey his triumph.

CHANGING ALLEGIANCES

Since his successes in Sicily, Pompey's loyalty to Sulla had never been questioned. Sulla had even strengthened the bond by arranging for his stepdaughter Aemelia to marry Pompey. It must have come as some surprise, then, when Pompey used his influence to have Lepidus, an opponent of Sulla's, elected to the consulship. What is even more surprising is that when the Senate feared that Lepidus was about to march on Rome, they declared a state of emergency, passing the *senatus consultum ultimum* and turned to Pompey for help. He was given *propraetorian imperium* to help the general Catulus put down the revolt.

During his short career, Pompey had given support to Sulla, Lepidus (an opponent of Sulla's) and then the Senate in opposing Lepidus. This changing allegiance was to become characteristic of Pompey. He supported whoever or whatever cause offered him the greatest reward and advancement.

Pompey and his army defeated Lepidus. The revolt was over and Pompey was seen by many as the saviour of the Republic. Once again he was asked to disband his troops; once again he refused. This time he wanted not a triumph, but a further command.

In Spain, Metellus Pius was fighting Sertorius, a most capable general who had won many victories against the Republic's commanders, including Metellus. The Senate agreed to send Pompey to help Metellus. They invested him with *proconsular imperium*, authority far beyond what was required. Pompey's campaign against Sertorius was not an easy one (the details can be read in Plutarch, *Pompey*, 18–19). Some historians suggest that Pompey's ultimate victory was due to the assassination of Sertorius by one of his own men rather than any brilliant strategy on Pompey's part.

EXPANDING INFLUENCE

The significance of the victory over Sertorius was that it enabled Pompey to increase his clients in Spain. As victor, he assumed the patronage of those he had defeated or who had surrendered to him. He was also responsible for establishing and administering new settlements. He organised towns, conferred citizenship, granted land and greatly extended the Pompeian clients established by his father. The consuls in Rome passed a law that ratified these arrangements. The strength of Spanish support for Pompey became evident later: Caesar estimates that one third of the legions he forced to surrender were made up of Spanish landowners. Later, Pompey's sons continued to make Spain a centre of resistance, not only against Caesar but also against Augustus.

THE SLAVE REVOLT

Pompey was recalled to Rome during the slave revolt led by Spartacus. The two consuls had been ineffective against the uprising and their legions had been crushed. The Senate appointed Crassus, who was then praetor, to take command. Despite Crassus having gained control of the situation by the time Pompey returned, the Senate (urged on by the people) commissioned Pompey to assist. Crassus did not really need Pompey's help, as he had just won the decisive battle in which he killed over 13 000 slaves. Pompey missed the battle but took care of 5 000 fugitives. According to Plutarch, Pompey then wrote to the Senate saying that although Crassus had defeated the gladiators in a pitched battle, he himself had finished off the war 'utterly and entirely'. In view of his success in Spain it seems unnecessary that he should have claimed for himself the honour due to Crassus. Crassus resented Pompey's action, but the people of Rome were happy to acknowledge Pompey as a hero.

Pompey used this popularity to his advantage. He wanted to stand for the consulship and would have had enough support from the people to be elected, but he was not eligible. Pompey had not disbanded his army since returning from Spain, claiming that he was keeping them together for his triumph. This may have been a legitimate reason, but the presence of his legions no doubt helped the Senate to decide to dispense with the constraints on holding office set out in the *Lex Annalis* and allow Pompey to stand for the consulship for 70 BC.

THE TRIUMPH

Towards the end of 71 BC, Pompey celebrated his Spanish triumph in a lavish fifteen-day spectacle. Crassus was rewarded with the lesser *ovatio*. Both men campaigned for the consulship. During this campaign Pompey revealed that he had switched political allegiance again—this time to the *populares*, a faction supported by the general populace. Plutarch tells us that the only fault his enemies could find in him at this time was that he had paid more attention to the people than to the Senate, promising to restore to the tribunes the powers which Sulla had removed from them. (*Pompey*, 21)

ELECTION AS CONSUL

Both Pompey and Crassus were elected as consuls for 70 BC, and before taking office had to disband their armies and relinquish their military authority. Pompey revealed a genius for self advertisement and used the occasion to his advantage.

But perhaps the most enjoyable of all spectacles to the people was the one which Pompey afforded himself when he appeared in person to ask for his discharge from military service. It is an old custom at Rome that those who belong to the propertied class outside the senate should, at the conclusion of the legal period of their military service, come into the forum, each leading his horse, and appear before the two officials called censors. Each man gives the names of the generals and imperators under whom he has served, and some account of his own actions in war, and then receives his discharge. According to his record he receives from the censors words either of praise or blame.

On this occasion the censors Gellius and Lentulus were sitting in state, and the gentlemen with their horses were passing in review in front of them when Pompey was seen coming down the hill into the forum. He had all the insignia of a consul, but he was leading his horse with his own hand. When he came nearer so that he could be seen by everyone, he ordered his lictors to make way for him and then led his horse up to the bench where the censors were sitting. The people were amazed and stood in complete silence; the censors too were awed and also delighted at the sight. Then the senior censor questioned him, "Pompey the Great, I require you to tell me whether you have taken part in all the military campaigns that the law demands." And in a loud voice Pompey replied: "I have taken part in all of them, and all under myself as imperator." These words were greeted with a great shout from the people, and indeed it became quite impossible to restrain their rapturous applause; the censors rose from their seats and led the procession escorting Pompey home, this giving great pleasure to the people who followed behind, shouting and clapping.

Plutarch, *Pompey*, 22

Crassus, who had followed the conventional path to the consulship, was a skilled orator, experienced with the workings of the courts and the Senate. Pompey, who made his first appearance in the Senate as a consul, was on unfamiliar ground. He was a poor speaker who had had no experience of senatorial debate or proceedings. Yet if the Senate thought that this inexperience would restrict Pompey's actions, they were very much mistaken. Also, the changes made to the Sullan constitution during 70 BC greatly weakened the Senate's position. The powers of the tribunes were restored, the courts were reconstituted so that the Senate had only one third of the places on the juries, the powers of the censor were revived and the senatorial rolls revised. Sixty-four senators were removed and new ones were admitted, especially from the equestrian order. Throughout Italy people were given citizenship which meant that there were masses of new voters not bound by established patron–client obligations.

Pompey and Crassus had much to gain from these new arrangements; although it is difficult to judge to what extent the two men co-operated in introducing them, Pompey is the one held most responsible. At the end of his term as consul, Pompey declined a proconsular command and instead waited in Rome for a more important command. Not surprisingly, the Senate did not fulfil his wishes: they were not prepared to give Pompey another opportunity to enhance his own position at their expense.

COMMAND AGAINST THE PIRATES

The next time Pompey was called upon to serve Rome was in 67 BC when pirates were making raids on Italy, pillaging shrines, taking Roman hostages and interfering with shipping in the Mediterranean to such an extent that Rome's corn supply was affected and prices rose sharply. When the tribune Gabinius proposed that Pompey be given a command against the pirates, the Senate violently opposed him. The only senator who spoke in favour was Caesar. There was strong popular support for Pompey and a crowd attacked the Senate when they heard of the rejection of Gabinius's proposal. Finally the Senate gave Pompey his command, which included extraordinary powers.

When the Romans could no longer endure the damage and disgrace they made Gnaeus Pompey, who was then their man of greatest reputation, commander by law for three years, with absolute power over the whole sea within the Pillars of Hercules, and of the land for a distance of 400 stades from the coast . . . They gave him power to raise troops and to collect money from the provinces, and they furnished a large army from their own muster-roll . . . Never did any man before Pompey set forth with so great authority conferred upon him by the Romans.

Appian, Civil Wars, 12.14.94

Part of that authority was the power to select twenty-four of his own legates, each of whom was to be invested with *praetorian imperium*. This was an ideal opportunity for Pompey to extend his patronage, to reward old supporters and attract new ones. Several of his legates later became consuls.

Pompey took just three months to clear the Mediterranean of pirates. Plutarch describes how he did it. (*Pompey* 26) The strategy which defeated the pirates demonstrated Pompey's military skill; his treatment of the defeated pirates demonstrated his political skill. Instead of slaughtering them, Pompey settled the pirates at various places in Asia Minor which were in need of additional population. By doing this, he encouraged the growth and prosperity of communities in key areas whose loyalty would be to Rome and to himself.

THE EASTERN COMMAND

In 66 BC the tribune Manilius, with the support of the *populares*, legislated to transfer the eastern command against Mithridates from Lucullus to Pompey. This time Pompey had an influential supporter in Cicero, who spoke in favour of the bill, arguing that the prolonged campaign under Lucullus was costing the business sector and tax farmers an enormous amount of revenue. Caesar also spoke in favour of the bill; the *optimates* (the faction traditionally supported by the nobility) resented Pompey being given even further powers. Despite the opposition of the *optimates*, the bill was eventually passed by a unanimous vote of all the tribes. Pompey was given the same unlimited powers as before,

. . . to make war and peace as he liked and to proclaim nations as friends or enemies according to his own judgment. They gave him command of all the forces beyond the borders of Italy. All these powers together had never been given to any one general before; and this is perhaps the reason why they call him Pompey the Great.

Appian, Civil Wars, 12.15.97

Lucullus was not impressed. Although he had not been able to end the war, he had won many victories against Mithridates and he now saw Pompey depriving him of the honour of his achievements. According to Plutarch, Lucullus accused Pompey of:

. . . following his usual custom of settling down, like some crazy carrion bird, on the bodies that had been killed by others and tearing to pieces the scattered remains of wars. It was in just this way that he had appropriated to himself the victories over Sertorius, Lepidus and the followers of Spartacus, though in fact these victories had been won by Metellus, Catulus and Crassus. There was therefore no reason to be surprised at his present plan of seizing for himself the glory of the Pontic and Armenian wars...

Plutarch, *Pompey*, 31

Plutarch devotes considerable attention to the battles of the eastern campaign, where Pompey showed great leadership and military skill. However, he dismisses lightly the complex range of settlements made by Pompey after the conquest: 'Having settled the affairs of the east and made what arrangements seemed good to him, Pompey started on his journey home.' (*Pompey*, 42) It was through these political and administrative arrangements that Pompey was able to consolidate his military conquests and achieve unprecedented wealth and honour.

In his settlements, Pompey followed where possible the traditional Roman practice of leaving administration to the dependent kings or city states. He recognised existing dynasties where they had proved loyal to Rome, and he reinstated or conferred authority on those leaders whom he felt could be trusted. In other areas, he annexed territory to Rome, reorganising existing provinces or creating new ones. In such cases he regulated the details of administration, as he did with his elaborate organisation for the new province of Pontus, which was divided into eleven communities, each with its own urban centre.

Through the creation and consolidation of provinces such as Pontus, Syria, Cilicia, Asia and Bithynia, Pompey was able to secure for Rome the coast of Asia Minor and the region south of the Black Sea. He also secured a network of tribute-paying client kingdoms. See Figure 3.1.

The wealth that accrued to the conqueror himself was sufficient to make him the richest man in Rome... But more than wealth Pompeius had acquired *clientelae* on a scale hitherto unwitnessed. Not merely individuals and cities but whole provinces and kingdoms acknowledged him as their patron.

Seager, *Pompey: A Political Biography*, 55

Velleius Paterculus indicates the value of this bond when he describes the forces Pompey summoned from the East to try to stop Caesar crossing the Adriatic. He lists 'legions from all the provinces beyond the sea, auxiliary troops of foot and horse, the forces of kings tetrarchs and other subject rulers', and also ships. (*Roman History*, 2.51.1) This support was all part of the patron–client relationship established through Pompey's eastern settlements.

THE FIRST TRIUMVIRATE

When Pompey returned from the East in 62 BC he was the wealthiest man in Rome, and with eight legions devoted to him, he was also the most powerful. He enjoyed immense popularity with the people but was still

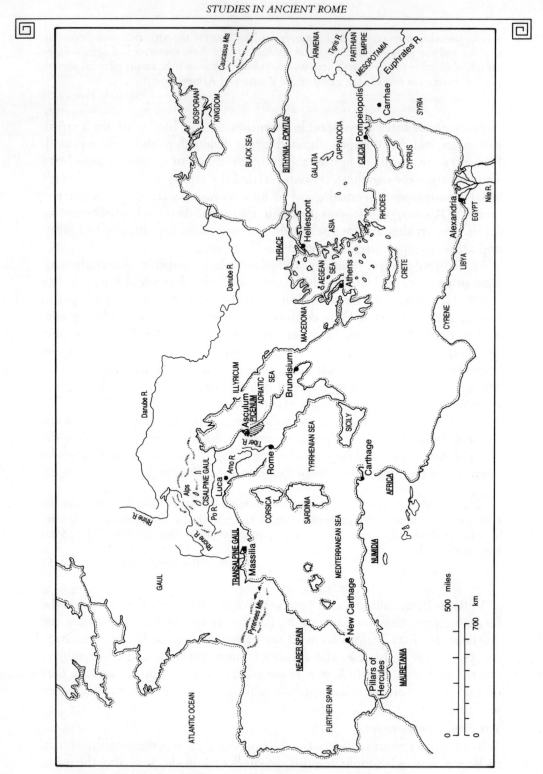

FIGURE 3.1 THE ROMAN EMPIRE IN POMPEY'S TIME
SHOWING AREAS WHERE HE ESTABLISHED EXTENSIVE CLIENTELA.

regarded with suspicion and perhaps fear by the *optimates*, who criticised his eastern settlements and refused to ratify them. They also refused to grant the land he desired for his veterans. Pompey was given no more military commands. There was a successful new general on the scene—Julius Caesar—and the Senate now favoured him with their appointments.

For the next two years Cato (a conservative member of the nobility) and the *optimates* continued to deny Pompey's requests. It was politically expedient, therefore, for Pompey to enter into an alliance with Caesar and Crassus, who both had grievances against the Senate.

Pompey benefited from this alliance, which came to be known as the 'First Triumvirate'. As consul, Caesar took the land bill to the *comitia* where it was passed, then had a tribune propose the bill confirming the eastern settlements. Pompey and Caesar assisted the passage of these bills through the public assemblies by filling Rome with their soldiers, where their presence as much as their votes was very influential.

Politics in Rome was degenerating, with mob violence, slander and intimidation being used by politicians against their opponents. After the triumvirs had used the tribune Clodius to remove two vocal opponents (Cato and Cicero) from the Senate, Clodius and his professional rioters turned against Pompey, attempting to drive him from public life. Pompey fought back. With his own legions posted elsewhere, he called on his family clients and veterans from Picenum and Gaul to support the tribune Milo in opposing Clodius. In defiance of the earlier decision of the triumvirate, Pompey tried to recall Cicero (according to Plutarch to bring about a reconciliation between Pompey and the Senate). Initially Clodius and his gangs blocked this appeal, but when Pompey called on his veterans and supporters from the Italian countryside to take up Cicero's cause in their own municipal assemblies or by coming to Rome, the recall was passed in both the Senate and the *comitia*.

In return, Cicero proposed that Pompey be given control of the grain supply. This office gave Pompey control of all ports and trading centres, *proconsular imperium* for five years, and fifteen legates. Despite opposition from Clodius, the Senate passed this bill, but rejected one proposing that Pompey be given a military command to go to Egypt.

At a meeting known as the 'Conference at Luca', the triumvirs decided that Pompey and Crassus were to be consuls for 55 BC. The 'election' campaign was marked by the violence which had become common in Roman politics and once more soldiers were implicated—this time Caesar's troops, whose furlough conveniently coincided with the election. The Conference at Luca decided that Pompey would receive four legions and proconsular command of Libya and the two Spains for five years. At the end of his term as consul, Pompey used his wealth to boost his popularity and prestige. He had built a grand theatre and at its opening staged spectacular games, including athletics, musical contests and wild animal fights in which 500 lions were killed.

While such amusements pleased the masses, not everyone was impressed. There was increasing criticism of Pompey for staying in Rome and governing his provinces through his legates. They found fault with him for spending too much time with his young wife, Julia, at the expense of his other duties. The death of Julia, who was Caesar's daughter, then that of Crassus brought an end to the triumvirate.

The relative balance of power that had existed was replaced by rivalry and suspicion. At the same time the political situation in Rome degenerated into anarchy. Violent riots prevented the election of consuls for 52 BC. Bribery was rife and rival gangs engaged in arson and open warfare in the streets. When Milo had Clodius murdered, Clodius's gangs burnt down the Senate House.

SOLE CONSUL

In the midst of this chaos the Senate turned to Pompey. Because of the emergency situation, there was much agitation for Pompey to be made dictator, a constitutional position which carried absolute power and authority. Instead, the *optimates* preferred to make him sole consul. In speaking for this extraordinary proposal, Cato, one of Pompey's longstanding opponents, argued that any government was better than none and that in such disturbed times Pompey was likely to govern better than anyone else. The Senate accepted the proposal and passed a decree empowering Pompey to levy troops for use in Rome.

Pompey had reached the height of his political career. He was sole consul, while still holding *proconsular imperium* as controller of the grain supply and proconsular command of Libya and the two Spains. He had immense wealth, loyal soldiers and many clients and supporters throughout the Empire. No other Roman had held such power.

➤ **List the ways in which Pompey's career was different from the normal Roman political career.**

➤ **Draw up a chart of events which demonstrate how Pompey advanced or consolidated his political position by means other than military conquest.**

➤ **How frequently did Pompey change his allegiance to particular people or parties? What did he gain each time?**

➤ **How did the following affect Pompey's career:**
  • **the impact of the battles and proscriptions of the civil war on available military talent and on the people of Rome?**
  • **the emergence of Caesar?**
  • **the deterioration of the domestic political situation in Rome?**

➤ **Discuss the extent to which Pompey was a 'user', and the extent to which he was used by others.**

POMPEY'S MARRIAGES

Marriage within the Roman nobility was not considered a life-long arrangement. Ambitious men often married to establish political alliances with important families, then divorced just as expediently. Pompey was no exception to this trend—he used women to further his political position. He married five times, each wife providing him with important connections and political influence at a vital time in his career.

At the age of twenty, Pompey became engaged to Antistia, daughter of Publius Antistius who was the magistrate presiding over Pompey's defence in court against misappropriation of funds charges (apparently inherited from his father). After Pompey's acquittal, he married Antistia. The marriage survived until the death of Antistius, when Pompey divorced Antistia in a manner Plutarch describes as dishonourable and pathetic. (*Pompey*, 9)

Pompey's next wife was Aemilia, who had superior family connections. Aemilia was from the Metelli family, and was stepdaughter of Sulla. While Pompey gained connections with Sulla and the influential Metelli, Sulla too gained from the match, as Pompey had proved to be a popular and successful general. (Plutarch suggests that the match was imposed by Sulla.) Aemilia's existing marriage was dissolved, even though she was pregnant, and she was married to Pompey. She died in childbirth shortly after her marriage.

Mucia was Pompey's third wife. She was daughter of Mucius Scaevola, who was closely related to the Metelli. While married to Mucia, Pompey's command in Spain was renewed and he was elected to the consulship, even though he was not eligible for either position. He was also given increasingly important military commands, first against the pirates, then against Mithridates. Although it is difficult to quantify the importance of the influence of the Metelli in the Senate, and it is necessary to consider the other forces at work, it is interesting to note that after Pompey divorced Mucia, his relationship with the Senate changed for the worse. They would not ratify his eastern settlements, nor would they give him the land he wanted for his veterans.

One of Pompey's main opponents in the Senate was Cato, who was described by Livy as 'the conscience of Rome'. Pompey tried to soften this opposition to him by offering to marry Cato's niece. Whatever had attracted Sulla and the Metelli to the prospect of a marriage alliance with Rome's greatest general obviously did not attract Cato—he refused.

After failing to neutralise Cato's opposition in the Senate, Pompey entered into an alliance with Crassus and Caesar in order to gain what he wanted from the Senate. Julius Caesar's daughter, Julia, became Pompey's fourth wife, thus strengthening the political alliance. From all accounts this was a happy marriage. Plutarch tells us that Pompey devoted so much attention to his young wife that he paid no attention to what was going on in the Forum.

Julia died in 54 BC and Crassus was killed in battle the following year. The triumvirate no longer existed, but Pompey and Caesar needed to maintain the support of Crassus' friends, the wealthy businessmen of Rome. One of Crassus' sons had been killed with his father at Carrhae and he left a young widow, Cornelia. She became Pompey's fifth wife, ensuring the support of many of Crassus' connections. Cornelia brought to the marriage considerable wealth, but more importantly, the support of the Metelli. The modern historian Rawson sees this marriage as Pompey's decisive commitment to the cause of the *optimates*.

❧List Pompey's five wives. Beside each one, indicate what Pompey gained from that particular marriage.

❧Which of the following descriptions of Pompey do you feel is most appropriate?

In fact Pompey, from the time when he first took part in public life, could not brook an equal at all. In undertakings in which he should have been merely the first he wished to be the only one. No one was ever more indifferent to other things or possessed a greater craving for glory; he knew no restraint in his quest for office, though he was moderate to a degree in the exercise of his powers. Entering upon each new office with the utmost eagerness, he would lay them aside with unconcern, and, although he consulted his own wishes in attaining what he desired, he yielded to the wishes of others in resigning it...

Velleius Paterculus, Roman History, 2.33

✻ ✻ ✻

His youth was spent in prosecuting through illegality and fraud, treachery and bloodshed the interests of Sulla and his own advancement. His maturity was consumed by a struggle to win recognition of his pre-eminence and acceptance by Sulla's oligarchy and its successors. Returning from the East he ostentatiously refused to imitate Sulla and sought accommodation and connection with the younger Cato. Cato's rebuff drove him into alliance with Caesar, from which he almost immediately tried to extricate himself and with which he was never easy. In the end it was the threat of Caesar in Gaul and the imminence of civil war which drove Cato and his faction, whose pretensions Pompey had overshadowed, whose relatives he had murdered and whose alliance he had desired, to accept and use him. It was their fault the accommodation was so late in coming. Ambitious and bloodthirsty, untrustworthy and devious, Pompey was yet no revolutionary.

Earl, The Moral and Political Tradition of Rome, 52

✻ ✻ ✻

Pompeius then did not want to destroy the republic...His ambitions are fairly clear...he wanted no more than to be treated with the respect that his standing and achievements deserved and in consequence to be able to advance and protect his friends and clients as the occasion demanded. To a certain extent these aims were those of any Roman *nobilis*. But Pompeius' character did not make matters easy. His conceit and hypocrisy inspired resentment, his deviousness bred distrust. As a result, even in emergencies, the senate would approach him only with reluctance, and took delight in pricking the bubble of his vanity whenever circumstances allowed.

Seager, Pompey: A Political Biography, 188

✻ ✻ ✻

But they cut off Pompey's head and threw the rest of his body naked out of the boat, leaving it there as a spectacle for those who desired to see such a sight. Philip, however, stayed by the body until they had had their fill of gazing at it. He then washed it in sea water and wrapped it in one of his own tunics. Then, since he had no materials, he searched up and down the coast until he found some broken planks of a small fishing boat, old and decaying, but enough to make a funeral pyre for a naked and mutilated body. As he was collecting the wood and building the pyre, an old man came up who was a Roman and who in his youth had served with Pompey in his first campaigns. "Who are you" he said, "who are preparing the funeral for Pompey the Great?" Philip said that he was Pompey's ex-slave and the old man said: "But you must not have this honour all to yourself. Let me too share in the pious work now that the chance has come to me. I shall not altogether regret my life in a foreign land if, in return for so many hardships, I find this happiness at last—to touch with my hands and to prepare for burial the body of the greatest Imperator that Rome has seen".

Plutarch, *Pompey*, 80

❋· ❋· ❋·

CONCLUSION

The ancient sources praise Pompey's military achievements, but some (such as Cicero) regard his moral values as his true greatness. Perhaps this is not surprising, considering the strife and corruption witnessed under Caesar's rule. Velleius Paterculus emphasises Pompey's military victories, but also admires his moral virtues, describing him as first among Roman citizens, and a most upright and eminent man. In *Annals* (3.20), Tacitus is less charitable. He denigrates Pompey's military achievements, accuses him of being a corrupt and incompetent politician and holds him responsible for the civil war and the long period of civil strife following his death.

What do you think? Do you agree with Tacitus that Pompey was a destroyer of the Republic—or do you see him as its defender? In assessing Pompey's career, consider not only how he acquired his power, but why he did so, and what he did with the power once he had it. Comparisons with Caesar are inevitable, and many historians see Caesar as a better general and more capable politician than Pompey. When comparing the two and the way they gained and used their power, keep in mind the fate of the Republic and Lucan's comment that Pompey 'was powerful without destroying freedom'.

LIST OF REFERENCES

ANCIENT SOURCES
Appian, *Appian's Roman History*, Vol. 3, *The Civil Wars*, Loeb Classical Library, 1958
Lucan, *Civil War*, Loeb Classical Library, 1957
Plutarch, 'Pompey' in *Fall of the Roman Republic*, Penguin, 1973
Sallust, 'The War with Jugurtha' in *Sallust*, Loeb Classical Library, 1965
Tacitus, *The Annals of Imperial Rome*, Penguin, 1971
Velleius Paterculus, *Compendium of Roman History*, Loeb Classical Library, 1979

SECONDARY SOURCES

Earl, D., *The Moral and Political Tradition of Rome*, Thames and Hudson, London, 1967

Rawson, B., *The Politics of Friendship*, Sydney University Press, Sydney, 1978

Seager, R., *Pompey: A Political Biography*, Basil Blackwell, Oxford, 1979

Syme, R., *The Roman Revolution*, Oxford University Press, Oxford, 1939

Taylor, L. Ross, *Party Politics in the Age of Caesar*, University of California Press, California, 1968

BIBLIOGRAPHY

ANCIENT SOURCES

Cicero, *Selected Works*, Penguin, 1975

CHAPTER FOUR

CRASSUS THE FORGOTTEN TRIUMVIR

JENNIFER LAWLESS

... a man distinguished among the Romans for birth and wealth
—Appian

c.115 BC	Crassus born
97	Father is consul
87	Crassus flees to Spain from Marian forces
84	Joins Sulla against Marians
78	Sulla dies
74	Revolt of Spartacus
73	Crassus is praetor
72 – 71	Crassus defeats Spartacus
70	Consulship of Crassus and Pompey
65	Crassus is censor
63	Catiline conspiracy
59	First Triumvirate Caesar is consul
56	Conference at Luca
55	Second consulship of Crassus and Pompey In November, Crassus leaves for Syria
54	Campaign against the Parthians
53	Crassus dies at the Battle of Carrhae

The importance and prominence of Marcus Licinius Crassus in the late Republic is often dismissed as being due to his wealth alone. This chapter examines how he achieved and used this wealth, and how he gained power and influence through the more traditional avenues of power available to the Roman nobility.

CRASSUS' EARLY CAREER

Marcus Crassus was probably born around 115 BC (the date favoured by Adcock) so his life spanned an interesting and turbulent period of the Roman Republic. He was the second son of Publius Licinius Crassus who had been tribune in circa 106 BC, consul in 97 BC, Governor of Further Spain and who celebrated a triumph over the Lusitanians.

Both his father and brother had fought and died in campaigns against Marius and Cinna during the civil war. Thus, at the beginning of his political career, Crassus was the only surviving male of an old noble family, inheriting the duty of equalling his father's achievements and preserving the status of his family's name. As a member of a noble family, he was expected to pursue political advancement and glory, through gaining political office of the highest standing.

After the death of his father and brother in the war against Marius, Crassus married his brother's widow, Tertulla, and fled to Spain. No doubt he saw in Spain a refuge, as his father, a previous governor, would have had many friends and clients and considerable property there. Plutarch points out:

> **H**e had been in Spain before, when his father was praetor there, and he had made friends in the country.
>
> Plutarch, *Crassus*, 4

After the death of Cinna in 84 BC, Crassus raised a small force and eventually joined Sulla against Marius in Italy. Directed by Sulla to march through enemy territory, Crassus asked for an escort, only to be cruelly reminded:

> **I** give you as an escort ... your father, your brother, your friends, and your relations who have been put to death without law or justice and whose murderers I am going to punish.
>
> Plutarch, *Crassus*, 6

Crassus displayed considerable military ability. During the last major battle at the gates of Rome, Sulla's army was defeated, but Crassus' right wing was victorious. However, in military matters, Crassus was already being overshadowed by the younger Pompey, who was preferred by Sulla and hailed as *imperator*.

Following Sulla's victory, Crassus accumulated great wealth during the proscriptions against the supporters of Marius. However, he apparently angered Sulla because of misconduct and disappeared from public life for several years.

It is said that in Bruttium he actually added a man's name to the proscription lists purely in order to get hold of his property and with no authority from Sulla; and that Sulla was so indignant at this that he never employed him again in public affairs.

Plutarch, *Crassus*, 6

How Crassus spent the years from circa 80 to 74 BC is not clear. It is probable that he consolidated his wealth, began business ventures and perhaps gained experience in the lower political offices.

THE SPARTACUS REVOLT

War and piracy had greatly increased the number of slaves working in Italy. From 105 BC, Romans expected annual games which included gladiatorial shows, so training schools were set up for these gladiators.

One of these gladiators—a Thracian slave called Spartacus—escaped from a training school in Capua with several others and seized Mount Vesuvius. They were quickly joined by other slaves and disgruntled herdsmen, eventually making up a considerable force. After overrunning Campania and Lucania, Spartacus and his followers defeated two Roman armies sent against them. They reached Northern Italy, from where Spartacus had hoped his followers could return to their homelands. However, the Gauls and Germans among his force refused to leave and continued to plunder Italy.

The Senate sent out both consuls of 72 BC with armies to fight Spartacus, but both were defeated. Having initially considered the uprising merely a nuisance, the Senate began to regard the situation as very serious: it was probably causing havoc to the rural economy as well as making a mockery of the Roman army. Crassus, who had become praetor in 73, was given a special proconsular command with six legions to quell the revolt.

Read the following sources and decide why Crassus was sent. Is it a possibility that he paid for these legions himself? Did he volunteer? Where was Pompey at this time?

This war, so formidable to the Romans (although ridiculed and despised in the beginning, as being merely the work of gladiators), had now lasted three years. When the election of new praetors came on, fear fell upon all, and nobody offered himself as a candidate until Licinius Crassus, a man distinguished among the Romans for birth and wealth, assumed the praetorship and marched against Spartacus with six new legions.

Appian, *Civil Wars*, 1.14.118

✽ ✽ ✽

The consuls [of 72 BC] were told to return to civilian life, and Crassus was appointed to the supreme command of the war. Because of his reputation or because of their friendship with him large numbers of the nobility volunteered to serve with him.

Plutarch, *Crassus*, 10

Considering that the nobility owned much of the land being devastated by Spartacus, it is little wonder that they supported Crassus! Within six months, Crassus crushed the rebellion; Spartacus was killed and 6 000 of his followers were crucified along the Appian Way. Some fugitives who escaped north were defeated by Pompey on his return from Spain. Pompey claimed credit for finishing the war, much to the disgust of Crassus. What further irritated Crassus was that Pompey was given a triumph for his defeat of Sertorius in Spain, while Crassus received only an *ovatio*, presumably because his success was not against a foreign enemy.

Read the account of the revolt in Plutarch, *Crassus*, 8–11.

THE CONSULSHIP OF 70 BC

In 71 BC, both Pompey and Crassus approached Rome with their armies and demanded the consulship. Who had the most legitimate claim?

Crassus
- had held the praetorship;
- was of the correct age;
- had defeated a dangerous enemy;
- was from a noble family;
- was strongly supported by business interests in Rome and presumably Italian land-owners, grateful for his crushing of the revolt.

Pompey
- had held none of the requisite offices;
- was too young for the consulship (for which the minimum age was forty-two);
- was not of a noble family;
- had defeated a dangerous enemy;
- had strong popular support in Rome.

Read the following accounts. Which man is seen as the most worthy?

The glory of ending this war belongs to Marcus Crassus, who was soon by unanimous consent to be regarded as the first citizen in the state.

Velleius Paterculus, *Roman History*, 2.30.6

❋ ❋ ❋

Crassus accomplished his task within six months, whence arose a contention for honours between himself and Pompey. Crassus did not dismiss his army, for Pompey did not dismiss his. Both were candidates for the consulship. Crassus had been praetor as the law of Sulla required. Pompey had been neither praetor nor quaestor, and was only thirty-four years old, but he had promised the tribunes of the people that much of their former power should be restored.

Appian, *Civil Wars*, 1.14.121

❋ ❋ ❋

. . . what seemed the most remarkable proof of his [Pompey's] extraordinary distinction was that Crassus, the richest statesman of the time, the best orator and the greatest man, Crassus, who looked down upon Pompey and everyone else, had not ventured to put himself forward as a candidate for the consulship until he had first asked Pompey to support him. Pompey was delighted to do so.

Plutarch, *Pompey*, 22

Was Crassus really in need of Pompey's aid at this stage in his career?

Once Crassus and Pompey were elected as consuls, their political friendship (*amicitia*) did not last long.

In fact they differed on practically every point that came up; they were constantly quarrelling, each trying to get the better of the other, and, as a result, they made themselves as consuls politically ineffective and achieved nothing.

Plutarch, *Crassus*, 12

Despite Plutarch's claim that they achieved nothing, under their consulship several changes were made to the Sullan constitution. They restored powers to the tribunate and revived the magistracy of censor. The censors promptly ejected sixty-four members of the Senate. They returned to the equestrians the privilege of farming taxes in Asia and a role in the law courts. Crassus gave three months corn dole to the people. Thus both men would have increased their popularity with the people of Rome and the wealthy equestrians. Urged on by the people, Pompey and Crassus staged a public reconciliation.

It was an interesting combination of political power, as Pompey and Crassus sought political influence and support in different ways.

In the senate Crassus was the more influential of the two, but Pompey had great power with the people.

Plutarch, *Pompey*, 22.

❋ ❋ ❋

CRASSUS AND POMPEY IN THE 60S

At the end of their consulship, neither man took a proconsular province but retired for some time to private life. Pompey gained great prestige in 67 – 66 BC when he was given unrestricted *imperium* to defeat the pirates interrupting the corn shipments to Rome. In 66 BC he was given a command in the East to fight against Mithridates.

Very little is known of Crassus' life during this period. He remained in Rome, probably trying to increase his influence there. At times, his methods appear somewhat unorthodox and his political aims difficult to follow. Presumably he was irritated by Pompey's success.

In 65 BC, Crassus became censor and Julius Caesar became aedile. Crassus had apparently assisted Caesar financially in staging magnificent games, which would have helped Caesar to attain this position. While censor, Crassus proposed that the Transpadanes (people who lived in the rich and fertile area between the Po River and the Alps) be granted citizenship. This would have given him a huge increase in his clientele at the expense of Pompey, who also had interests in the area. However, Crassus' ambitious proposal was opposed by Catulus, his fellow censor.

Crassus also suggested the annexation of Egypt, the main supplier of grain to Rome. The resultant increase in trade would have meant an increase in wealth for the equites and others involved in these activities, such as Crassus himself. Again, this move was opposed by Catulus.

Crassus and Caesar were both suspected of having been involved in the Catiline conspiracy of 63 BC (see chapter five). Lucius Tarquinius made accusations to this effect in the Senate.

> **A**s soon, however, as Tarquinius named Crassus, a noble of great wealth and of the highest rank, some thought the charge incredible; others believed it to be true, but thought that in such a crisis so powerful a man ought to be propitiated rather than exasperated. There were many, too, who were under obligation to Crassus through private business relations. All these loudly insisted that the accusation was false, and demanded that the matter be laid before the senate. Accordingly, on the motion of Cicero, the senate in full session voted that the testimony of Tarquinius appeared to be false ...
>
> Sallust, *The War with Catiline*, 48.5

> ╲**Compare this account with Plutarch,** *Cicero* **(14 – 22). What are the differences between the two accounts?**

It is likely that when Crassus left Rome he visited Pompey in the East. They may have made plans for the future at this time. Thus it was a surprise to many that, on landing at Brundisium from the Mithridatic War in 62, Pompey dismissed his troops and in 61 held his third triumph. However, on divorcing his wife, he asked permission to marry Cato's daughter. This would have given him powerful connections with the old nobility and within the Senate. Cato refused his request—and Pompey felt rebuffed.

THE 'FIRST TRIUMVIRATE'

In 60 BC the Senate rejected the various demands of Crassus, Pompey and Caesar. Crassus had suggested compensation be paid to equestrians who had lost investment opportunities in tax-gathering in the East due to the Mithridatic War. Caesar, on returning from Spain, wanted a triumph and the consulship *in absentia*. Pompey wanted ratification of his eastern settlements and land for his veterans. The stage was set to throw together the three most powerful and ambitious men in Rome in a political alliance.

For the three to achieve their ends, they had to ensure a sympathetic consul was elected for the following year. The three formed a political *amicitia*, known by later historians as the 'First Triumvirate', to further their own demands. Caesar was elected consul for 59, so the three achieved their main objective.

Read the following extracts and answer these questions:

╲**How do the accounts differ?**

╲**What does each man want?**

╲**Why is Crassus asked to join?**

╲**Is he the least powerful of the three?**

He [Caesar] observed that Pompey and Crassus were once again on bad terms with each other and, while he had no wish to make an enemy of one of them by seeking support from the other, he felt that without the help of either of them, his own prospects would be hopeless. He therefore set to work to reconcile them.

Plutarch, *Crassus*, 14

❋ ❋ ❋

Pompey was indignant and made friends with Caesar and promised under oath to support him for the consulship. The latter thereupon brought Crassus into friendly relations with Pompey. So these three most powerful men pooled their interests.

Appian, *Civil Wars*, 2.2.9

❋ ❋ ❋

He [Caesar]... actually reconciled the men themselves, not because he was desirous that they should agree, but because he saw that they were most powerful. He understood well that without the aid of both, or at least one, he could never come to any great power... Pompey and Crassus, the moment they really set about it, made peace with each other, for reasons of their own and they took Caesar into partnership in their plans.

Cassius Dio, *Roman History*, 37.55.1–2

❋ ❋ ❋

Pompey, Caesar and Crassus now formed a triple pact, jointly swearing to oppose all legislation of which any one of them might disapprove.

Suetonius, *Julius Caesar*, 19

❋ ❋ ❋

It was in Caesar's consulship that there was formed between himself, Gnaeus Pompeius and Marcus Crassus the partnership in political power which proved so baleful to the city, to the world, and subsequently at different periods to each of the triumvirs themselves... while Crassus hoped that by the influence of Pompey and the power of Caesar he might achieve a place of pre-eminence in the state which he had not been able to reach single-handed.

Velleius Paterculus, *Roman History*, 2.44.1–2

The records of the next few years are confused and events obscure. It is difficult to understand fully Crassus' role during this period. After his consulship, Caesar left Rome for his command in Gaul and Illyricum and relations between Crassus and Pompey declined rapidly. Clodius, as tribune of 58, began attacking Pompey politically. Were the *optimates* trying to force a wedge between Pompey and Crassus?

Clashes between the supporters of Crassus and Pompey became frequent. Pompey accused Crassus of plotting against his life. In 56, after his recall from exile a year before, Cicero began to attack Caesar's earlier legislation. Worried by the decline in the triumvirate's position, Crassus hurriedly met Caesar at Ravenna. Obviously, a reconciliation between the three had to be made and the *amicitia* strengthened.

THE CONFERENCE AT LUCA, 56 BC

A meeting between the three—and a bevy of senators—occurred at Luca.

Read the following extracts. What would Caesar, Pompey and Crassus each gain from the agreement?

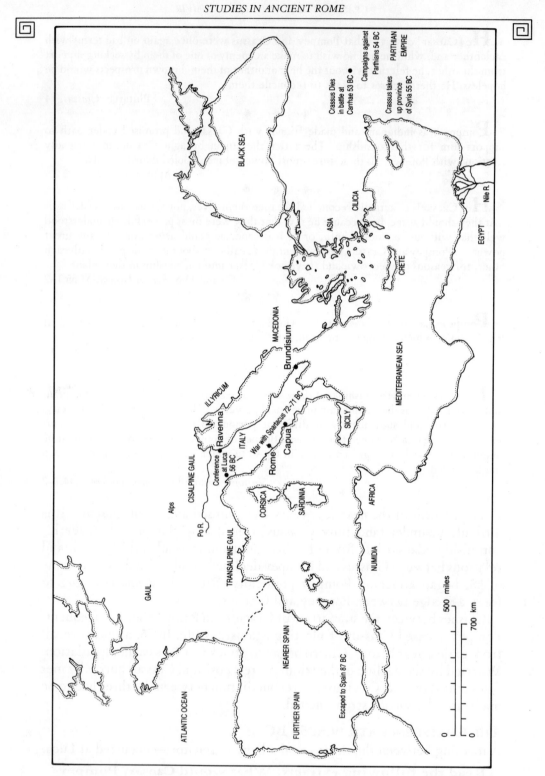

FIGURE 4.1   ROME IN CRASSUS' TIME

When Caesar came south from Gaul to the city of Luca a great many Romans went there to meet him. Among these were Pompey and Crassus. At the private conferences which the three men held together they decided to tighten their grip on public affairs and to take over the entire control of the state. Caesar was to retain his army and Pompey and Crassus were to have other provinces and armies. The only way to carry out this plan was to stand for a second consulship. Pompey and Crassus were to put themselves forward as candidates, and Caesar was to cooperate by writing to his friends and sending back large numbers of his soldiers to support them at the elections.

Plutarch, Crassus, 14

* * *

Pompey and Crassus, his partners in the triumvirate, came also. In their conference it was decided that Pompey and Crassus should be elected consuls again and that Caesar's governorship over his provinces should be extended for five years more.

Appian, Civil Wars, 2.3.17

Pompey and Crassus were elected to their second consulships in 55 BC. Presumably the violent behaviour of their supporters kept political opposition at bay.

\How did the second consulship further the political careers of Pompey and Crassus?

\Compare the account below with Plutarch, *Crassus* (15).

Gnaeus Pompeius and Marcus Crassus, who had once before been consuls together, now entered upon their second consulship, which office they not only won by unfair means, but also administered without popular approval. In a law which Pompey proposed in the assembly of the people, Caesar's tenure of office in his provinces was continued for another five years, and Syria was decreed to Crassus, who was now planning to make war upon Parthia.

Velleius Paterculus, Roman History, 2.46.1–2

At the end of his consulship, with Caesar back in his province and Pompey at Rome attending to matters there, Crassus prepared to leave for his Syrian province and a war with Parthia. It seems that with the possibility of increasing his wealth, prestige and clients in a war, Crassus stood to gain most from the Conference at Luca.

WHY A PARTHIAN WAR?

In pursuing war with Parthia, Crassus may have been trying to prove himself a military leader as great as Pompey and Caesar, his younger rivals. He had achieved the highest offices in Rome, but perhaps felt the need to achieve similar military glory, as the following extracts suggest.

• • • in the case of Crassus a new passion, in addition to his old weakness of avarice, began to show itself. The glorious exploits of Caesar made Crassus also long for trophies and triumphs—the one field of activity in which he was not, he considered, Caesar's superior.

Plutarch, Crassus, 14

* * *

Now, however, he seemed to be transported right out of his senses. He had no intention of making Syria or even Parthia the limit of his successful enterprises. What he proposed to do was to make the campaigns of Lucullus against Tigranes and those of Pompey against Mithridates appear as mere child's play, and in his hopes he saw himself penetrating as far as Bactria and India and the Outer Ocean.

ibid., 16

✦ ✦ ✦

Crassus took Syria and the adjacent country because he wanted a war with the Parthians, which he thought would be easy as well as glorious and profitable.

Appian, Civil Wars, 2.3.18

Another possible consideration was a desire to control the new Chinese silk-trade route in the East—a lucrative venture if successful. (Adcock, *Marcus Crassus*, 48–9)

Whatever the reasons behind the war, it was not a popular campaign. When the Senate gave the command of Syria to Crassus, there had been no reference to a war with Parthia. Indeed, Plutarch says that there was opposition because Rome had treaties of friendship with Parthia and there was no reason to go to war. (*Crassus*, 16) Crassus left Rome for Syria to curses pronounced by the tribune Ateius, and many people feared the outcome.

Read the account of the Parthian War in Plutarch, *Crassus* (16–33) and answer these questions.

❧ **Why was Crassus defeated?**

❧ **How did his death affect Rome, and the relationship between Pompey and Caesar?**

SOURCES OF POWER

To be successful in the political arena in Rome, a noble had to exhibit certain virtues and had to have access to many avenues of power. In varying degrees, Crassus had all of the prerequisites. As well as being one of the wealthiest men of Rome, he also understood the need to exploit the traditional forms of political power and influence, such as:

- family connections;
- personality and character;
- wealth;
- patronage and a large clientele;
- success in the courts and as an orator;
- influence in the Senate—*auctoritas*;
- magistracies following in the *cursus honorum*;
- military honours;
- political friendships.

Each of these factors will now be examined.

FAMILY CONNECTIONS

Crassus came from one of the noblest families. He was expected to uphold the family's honour and traditions, and to seek glory through political advancement. He had quite a lot to live up to, his father being tribune, praetor, consul, censor, Governor of Spain and having been given a triumph. After his father and brother were killed, he was the only surviving male member of the family.

Crassus had married his brother's widow, Tertulla, and apparently remained faithful to her for the rest of his life, even though it had been rumoured (probably by his enemies) that she had been unfaithful to him with Caesar. That the marriage survived his lifetime was remarkable in a period when the nobility often married several times to gain political advancement or to strengthen political ties.

The marriage produced two sons who Crassus married into established noble families. His eldest son, Marcus, married the daughter of Metellus Creticus, and his younger son, Publius, married the daughter of P. Scipio Nasica. Thus, important links were formed with the Metelli and Scipionic families.

PERSONALITY AND CHARACTER

To gain political supremacy, it was important to be popular in all levels of society. Methods of achieving popularity varied, but it was an advantage to be seen to exhibit a range of virtues that would appeal to all social classes.

Read the following source extracts. What qualities in Crassus are emphasised?

How could his attitude to people have helped his political career?

Crassus was so temperate and moderate in his way of life...with regard to his relations with women his conduct was as exemplary as that of anyone in Rome.

Plutarch, *Crassus*, 1

✤   ✤   ✤

Crassus was eager to show kindness and hospitality. His house was open to all, and he used to lend money to his friends without interest...The people he invited to his dinner parties were usually ordinary people and not members of the great families; and these meals were not expensive, but they were good and there was a friendliness about them which made them more agreeable than more lavish entertainments...Another thing which made him more popular was the courteous unaffected way in which he greeted people and spoke to them. However humble and obscure a man might be, Crassus, on meeting him, would invariably return his greeting and address him by name.

ibid., 3

✤   ✤   ✤

Crassus...was continually ready to be of use to people, always available and easy to be found; he had a hand in everything that was going on, and by the kindness which he was prepared to show to everyone he made himself more influential than Pompey was able to do with his high-handed manners.

ibid., 7

✤   ✤   ✤

WEALTH

It is interesting to discover how Crassus gained his enormous wealth, and how he used it for advancing his political reputation.

Crassus' most famous 'quality' was avarice—the desire to accumulate wealth. Plutarch points out that he began his career with only 300 talents and yet by his consulship of 55:

> • • • he dedicated a tenth of his property to Hercules, he provided a banquet for the people, and he gave out of his own funds to every Roman citizen enough to live on for three months; yet after all this, when he made up his accounts before setting out on the expedition to Parthia, he found that he was worth 7 100 talents . . . he amassed most of this property by means of fire and war; public calamities were his principal source of revenue.
>
> ibid., 2

Crassus made his fortune from a range of activities:
- During Sulla's proscriptions, he bought up many properties very cheaply and sold them at high prices when conditions stabilised.
- He acquired properties either affected or threatened by the frequent fires in Rome. He owned over 500 slaves whom he used as architects and builders to rebuild many of these properties, and eventually 'most of Rome came into his possession'. (ibid., 2)
- He owned many silver mines, lent money at varying interest rates, and was apparently involved with many commercial undertakings.
- He owned and farmed large tracts of land.
- He bought, educated and then sold numerous high-quality slaves.

Such wealth could easily be put to advantage, as political activity in Rome needed ready cash. It seems that most senators had money tied up in land, so often needed to borrow cash for various reasons: to sustain an expensive life-style, subsidise friends, and to provide games, contests, gifts and bribes for electors and jurors. Enormous debts were often incurred. Thus money-lending, at varying rates of interest, was always in demand. Before the consular elections for 53 BC, the interest rate rose from four per cent to eight per cent due to the demand for cash.

Crassus, by lending money whenever requested, ensured that many senators were grateful and indebted to him. He could easily speculate in a man's career, 'buying' him victory in an election or in the law courts. This is shown by the generous help often given to Caesar throughout his career. When Caesar was setting out to govern Spain in 61 BC, he was detained by creditors demanding that bills be paid.

> **H**e therefore turned for help to Crassus, who was the richest man in Rome . . . Crassus met the demands of those creditors who were most difficult to deal with and would not be put off any longer, and gave his personal guarantee for 830 talents.
>
> Plutarch, *Caesar*, 11

How important a role did Crassus' money play in the political careers of the three triumvirs?

It is interesting to note that Pompey returned from the Mithridatic War with even greater wealth than Crassus. Therefore Crassus' involvement in the triumvirate was not solely due to his money.

PATRONAGE AND CLIENTELE

The relationship of a patron to his clients was very important in Roman society. Patronage (a duty to aid the client in whatever manner was available in return for loyalty, support and votes) could extend from:

- a former master to his freedman;
- an advocate in court to his client;
- an important Roman to members of the lower classes, provinces, municipia, colonies and individuals in these communities.

Aid could come in the form of gifts of money, loans or legal and political assistance.

Crassus had cultivated an enormous number of clients. He was popular with the lower classes in Rome, had supported the equestrians in various business ventures, probably inherited many clients from his father's Spanish province and had attempted to add the Transpadanes to his list by offering them citizenship. He had also gained powerful support by lending money to influential senators. If he had been successful in Parthia, the increase in wealthy clients would have been enormous.

Crassus understood the power and influence of a large clientele and also understood how to acquire them. He worked assiduously in Rome, in the courts and beyond the city to acquire clients in all classes of society.

THE LAW COURTS

The influence of a Roman noble could be considerable in the courts. Often political battles were fought in the courts of law, and it was here that Crassus won himself much support and many clients. In order to excel, he prepared himself well, polished his skills of oratory and often helped people whom Pompey and Caesar would not bother to aid.

So far as his general culture was concerned, he gave most attention to the art of speaking and to those aspects of it which would be useful in dealing with numbers of people. He became one of the best speakers of Rome and, by care and application, was able to surpass those who were more highly gifted by nature. He never appeared in the law courts without having prepared his speech beforehand, however small or inconsiderable the case might be with which he was dealing, and often when Pompey and Cicero and Caesar were reluctant to speak, he undertook the whole management of the case himself, thereby gaining an advantage over them in popularity, since people thought of him as a man willing to take trouble and to help others.

Plutarch, *Crassus*, 3

✳   ✳   ✳

THE SENATE AND *AUCTORITAS*

As a member of one of the most noble families in Rome, Crassus would have felt quite at home dealing with other senators (in contrast to Pompey, who apparently needed a guide written for him on senatorial dealings). It is often suggested that he had great influence and prestige—*auctoritas*—within the Senate. It would have helped that many senators also owed him money!

Analyse the following sources. How important was this *auctoritas*?

On Crassus' involvement in the Catiline conspiracy:

> ... others regarded it as a story trumped up by the accused, in order that they might thereby receive some aid from him, because he possessed the greatest influence.

Cassius Dio, Roman History, 37.35.1–2

✦　✦　✦

Here by taking pains, by helping people in the law courts or with loans, or in the canvassing and questioning which has to be done and undergone by candidates for office, he acquired an influence and a reputation equal to that which Pompey had won by all his great military expeditions... when he [Pompey] was present [in Rome], he was often less important than Crassus.

Plutarch, Crassus, 7

✦　✦　✦

In the senate Crassus was the more influential of the two, but Pompey had great power with the people.

Plutarch, Pompey, 22

✦　✦　✦

MAGISTRACIES OF THE *CURSUS HONORUM*

The path to political advancement in Rome was through the natural progression up the political ladder—the *cursus honorum*. Crassus, like his father, reached the pinnacle of success at Rome, by being praetor, consul (twice), and censor. It was acknowledged that he had great *auctoritas* in the Senate, but also used the *popularis* method of having bills presented to the people by the tribunes. He also showed a shrewd ability to compromise to advance his ambitions. In 71 BC he compromised with his rival, Pompey, to gain the consulship of 70; he did so again in 56 to share their second consulship and to gain Syria and the Parthian War.

MILITARY HONOURS

Crassus performed well in his early military career under Sulla and later against Spartacus. However, he couldn't compete with the extraordinary military victories of Pompey and, later, Caesar. Crassus' father had gained a triumph; Crassus, the lesser honour of an *ovatio*. Perhaps his desire for greater glory in the military field was the impetus behind his pursuit of war against Parthia.

Read the accounts of Crassus' military career in Plutarch, *Crassus*, 6.8–11.

POLITICAL FRIENDSHIPS

Political friendships (*amicitia*) enabled people to work together for their common advancement:

Pompey, Caesar and Crassus now formed a triple pact, jointly swearing to oppose all legislation of which any one of them might disapprove.

Suetonius, *Julius Caesar*, 19

Such a political clique was sometimes called a *factio*. In *The War with Catiline* (32.2), Sallust refers to the Catiline conspirators as such. Thus the formation of the triumvirate by the three men was not an extraordinary step. With other avenues closed to them, their demands rebuffed by the Senate, forming a political pact with others was one way around the obstacle.

CONCLUSION

It is too simple to say that Crassus' power lay solely in his wealth. He worked industriously to acquire it, knowing that enormous power and influence followed its acquisition. He also used his wealth astutely to gain influence over many other Romans. However, he also gained great influence and support through his family connections, patronage, his *auctoritas* in the Senate, the magistracies that he held and his *amicitia* with Pompey and Caesar.

In another time, Crassus' political career, background and clientele would have ensured that he gained the position of first citizen at Rome. However, he found himself competing for glory and recognition against two men who exhibited great talents in the military field, particularly Pompey, with his extraordinary commands and popularity.

Having reached the pinnacle of power in Rome, Crassus then looked to the campaign in Parthia to achieve similar military glory. His ambition could be said to have been the death of him.

Although Crassus was, in his general character, entirely upright and free from base desires, in his lust for money and his ambition for glory, he knew no limits, and accepted no bounds.

Velleius Paterculus, *Roman History*, 2.46.2

❋   ❋   ❋

LIST OF REFERENCES

ANCIENT SOURCES

Appian, *Appian's Roman History, Vol 3: The Civil Wars*, Loeb Classical Library, 1972

Cassius Dio, *Dio's Roman History*, Vol. 3, Loeb Classical Library, 1980

Plutarch, 'Caesar', 'Cicero', 'Crassus' and 'Pompey' in *Fall of the Roman Republic*, Penguin, 1973

Sallust, 'The War with Catiline' in *Sallust*, Loeb Classical Library, 1965

Suetonius, 'Julius Caesar' in *The Twelve Caesars*, Penguin, 1973

Velleius Paterculus, *Compendium of Roman History*, Loeb Classical Library, 1979

SECONDARY SOURCES

Adcock, F.E., *Marcus Crassus: Millionaire*, W. Heffer & Sons Ltd, Cambridge, 1966

BIBLIOGRAPHY

SECONDARY SOURCES

Gelzer, M., *The Roman Nobility*, Basil Blackwell, Oxford, 1969

Marshall, B.A., *Crassus: A Political Biography*, Adolf M. Hakkert, Amsterdam, 1976

Scullard, H.H., *From the Gracchi to Nero*, Methuen, London, 1979

Seager, R., *Pompey: A Political Biography*, Basil Blackwell, Oxford, 1979

Taylor, L.R., *Party Politics in the Age of Caesar*, University of California Press, 1968

Ward, A.M., *Marcus Crassus and the Late Roman Republic*, University of Missouri Press, Columbia, 1977

CAESAR
ULTIMATE POWER

DIANNE HENNESSY

It is more important for Rome than for myself that I should survive
—Caesar

100 BC	July 13, Caesar born into a patrician (noble) family
84	Marries Cornelia, the daughter of Cinna who had been consul four times
81	Sent as a *legate* (lieutenant) to King of Bithynia to help in the collection of a fleet
80	Wins the *civic crown* (awarded for bravery in battle, particularly for saving the life of a Roman citizen) while on military service in Asia
75	Leaves Rome for Rhodes; on the way he is captured by pirates who hold him for ransom
74	Punishes pirates on his own initiative; assists in military activities in Asia Minor
73	Becomes a member of the college of pontiffs (a pontifex) Returns to Rome
72	Delivers a speech in the extortion court on behalf of the Bithynians
71	Becomes a military tribune
70	Speaks in favour of a bill to grant amnesty to the followers of Lepidus and Sertorius
69	Quaestor in Further Spain; before his departure for Spain he speaks at the funerals of his aunt Julia and his wife Cornelia
68	Goes to Transpadane Gaul where he has a strong patron–client base
67	Curator of the Appian Way Speaks in support of the Gabinian Law
66	Supports the Manilian Bill giving additional powers to Pompey

65	Curule aedile; while in this position falls into great debt entertaining the Romans with magnificent games.
64	Appointed magistrate in charge of one of the courts in Rome Supports an agrarian bill which would have benefited Rome's unemployed
63	Takes Rabirius to trial for treason Prosecutes an ex-consul (Piso) for the unjust execution of a Transpadane citizen Caesar is elected *pontifex maximus* (chief priest) Year of the Catilinarian conspiracy; Caesar speaks in the Senate against using the death penalty on conspirators
62	Becomes Praetor Divorces Pompeia because of Clodius's sacrilegious acts in Caesar's home
61	Becomes Governor of Further Spain (using title proconsul); has great military success and accrues enough wealth to pay back his debts
60	Stands for and is elected consul for 59 BC Formation of the 'First Triumvirate'
59	Consul with Bibulus Honours his commitments to his co-triumvirs and puts through an agrarian bill Receives command of Cisalpine Gaul and Illyricum—later extended to Transalpine Gaul Caesar marries Calpurnia; Pompey marries Caesar's daughter, Julia
58	Proconsul Military action against the *Helvetii* and Ariovistus and his Germans
57 – 56	Further campaigns in Gaul
56	Conference at Luca Extension of Caesar's command agreed upon
55	Further campaigns in Gaul; first expedition to Britain
54	Second expedition to Britain; campaigns in Northern Gaul
53	Campaigns in Northern Gaul continue
52	Gallic revolt under Vercingetorix occupies Caesar militarily In Rome, efforts being made to allow Caesar to stand for the consulship *in absentia*
51	Final pacification of Gaul Attempts to make Caesar return to Rome
50	Attempts to bring Caesar home continue
49	Caesar crosses the Rubicon and civil war erupts First period of dictatorship (eleven days)

48	Caesar is consul; takes battle to Greece and Egypt
	Caesar is dictator for a year, beginning in October
47	War in Alexandria; defeats Pharnaces, King of Pontus
46	Caesar is consul; wins Battle of Thapsus in Africa
	Dictator for ten years
45	Consul; wins Battle of Munda in Spain
	Dictator for life
44	Consul
	Assassinated on 15 March

Gaius Julius Caesar is probably one of the best known figures of the ancient world. While many people know that he was famous, and that Shakespeare wrote a play about him, few know the origins of this fame.

Caesar was a general, politician, statesman and writer who became enormously powerful in ancient Rome. Ultimately, his use of power cost him his life. This chapter investigates Caesar's power, both its sources and the uses he made of it.

BORN TO RULE?

While speaking at the funeral of his aunt and wife, Caesar claimed descendancy from the gods.

During his quaestorship he made the customary funeral speeches from the Rostra in honour of his aunt Julia and his wife Cornelia; and while eulogizing Julia's maternal and paternal ancestry, did the same for the Caesars too. "Her mother", he said, "was a descendant of kings, namely the Royal Marcians, a family founded by the Roman King Ancus Marcius; and her father, of gods—since the Julians (of which we Caesars are a branch) reckon descent from the Goddess Venus. Thus Julia's stock can claim both the sanctity of kings, who reign supreme among mortals, and the reverence due to gods, who hold even kings in their power."

Suetonius, *Julius Caesar*, 6

Caesar's parents were from two important Roman families—the Julian and the Aurelian. (See Table 5.1) Although the Julian family was patrician, it is unlikely that a member of the family had ever been consul; Caesar's own father was only ever praetor. When Caesar's aunt Julia married C. Marius, the consulship came within the grasp of the Julii (even though Marius was a *novus homo*, a 'new man' to the Senate). The Aurelians were part of the plebeian nobility, with many consuls among their ranks. In 83 BC, Caesar extended his political ties by marrying Cornelia, who was from another patrician family—the Cornelii. His new father-in-law, Cinna, had been consul four times.

TABLE 5.1 CAESAR'S FAMILY

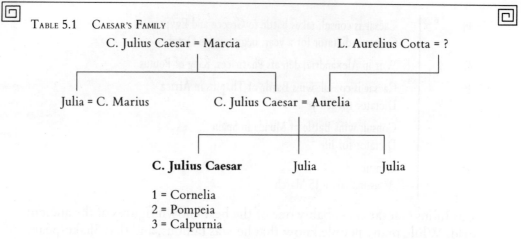

Both Marius and Cinna had a strong influence on the young Julius Caesar. Although both were from the senatorial class they strongly opposed the dictator Sulla, who tried to reassert the Senate as an unquestionable force in the state.

Julius Caesar's background met the criteria for success in Roman politics. While his early career was unspectacular, members of the aristocracy—his peers—became troubled when, like his uncle Marius, Caesar became a champion of the people.

CAESAR: THE MAN

One way of trying to understand the people of the past is to conjure up an image of them in your mind. Study the statue of Caesar, then read this description from Suetonius. What assumptions can you make about the character of Caesar from this evidence?

Caesar is said to have been tall, fair, and well-built, with a rather broad face and keen, dark-brown eyes. His health was sound, apart from sudden comas and a tendency to nightmares which troubled him towards the end of his life; but he twice had epileptic fits while on campaign. He was something of a dandy, always keeping his head carefully trimmed and shaved; and has been accused of having certain other hairy parts of his body depilated with tweezers. His baldness was a disfigurement which his enemies harped upon, much to his exasperation; but he used to comb the thin strands of hair forward from his poll, and of all the honours voted by the Senate and People, none pleased him so much as the privilege of wearing a laurel wreath on all occasions—he constantly took advantage of it. His dress was, it seems, unusual: he had added wrist-length sleeves with fringes to his purple-striped senatorial tunic, and the belt which he wore over it was never tightly fastened—hence Sulla's warning to the aristocratic party: "Beware of that boy with loose clothes!"

Suetonius, *Julius Caesar*, 45

✳ ✳ ✳

Statue of Caesar, Historical Picture Services, Chicago

THE FORMATIVE YEARS

Plutarch relates the following story about Caesar:

. . . in Spain, when he was at leisure and was reading from the history of Alexander, he was lost in thought for a long time, and then burst into tears. His friends were astonished, and asked the reason for his tears. "Do you not think", said he, "It is a matter for sorrow that while Alexander, at my age, was already king of so many peoples, I have as yet achieved no brilliant success?".

Plutarch, Caesar, 11

Suetonius gives a totally different picture of Caesar's power nine years later, in 60 BC, when Caesar was standing for election to the consulship for 59 BC.

Read the following extract—it provides clear evidence that the Senate did not like Caesar's methods of acquiring power. What methods were most unwelcome by the Senate?

The province of Western Spain was now allotted to Caesar. He relieved himself of the creditors who tried to keep him in Rome until he had paid his debts, by providing sureties for their eventual settlement. Then he took the illegal and unprecedented step of hurrying off before the Senate had either formally confirmed his appointment or voted him the necessary funds. He may have been afraid of being impeached while still a private citizen, or he may have been anxious to respond as quickly as possible to the appeals of our Spanish allies for help against aggression. At any rate, on his arrival in Spain he rapidly subdued the Lusitanian mountaineers, captured Brigantium, the capital of Galicia, and returned to

Rome in the following summer with equal haste—not waiting until he had been relieved—to demand a triumph and stand for the consulship. But the day of the consular elections had already been announced. His candidacy could therefore not be admitted unless he entered the City as a civilian; and when a general outcry arose against his intrigues to be exempted from the regulations governing candidatures, he was faced with the alternative of forgoing the triumph or forgoing the consulship.

There were two other candidates; Lucius Lucceius and Marcus Bibulus. Caesar now approached Lucceius and suggested that they should join forces; but since Lucceius had more money and Caesar greater influence, it was agreed that Lucceius should finance their joint candidacy by bribing the voters. The aristocratic party got wind of this arrangement and, fearing that if Caesar were elected Consul, with a pliant colleague by his side, he would stop at nothing to gain his own ends, they authorized Marcus Bibulus to bribe the voters as heavily as Lucceius had done. Many aristocrats contributed to Bibulus's campaign funds, and Cato himself admitted that this was an occasion when even bribery might be excused as a legitimate means of preserving the Constitution.

Caesar and Bibulus were elected Consuls...

Suetonius, *Julius Caesar*, 18–19

The Senate had indeed become wary of Caesar. Since they had given him support in his election to the pontificate in 73 BC, Caesar had shown populist tendencies, courting the favour of the people whenever possible.

Both Plutarch and Suetonius tell us that, after laying down his quaestorship in 68 BC, Caesar visited the colonists beyond the Po River who were discontented with their lack of citizenship. The Senate believed that Caesar supported an armed revolt to further their cause. Later, as aedile in 65 BC, Caesar put on a huge gladiatorial display at games in Rome to honour his father, who had died many years earlier. The Senate was so concerned at the number of gladiators being used that they passed a 'hurried bill' limiting the number of gladiators allowed to be kept in Rome.

Caesar went even further when, in 65 BC, he had statues and monuments of his uncle Marius and his victories displayed around the streets of Rome, even though the Senate had forbidden such actions. These activities paid off, as the people elected Caesar *pontifex maximus* in 63 BC. He had used his earlier offices wisely and had effectively courted the people's favour. This position held great prestige in Rome and was very important to Caesar. In achieving this goal, Caesar defeated two other candidates, both of whom had already held the consulship. The Senate certainly had reason to fear Caesar—what might happen if this popularity were misused by an unscrupulous man?

THE CATILINARIAN CONSPIRACY

In 63 BC the consul Marcus Tullius Cicero uncovered a plot to overthrow the government. In a speech delivered to the Senate, he named the leader, Catiline, and called for prompt action:

I wish, Conscript Fathers, to be merciful. I wish not to seem lax when the perils of the state are so great, but now I condemn myself for inaction and remissness. There is in Italy a camp of enemies of the Roman people, situated in the passes of Etruria, their number is increasing daily; but you behold the commander of that camp and the leader of the enemy inside the walls and even in the senate plotting daily from within the city the destruction of the state. But if, Catiline, I shall order you to be seized, to be executed, I shall have to fear, I suppose, not that all respectable people may say I acted too tardily, but that someone may say that I acted too cruelly!

Cicero, *In Catilinam*, 1.2.4–5

Caesar came under the scrutiny of the Senate when his recommendations on the punishment of the conspirators set him apart from many of his peers.

The greater number of those who have expressed their opinions before me have deplored the lot of the commonwealth in finished and noble phrases; they have dwelt upon the horrors of war, the wretched fate of the conquered, the rape of maidens and boys, children torn from their parents' arms, matrons subjected to the will of the victors, temples and homes pillaged, bloodshed and fire; in short, arms and corpses everywhere, gore and grief. But, O ye immortal gods! what was the purpose of such speeches? Was it to make you detest the conspiracy? You think that a man who has not been affected by a crime so monstrous and so cruel will be fired by a speech! Nay, not so; no mortal man thinks his own wrongs unimportant; many, indeed, are wont to resent them more than is right. But not all men, Fathers of the Senate, are allowed the same freedom of action. If the humble, who pass their lives in obscurity, commit any offence through anger, it is known to few; their fame and fortune are alike. But the actions of those who hold great power, and pass their lives in a lofty station, are known to all the world. So it comes to pass that in the highest position there is the least freedom of action. There neither partiality nor dislike is in place, and anger least of all; for what in others is called wrath, this in a ruler is termed insolence and cruelty.

For my own part, Fathers of the Senate, I consider no tortures sufficient for the crimes of these men; but most mortals remember only that which happens last, and in the case of godless men forget their guilt and descant upon the punishment they have received, if it is a little more severe than common . . .

For my own part, I fear nothing of that kind for Marcus Tullius or for our times, but in a great commonwealth there are many different natures. It is possible that at another time, when someone else is consul and is likewise in command of an army, some falsehood may be believed to be true. When the consul, with this precedent before him, shall draw the sword in obedience to the senate's decree, who shall limit or restrain him? . . .

Do I then recommend that the prisoners be allowed to depart and swell Catiline's forces? By no means! This, rather, is my advice: that their goods be confiscated and that they themselves be kept imprisoned in the strongest of the free towns; further, that no one hereafter shall refer their case to the senate or bring it before the people, under pain of being considered by the senate to have designs against the welfare of the state and common safety.

Sallust, *The War with Cataline*, 51

➲ **What does Caesar recommend?**

➲ **What arguments could be mounted against Caesar's suggestions?**

Caesar's advice was fair and was supported by some sections of the Senate. However, clear and rational thought in a time of crisis was not always welcomed. Some senators were convinced that Caesar was a part of the conspiracy; his speech further confirmed their suspicions. The people, on the other hand, rallied to his support. According to Plutarch, when Caesar returned to the Senate to clear himself of any complicity with the conspirators, the people feared for his safety and surrounded the Senate House, calling for his release.

↘ **What levels of support had Caesar mustered in the twenty years prior to his election as consul?**

↘ **Why did his actions during this time cause such great concern among senators?**

THE 'FIRST TRIUMVIRATE' AND THE CONSULSHIP

In 60 BC two major events happened: Caesar joined Pompey and Crassus in an alliance known as the 'First Triumvirate', and he was elected consul for 59.

THE 'FIRST TRIUMVIRATE'

↘ **Read each of the following sources to establish each partner's motives in joining the alliance. Refer also to chapters three and four. What can be said of the role of the Senate? Does there appear to be a dominant member at this formative stage? How long would you expect such a partnership to last?**

But to resume. It was in Caesar's consulship that there was formed between himself, Gnaeus Pompeius and Marcus Crassus the partnership in political power which proved so baleful to the city, to the world, and, subsequently at different periods to each of the triumvirs themselves. Pompey's motive in the adoption of this policy had been to secure through Caesar as consul the long delayed ratification of his acts in the provinces across the seas, to which, as I have already said, many still raised objections; Caesar agreed to it because he realized that in making this concession to the prestige of Pompey he would increase his own, and that by throwing on Pompey the odium for their joint control he would add to his own power; while Crassus hoped that by the influence of Pompey and the power of Caesar he might achieve a place of pre-eminence in the state which he had not been able to reach single-handed. Furthermore, a tie of marriage was cemented between Caesar and Pompey, in that Pompey now wedded Julia, Caesar's daughter.

In this consulship, Caesar, with Pompey's backing, passed a law authorizing a distribution to the plebs of the public domain in Campania. And so about twenty thousand citizens were established there, and its rights as a city were restored to Capua one hundred and fifty-two years after she had been reduced to a prefecture in the Second Punic War. Bibulus, Caesar's colleague, with the intent rather than the power of hindering Caesar's acts, confined himself to his house for the greater part of the year. By this conduct, whereby he hoped to increase his colleague's unpopularity, he only increased his power. At this time the Gallic provinces were assigned to Caesar for a period of five years.

Velleius Paterculus, *Roman History*, 2.44

✤ ✤ ✤

In the meantime Pompey, who had acquired great glory and power by his Mithridatic war, was asking the Senate to ratify numerous concessions that he had granted to kings, princes, and cities. Most Senators, however, moved by envy, made opposition, and especially Lucullus, who had held the command against Mithridates before Pompey, and who considered that the victory was his, since he had left the king for Pompey in a state of extreme weakness. Crassus co-operated with Lucullus in this matter.

Pompey was indignant and made friends with Caesar and promised under oath to support him for the consulship. The latter thereupon brought Crassus into friendly relations with Pompey. So these three most powerful men pooled their interests. This coalition the Roman writer Varro treated of in a book entitled *Tricaranus* (the three-headed monster).

Appian, *Civil Wars*, 2.2.9

✳ ✳ ✳

Caesar and Bibulus were elected Consuls, but the aristoctrats continued to restrict Caesar's influence by ensuring that when he and Bibulus had completed their term, neither should govern a province garrisoned by large forces; they would be sent off somewhere "to guard mountain-pastures and keep forests clear of brigands". Infuriated by this slight, Caesar exerted his charm on Gnaeus Pompey, who had quarrelled with the Senate because they were so slow in approving the steps that he had taken to defeat King Mithridates of Pontus. He also succeeded in conciliating Pompey and Marcus Crassus—they were still at odds after their failure to agree on matters of policy while sharing the consulship. Pompey, Caesar, and Crassus now formed a triple pact, jointly swearing to oppose all legislation of which any one of them might disapprove.

Suetonius, *Julius Caesar*, 19

✳ ✳ ✳

[Caesar] reconciled the men themselves, not because he was desirous that they should agree, but because he saw that they were most powerful. He understood well that without the aid of both, or at least of one, he could never come to any great power; and if he made a friend of either one of them alone, he would by that very fact have the other as his opponent and would meet with more failures through him than successes through the support of the other ... For he understood perfectly that he would master others at once through their friendship, and a little later master them through each other.

Cassius Dio, *Roman History*, 37.55–6

✳ ✳ ✳

ELECTION TO THE CONSULSHIP

Caesar's attempts to win the consulship were fraught with difficulties. He had been voted a triumph for his military successes in Spain (which had brought great wealth to Rome) but did not have the time to return with his army to Italy, prepare and celebrate his triumph and then enter Rome as a civilian to stand for the consulship. Caesar had requested permission to stand for the consulship *in absentia*—the perfect compromise from his point of view—but the Senate had not agreed. He was forced to forgo his triumph to put all his efforts and whatever finances he could raise into the consular elections.

The Senate had shown itself to be intractable on this occasion, but added insult to injury when it announced the consular provinces for 58 BC. So as not to favour any particular person, the Senate traditionally allocated provinces before the consular elections took place. Believing that Caesar would be elected consul, the Senate nominated 'the woods and pastures' as the province for the two consuls, the highest government officials. This, of course, was a means of denying Caesar an army! In due course, Caesar was elected consul, with Bibulus as his partner.

Caesar set to work as consul, honouring the promises to his colleagues. But he could not run the risk of failure. Caesar's plan was clear: his promises must be kept; his own future must be secured; his other legislative work must be carried out. He would not tolerate any individual or any institution standing in his way. Caesar's consulship was going to be an eventful one!

CAESAR'S CONSULSHIP—THE EARLY DAYS

In the following extract, Appian tells of Caesar's determination and tactics employed to carry out his work as consul.

Caesar, who was a master of dissimulation, made speeches in the Senate in the interest of concord to Bibulus, insinuating that any differences between them might have serious results for the state. As he was believed to be sincere, Bibulus was thrown off his guard, and while he was unprepared and unsuspecting Caesar secretly got a large band of soldiers in readiness and brought before the Senate measures for the relief of the poor by the distribution of the public land to them. The best part of this land especially round Capua, which was leased for the public benefit, he proposed to bestow upon those who were the fathers of at least three children, by which means he bought for himself the favour of a multitude of men, for twenty thousand, being those only who had three children each, came forward at once. As many senators opposed his motion he pretended to be indignant at their injustice, and rushed out of the Senate and did not convene it again for the remainder of the year, but harangued the people from the rostra. In a public assembly he asked Pompey and Crassus what they thought about his proposed laws. Both gave their approval, and the people came to the voting-place carrying concealed daggers.

The Senate (since no one called it together and it was not lawful for one consul to do so without the consent of the other) assembled at the house of Bibulus, but did nothing to counteract the force and preparation of Caesar. They planned, however, that Bibulus should oppose Caesar's laws, so that they should seem to be overcome by force rather than to suffer by their own negligence. Accordingly, Bibulus burst into the forum while Caesar was still speaking. Strife and tumult arose, blows were given, and those who had daggers broke the fasces and insignia of Bibulus and wounded some of the tribunes who stood around him ... Then Cato was summoned to the spot, and being a young man, forced his way to the midst of the crowd and began to make a speech, but was lifted up and carried out by Caesar's partisans. Then he went around secretly by another street and again mounted the rostra; but as he despaired of making a speech, since nobody would listen to him, he abused Caesar roundly until he was again lifted up and ejected by the Caesarians, and Caesar secured the enactment of his laws.

The plebeians swore to observe these laws for ever, and Caesar directed the Senate to do the same. Many of them, including Cato, refused, and Caesar proposed and the people enacted the death penalty to the recusants. Then they became alarmed and took the oath, including the tribunes, for it was no longer of any use to speak against it after the law had been confirmed by the others ... The people furnished him [Caesar] a guard to protect him against conspirators, and Bibulus abstained from public business altogether, as though he were a private citizen, and did not go out of his house for the remainder of his official term.

He [Caesar] brought forward new laws to win the favour of the multitude, and caused all of Pompey's acts to be ratified, as he had promised him. The knights, who held the middle place in rank between the Senate and the plebeians, and were extremely powerful in all ways by reason of their wealth, and of the farming of the provincial revenues which they contracted for, and who kept for this purpose multitudes of very trusty servants, had been asking the Senate for a long time to release them from a part of what they owed to the treasury. The Senate regularly shelved the question. As Caesar did not want anything of the Senate then, but was employing the people only, he released the publicans from the third part of their obligations. For this unexpected favour, which was far beyond their deserts, the knights extolled Caesar to the skies. Thus a more powerful body of defenders than that of the plebeians was added to Caesar's support through one political act. He gave spectacles and combats of wild beasts beyond his means, borrowing money on all sides, and surpassing all former exhibitions in lavish display and splendid gifts, in consequence of which he was appointed governor of both Cisalpine and Transalpine Gaul for five years, with the command of four legions.

Appian, *Civil Wars*, 2.2.10–14

What inferences in the extract suggest that Caesar's use of violence was premeditated?

Comment on Appian's opinion of the Senate's actions: 'They [the Senate] planned, however, that Bibulus should oppose Caesar's laws, so that they should seem to be overcome by force rather than to suffer by their own negligence.' Do you think the Senate at this early stage would have been so convinced of Caesar's superiority?

Assess Caesar's long-term objectives on the basis of his first consulship in 59 BC, as summarised in Table 5.2.

The following list of events demonstrates the extent to which Caesar would go to achieve his objectives, his disregard of the Roman constitution, and his desire to rid himself of opposition.

- When the Senate refused to agree to his agrarian bill he took it straight to the people through the plebeian assembly and did not use the Senate again.
- He set up in public a conversation with Pompey wherein Pompey declared his intention to use violence if any resistance to the agrarian bill arose. Pompey then filled the city with soldiers and held everyone down by force.
- The violent treatment of Bibulus at the assembly when he came to speak against the agrarian bill was a warning to others who might have considered speaking out. Tribunes were wounded and Cato was 'carried off'.
- After being driven from the forum, Bibulus refused to leave his own home, claiming that he was observing the heavens. When the assembly continued to meet to pass legislation, it was acting unconstitutionally.
- The agrarian bill was made law even though it had been vetoed by the tribunes.
- Senators did not go to Senate meetings for fear of Pompey's soldiers.
- A private citizen who called Pompey *privatus dictator* was bashed so severely by Pompey's bodyguard that he almost died.

Most of these acts occurred in January 59 or were a product of the events surrounding the introduction of the first agrarian law. They set the scene of Caesar's consulship: people learnt quickly that they were not free to oppose him in any way.

TABLE 5.2   CAESAR'S CONSULSHIP 59 BC (JANUARY–MAY)

ACTION	AGENT	PURPOSE	RESULT
Publication of records of senatorial procedures and public events (January)	Caesar	To allow the ordinary people insight into decisions made by senators	Caesar used this as political propaganda • **bill passed**
First agrarian bill: • land to be bought up at market value and redistributed to the poor, to ex-soldiers or to Pompey's veterans • commission of twenty to be established to administer all work • clause included requiring all senators to take an oath to observe the bill	Caesar to the Senate	To: • win popular support • fulfil one part of obligation to Pompey • provide additional support for himself from ex-soldiers	• Senate objected to bill so Caesar took it directly to the plebeian assembly (*concilium plebis*), which he continued to do from this time • Bibulus treated violently in the assembly and refused to take part in public business again • **bill passed**
Clodius adopted in plebeian family (March)	Caesar as *pontifex maximus* presiding over curiate assembly (*comitia curiata*) for law to go through	To allow Clodius to become tribune in 58 BC so that he could carry out his plans against Cicero	• **bill passed** • Clodius adopted
Asiatic tax-farmers received back ⅓ of what they paid for their contract (March)	Vatinius (tribune)	Fulfil obligation to Crassus	• Equestrians were 'won over' to Caesar • **bill passed**
Ptolemy Auletes recognised as King of Egypt (April)	Caesar	To provide stability to a reign which had been in jeopardy since 80 BC	• Caesar and Pompey and possibly Crassus were paid huge sums to agree to this • **bill passed**

ACTION	AGENT	PURPOSE	RESULT
Law on extortion which was directed against governors (April)	Caesar	Further attack on *optimates*	Equestrian support continued as they were not included in the law • **bill passed**
Pompey's 'eastern settlement' ratified (May)	Vatinius	To fulfil obligation to Pompey	Support of Pompey and his veteran soldiers ensured • **bill passed**
Second agrarian bill: *ager publicus* in Campania which was leased to wealthy tenants to be reclaimed and redistributed to the poor, particularly those with three or more children (May)	Caesar	To benefit the urban poor or the rural landless	Great animosity among the *optimates* towards the 'triumvirs' • **bill passed**
Caesar's provincial command amended to provide Caesar with two new provinces: 1) Cisalpine Gaul 2) Illyricum for five years. This was later further amended to include: 3) Transalpine Gaul (May)	Vatinius Pompey	To provide Caesar with a provincial command which offered an army command, a chance for military glory and financial remuneration	

CAESAR'S CONSULSHIP—THE SECOND HALF

The partnership was not well-liked by mid-59.

⟍Read the following extract and decide who it was that the population blamed most for what Cicero calls 'this present state of affairs'. How do you account for this?

Cicero in Rome to Atticus in Epirus:

. . . nothing was ever so scandalous, so disgraceful, and so objectionable to every rank and class of men young or old as this present state of affairs, far more so than I expected, nay, upon my soul it is more so than I could wish. The popular party have taught even the moderate men to hiss. Bibulus is exalted to the sky, though I don't know why. However, he is as much bepraised as though "His wise delay alone did save the State."

To my infinite sorrow, my pet, Pompey, has shattered his own reputation. They have no hold on anyone by affection: and I am afraid they may find it necessary to try the effect of fear. I do not quarrel with them on account of my friendship for him, though I refrain from showing approval not to stultify all my previous actions. I keep to the high-road. The popular feeling can be seen best in the theatre and at public exhibitions. For at the gladiatorial show both the leader and his associates were overwhelmed with hisses: at the games in honour of Apollo the actor Diphilus made an impertinent attack on Pompey, "By our misfortunes thou art Great," which was encored again and again. "A time will come when thou wilt rue that might" he declaimed amid the cheers of the whole audience, and so on with the rest. For indeed the verses do look as though they had been written for the occasion by an enemy of Pompey: "If neither law nor custom can constrain," etc., was received with a tremendous uproar and outcry. At Caesar's entry the applause dwindled away; but young Curio, who followed, was applauded as Pompey used to be when the constitution was still sound. Caesar was much annoyed: and it is said a letter flew post haste to Pompey at Capua.

They are annoyed with the knights who stood up and clapped Curio, and their hand is against every man's. They are threatening the Roscian law and even the corn law. Things are in a most disturbed condition. I used to think it would be best silently to ignore their doings, but I am afraid that will be impossible. The public cannot put up with things, and yet it looks as though they would have to put up with them. The whole people speak now with one voice, but the unanimity has no foundation but common hate . . .

Cicero, *Letters to Atticus*, 2.19

After his appointment to the province of Gaul for five years, Caesar spent the remainder of his consulship year making arrangements for his departure from Rome. These arrangements included protection of his legislation and his position while away in his province, and military preparations in readiness for his provincial command. He also had to leave trusted allies in key positions in the Roman government.

Using the following extracts, make a list of Caesar's 'arrangements'.

And it was decided that the consuls for the ensuing year should be Piso [Lucius Calpurnius Piso], the father-in-law of Caesar, and Gabinius [Aulus Gabinius, tribune of 67 BC], who was the most extravagant of Pompey's flatterers.

Plutarch, *Pompey*, 48.3

❋ ❋ ❋

As Caesar saw that he would be away from home a long time, and that envy would be greater in proportion to the greatness of the benefits conferred, he gave his daughter in marriage to Pompey, although she was betrothed to Caepio, because he feared that even a friend might become envious of his great success. He also promoted the boldest of his partisans to the principal offices for the ensuing year. He designated his friend Aulus Gabinius as consul, with Lucius Piso as his colleague, whose daughter, Calpurnia, Caesar married, although Cato cried out that the empire was become a mere matrimonial agency. For tribunes he chose Vatinius and Clodius Pulcher, although the latter had been suspected of an intrigue with the wife of Caesar himself during a religious ceremony of women. Caesar, however, did not bring him to trial owing to his popularity with the masses, but divorced his wife. Others prosecuted Clodius for impiety at the sacred rites, and Cicero was the counsel for the prosecution. When Caesar was called as a witness he refused to testify against Clodius, but even raised him to the tribuneship as a foil to Cicero, who was already decrying the triumvirate as tending toward monarchy. Thus Caesar turned a private grievance to useful account and benefited one enemy in order to revenge himself on another. It appears, however, that Clodius had previously requited Caesar by helping him to secure the governorship of Gaul.

Appian, *Civil Wars*, 2.14

(*Note*: Vatinius was *not* the tribune for 58 BC as mentioned here—he had held that office in 59 BC. It was Vatinius who had put forward the law to help Caesar secure 'the governorship of Gaul'.)

In the opening weeks of 58 BC, Caesar's two main opponents had been dealt with by Clodius: Cicero had been forced into exile and Cato had been offered a provincial command to Cyprus which, as a true patriot, he felt he could not refuse.

CAESAR THE PROCONSUL

In 59 BC, Caesar was voted four legions for his proconsulship. He was allowed to appoint his own legates (usually members of provincial governors' staff but used by Caesar as commanders of his legions) and was provided with an allowance appropriate to a force of this size. By 53 BC, Caesar increased his number of legions to eleven.

It is difficult to assess exactly what Caesar had in mind when Gaul was voted to him. Certainly he wanted military glory, which this province could readily provide, along with the opportunity to improve his financial standing. But to what extent he planned the extension of the Roman Empire to include all of Gaul can only be guessed at.

CAESAR IN GAUL

The area known as Gaul was far larger than the existing Roman provincial holdings. It was peopled by many tribal groups. One of these tribes, the *Aedui*, was a 'friend of Rome' and even though their land lay well to the north of Transalpine Gaul, the Roman governor was permitted to enter into this 'Free Gaul' territory in support of Rome's ally.

The *Helvetii*, a tribe to the north of Transalpine Gaul, requested permission of Caesar to move west through this Roman province as part of their migration to the Atlantic coast. Caesar refused to comply, provoking the *Helvetii* to threaten the *Aedui* and thereby provide Caesar with his cause for interference in affairs outside his province. The *Helvetii* were defeated in battle and sent back to their homeland.

The Germans were another migratory group. Led by Ariovistus, this group had allied itself to two powerful tribes, the *Suebi* and the *Sequani*, and was infiltrating Gaul at a great rate. Soon Ariovistus's demands for *Aedui* hostages and his encroachment onto the land of the *Sequani* came to be viewed as a potential threat to Rome. Caesar stepped in, defeating Ariovistus in battle. See Figure 5.1.

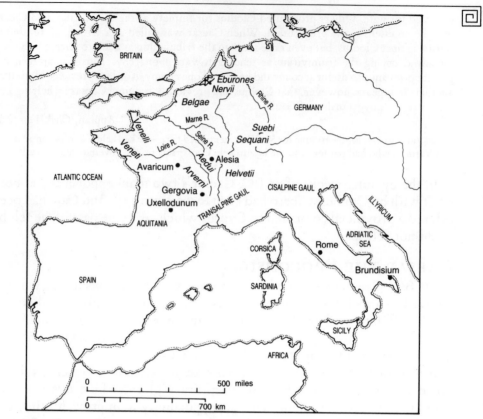

FIGURE 5.1   CAESAR'S PROVINCIAL DOMAIN

So ended Caesar's first proconsular year. His second proved to be even more successful.

After these events Caesar had every reason to suppose that Gaul was at peace again, for the Belgae were defeated, the Germans driven out, and the Seduni in the Alpine region conquered; therefore after the beginning of winter he had set out for Illyricum, desiring to visit the tribes there also and to become acquainted with the country.

Caesar, *Gallic War*, 3.7

✦   ✦   ✦

ROME DURING CAESAR'S ABSENCE

Rome in 58 BC was still under the shadow of the violence of the previous year. The legislation of 59 BC was largely secure, the new consuls had been hand-picked and opposition was dealt with effectively. To understand events in Rome during Caesar's absence, the roles of two key people must be examined.

Marcus Tullius Cicero was a member of the senatorial group known as the *optimates*. He had worked his way to prominence in Rome by following the Sullan *cursus honorum* even though he was a *novus homo*. He had made a name for himself through his advocacy in the Roman courts, but the pinnacle of his career came with his consulship in 63 BC when he was acclaimed the 'saviour of Rome' for bringing the Catilinarian conspirators to 'justice'. Until 59 BC, he had been a strong supporter of Pompey. Cicero's pre-eminence was recognised by Caesar, who tried to entice him to join the faction organised to force Caesar's legislation through the processes of government. Cicero often voiced his disgust at the methods employed by the triumvirs to impose their will upon the state. His great disappointment was Pompey. However, in 62 BC Cicero had made an arch enemy, P. Clodius Pulcher.

Publius Clodius Pulcher was a patrician who started his career as a member of staff for his brother-in-law, Lucullus, who commanded an army in Armenia. When Lucullus's army mutinied, Clodius did not stand at his side. For this he should have been prosecuted but he was not. Cicero accused Clodius of all manner of wickedness, and he may have been correct. But the act for which Clodius gained great notoriety in Rome was his involvement in sacrilege.

In 62 BC, the year of Caesar's praetorship, Clodius was accused of invading the precincts of a sacred religious ceremony open only to women. The observances, held at the home of Caesar, were considered to have been defiled. Rumours spread through Rome that Clodius, dressed in female garb, had gone to the house to continue his affair with Caesar's wife Pompeia. Caesar divorced his wife without even consulting her and Clodius was brought to trial by the distinguished senator, Cato. Further charges were added: incest with his sister and provoking mutiny against Lucullus. During the trial Clodius claimed he was not even in Rome, but Cicero testified that he had seen Clodius on the very evening in question. The jury, bribed by Crassus, acquitted Clodius. Three years later a plebeian family adopted Clodius, and he was elected to the tribuneship for the year 58 BC.

Very early in 58 BC while Caesar's army was preparing to leave Rome for Gaul, Clodius put before the people a bill calling for the passing of the death sentence on any person who had put to death a Roman citizen without proper trial. The law was to be made retrospective. This was aimed directly at Cicero, who, as consul in 63 BC, had ordered the death of five of the conspirators who had joined Catiline in his attempt to overthrow the government. Cicero left Rome immediately. Cato, who had accepted the governorship of Cyprus, was also out of the way.

Erich Gruen challenges the view of Plutarch and Cassius Dio that these acts were in accordance with the wishes of Pompey, Crassus and Caesar.

There was no reason why they should have insisted upon Cicero's elimination. Caesar had his five-year command in Gaul, Pompey's eastern *acta* had been confirmed, and his troops presumably resettled; nor did Crassus show any signs of discontent. If Cicero were to cause any trouble it would have been trouble for Clodius... As for Cicero, the same could be said for Cato. He had been handled in 59, in 58 he represented a stumbling-block for the tribune, not for the dynasts.

Gruen, *P. Clodius*, 126–7

STUDIES IN ANCIENT ROME

  Does the inaction and silence of the triumvirs indicate their approval of Clodius's bills?

  Would it not be equally beneficial to the triumvirs as to Clodius to have Cato and Cicero out of the way?

  To what extent would the potential realignment of Cicero and Pompey, whose veterans were close at hand, be a threat to Caesar in his absence?

  Was Clodius, who had become a true leader of the masses, now more of a danger to the triumvirs with Cicero and Cato gone?

Clodius continued to win favour with the people. He gave them free corn and controlled Rome with his armed gang, constantly intimidating Pompey.

In 57 BC, Clodius was out of public office and the consulship was no longer controlled by Caesar. A rival gang had been created, led by a new tribune, Milo, and Rome was often in open conflict. Cicero was recalled to Rome and the friendship between him and Pompey was renewed. The great grain shortage prompted a law to be passed in the Senate, giving Pompey complete control of the corn-supply for five years, and providing him with a fleet and an army.

By 56 BC it appeared that Caesar had been away from Rome for too long. Attacks upon him were being raised in the Senate. A new meeting between himself and his partners was called.

Therefore when he crossed the Alps and spent the winter in Luca, a great crowd of ordinary men and women gathered there in eager haste to see him, while two hundred men of senatorial rank, among whom were Pompey and Crassus, and a hundred and twenty fasces of proconsuls and praetors were seen at Caesar's door. Accordingly, he filled all the rest with hopes and loaded them with money, and sent them away; but between himself, Pompey, and Crassus the following compact was made: these two were to stand for the consulship, and Caesar was to assist their candidacy by sending large numbers of his soldiers home to vote for them; as soon as they were elected, they were to secure for themselves commands of provinces and armies, and to confirm Caesar's present provinces to him for another term of five years. When all this was publicly known, it gave displeasure to the chief men of the state, and Marcellinus rose in the assembly and asked Pompey and Crassus to their faces whether they were going to be candidates for the consulship. As the majority of the people bade them answer, Pompey did so first, and said that perhaps he would be a candidate, and perhaps he would not; but Crassus gave a more politic answer, for he said he would take whichever course he thought would be for the advantage of the common-wealth. And when Marcellinus persisted in his attack upon Pompey and was thought to be making a strong speech, Pompey remarked that Marcellinus was of all men most unjust, since he was not grateful to him for making him eloquent instead of speechless, and full to vomiting instead of famished.

However, though all the rest declined to be candidates for the consulship, Cato encouraged and persuaded Lucius Domitius not to desist, for the struggle with the tyrants, he said, was not for office, but for liberty. But Pompey and his partisans, seeing the firmness of Cato, and fearing lest, having all the senate with him, he should draw away and pervert the sound-minded among the people, would not suffer Domitius to go down into the forum, but sent armed men and slew the link-bearer who was leading his company, and put the rest to flight; Cato was the last to retire, after being wounded in the right arm while he was fighting to defend Domitius.

By such a path they made their way into the office they sought, nor even then did they behave more decently. But first of all, while the people were casting their votes for the election of Cato to the praetorship, Pompey dissolved the assembly, alleging an inauspicious omen, and after corrupting the tribes with money, they proclaimed Vatinius praetor instead of Cato. Then, by means of Trebonius, a tribune, they introduced laws which, according to the agreement, continued his provinces to Caesar for a second term of five years, gave Crassus Syria and the expedition against the Parthians, and to Pompey himself the whole of Africa, both Spains, and four legions; of these he lent two to Caesar, at his request, for the war in Gaul. But although Crassus went out to his province at the expiration of his consulship, Pompey opened his theatre and held gymnastic and musical contests at its dedication, and furnished combats of wild beasts in which five hundred lions were killed, and above all, an elephant fight, a most terrifying spectacle.

Plutarch, *Pompey*, 51–2

⟍**What did each of the triumvirs require from this new agreement?**

⟍**In what ways were the methods employed to achieve the objectives of the triumvirs reminiscent of 59 BC?**

⟍**Can any one triumvir be singled out at this time as having superior power?**

CAESAR RETURNS TO GAUL

During Caesar's absence, trouble was brewing in Gaul. When he returned to his province in 56 BC, revolts had to be put down in Aquitania and in the land of the *Veneti* and the *Venelli*. In 55 BC, attempts by German tribes to cross the Rhine and migrate into Gallic territory were stopped ruthlessly by Caesar—the Germans never tried to cross the Rhine border again. However, all of this was overshadowed by Caesar's decision to invade Britain.

The first Roman invasion of Britain in 55 BC was poorly prepared and achieved little. The second, in 54 BC, had greater military success but there were no long-term benefits; Caesar returned to Gaul claiming victory but did not return to Britain.

Caesar's arrival in Gaul and settlement in winter quarters signalled the opening of a new campaign. Having split his forces, Caesar had played into the hands of the Gallic leader Ambiorix (from the tribe of the *Eburones*) who attacked one of the camps and killed fifteen cohorts and two commanders. In the following year, the *Eburones* felt the full weight of Caesar's wrath— but the leader remained out of his grasp.

Caesar's work in Gaul, which he believed he had completed some years earlier, now had to begin again. By 52 BC, individual Gallic tribes had risen against the Romans and had been beaten by the highly skilled Roman army. In 52 BC, Vercingetorix, a leader from the *Arverni* tribe, unified the Gauls and became a real menace to Caesar.

Vercingetorix suggested to the Gauls that they burn their homelands to stop the Romans using them as a source of food. The policy was adopted with the exception of the city of Avaricum—a decision which proved to be a tragic mistake, as the Romans besieged the town and massacred the inhabitants. Reverses followed for Caesar, but his revenge came at the town of Alesia into which Vercingetorix had moved a large force. It was here that the Roman expertise in siege warfare was used most effectively. Caesar set about encircling the town with rows of trenches, a series facing Alesia and another facing outwards. Into these he placed various devices to reduce the possibility of anyone escaping and any reinforcements arriving. The Romans were encamped in the centre of these rows of trenches so that they could fight a force from both directions simultaneously if necessary. For days they did just that. Eventually the siege was successful and Vercinge-torix surrendered.

But the conquest of Gaul was not finished. To the south-west the last important stand took place at Uxellodunum in 51 BC. Once again siege works were constructed, but the people inside the town could easily maintain themselves indefinitely and their position on a hill made it impossible for the Romans to gain a victory. Caesar finally cut off the townspeople from their source of water, forcing them to surrender.

By the end of 51 BC, Caesar's conquest of Gaul was over. In nine years he had achieved a great deal. Suetonius tells us:

He reduced to the form of a province the whole of Gaul enclosed by the Pyrenees, the Alps, the Cevennes, the Rhine, and the Rhone—about 640,000 square miles—except for certain allied states which had given him useful support; and exacted an annual tribute of 400,000 gold pieces. Caesar was the first Roman to build a military bridge across the Rhine and cause the Germans on the farther bank heavy losses. He also invaded Britain, a hitherto unknown country, and defeated the natives, from whom he exacted a large sum of money as well as hostages for future good behaviour. He met with only three serious reverses: in Britain, when his fleet was all but destroyed by a gale; in Gaul, when one of his legions was routed at Gergovia among the Auvergne mountains; and on the German frontier, when his generals Titurius and Aurunculeius were ambushed and killed.

Suetonius, *Julius Caesar*, 25

The Forum of Caesar, Rome (Mansell Collection)

In Rome, Caesar's successes and name were publicised widely.

He began building a new Forum with the spoils taken in Gaul, and paid more than a million gold pieces for the site alone. Then he announced a gladiatorial show and a public banquet in memory of his daughter Julia—an unprecedented event; and, to create as much excitement among the commons as possible, had the banquet catered for partly by his own household, partly by the market contractors...He fixed the daily pay of the regular soldiers at double what it had been, for all time. Whenever the granaries were full he would make a lavish distribution to the army, without measuring the amount, and occasionally gave every man a Gallic slave.

Suetonius, Julius Caesar, 26

He had even freely lent money to influential people in Rome, such as Cicero; the fortune Caesar had made in Gaul was now going to work for him in Rome! Caesar's documentation of his experiences in Gaul had been sent in instalments to the Senate. Now he released all seven books of his *Gallic Wars* to tell the people of the hardships he and his men had suffered and the great rewards brought to Rome with the conquest of Gaul.

❧**Examine each of the methods of propaganda employed by Caesar at this time. What was he trying to achieve?**

❧**Which group/s of people was he trying to reach with each measure taken? How effective would you expect each to be?**

STEPS TO CIVIL WAR

While Caesar had been in his province, the situation in Rome had become very fragile. A number of events had occurred which eventually placed Caesar at loggerheads with Pompey and the Senate and brought about the civil war of 49 – 45 BC. Read Figure 5.2, then answer the following questions.

❧**Had Pompey and Caesar always maintained their equality in accordance with the agreement of 56 BC?**

❧**In 52 BC, Milo was condemned to death for his role in the murder of Clodius. Even though Milo was defended by Clodius's enemy Cicero, the verdict had to be approved by Pompey. Later that same year many of Clodius's supporters were also brought to trial and condemned. These trials were brought about by the strong anti–Caesar section of the Senate. Comment on the role played by the Senate and its leaders in this year and other years leading up to the outbreak of civil war. Could the Senate have played a more conciliatory role? What actions might the Senate have taken to avoid the forthcoming conflict?**

CAESAR CROSSES THE RUBICON

Caesar had repeatedly offered to make concessions, including, finally, the dismissal of all but two legions if the Senate would adhere to the law allowing him to stand for the consulship. As tribune, Curio had worked tirelessly for Caesar but he had only delayed the inevitable. In January of 49

Figure 5.2   Steps to Civil War

56 BC	54 BC	53 BC	52 BC	52 BC	51 BC	50 BC
RENEWAL OF AGREEMENT BETWEEN CAESAR, POMPEY AND CRASSUS AT LUCA	DEATH OF JULIA	DEATH OF CRASSUS AT CARRHAE	DEATH OF CLODIUS	POMPEY'S SOLE CONSULSHIP	CONSULSHIP OF MARCELLUS	TRIBUNESHIP OF CURIO

56 BC — RENEWAL OF AGREEMENT BETWEEN CAESAR, POMPEY AND CRASSUS AT LUCA

- All demands were met but the potential for conflict was already evident.
- Pompey and Caesar had to be seen to be equal.
- Crassus was fighting for equal status.
- The Senate was split in its support for the three.

54 BC — DEATH OF JULIA

- As Julia was the daughter of Caesar and the wife of Pompey, an important bond was broken.
- Caesar later made attempts to create a new marriage agreement to unite himself and Pompey, but decided against divorcing his wife Calpurnia, whose family was from the senatorial aristocracy.

53 BC — DEATH OF CRASSUS AT CARRHAE

- What had been a partnership of three was reduced to two.
- While Crassus lived, the chance of any kind of civil war was minimal—no one person was prepared to take on the other two.

52 BC — DEATH OF CLODIUS

- Clodius died at the hands of the gang of his rival, Milo. This was the culmination of twelve months of violence and upheaval in Rome, which resulted in the consular elections of 53 BC not being held.
- At Clodius's funeral the Senate House was burnt down. The Senate perceived the situation to be so desperate they elected Pompey as sole consul.

52 BC — POMPEY'S SOLE CONSULSHIP

- The Senate ordered Pompey to recruit troops to be kept outside city limits.
- In a meeting with Caesar, Pompey agreed to support the 'bill of the ten tribunes', to allow Caesar to stand for the consulship of 48 BC *in absentia* (while not in Rome). This would allow Caesar to remain in his province as proconsul until the end of 49 BC and thereby avoid a period of time in which he held no office and could be prosecuted for the illegal acts of his first consulship.
- Pompey proposed a law to change the method of appointment of provincial governors. Ordinarily, provincial governors came from the ranks of consuls and praetors who had held office in the year directly preceding their provincial command. Now they could be appointed only from the ranks of ex-consuls or ex-praetors who had not held a governorship. Hence Caesar could be replaced at any time.
- Pompey proposed a law that all candidates for election must appear in person. Caesar later given exemption.
- Pompey's proconsulship in Spain was extended five years. He was concurrently consul and proconsul.

51 BC — CONSULSHIP OF MARCELLUS

- Caesar's request for an extension on his proconsulship was rejected.
- Marcellus led the call for Caesar's immediate recall; this was vetoed.
- A decision was made in the Senate that discussions of Caesar's position in Gaul would take place in March 50 BC.
- It was perfectly clear in this year that the senatorial *optimates* would go to any lengths to break Caesar's power and bring him back to Rome, to the courts.

50 BC — TRIBUNESHIP OF CURIO

- Curio was originally an enemy of Caesar but became his supporter following Caesar's generous offer to pay off his enormous debts.
- He vetoed all attempts to appoint a successor to Caesar.
- It was proposed that both Pompey and Caesar should give up their armies and provinces. This was finally agreed to but never enacted.
- The Senate decided to send two legions to deal with trouble in Parthia—one legion from Pompey, one from Caesar. Pompey requested Caesar to send the legion he had lent him in 53 BC. Hence Caesar lost two legions.

BC, the Senate met again and voted that Caesar had to disband his army or be declared a public enemy. As the consular elections were held in the middle of the year, this would leave Caesar open to criminal proceedings while he did not hold an official position. Two of the new tribunes attempted to veto this bill, but a state of emergency was declared, thereby proclaiming Caesar an enemy unless he complied. The tribunes and any senatorial supporters of Caesar left Rome to join him.

Although the Rubicon was little more than a stream to the north of Italy, Caesar's decision to cross it was the signal for the outbreak of civil war. Why did Caesar make this decision? Read the following and make your own assessment of Caesar's motives.

Since the Senate refused to intervene on his behalf in a matter of such national importance, Caesar crossed into Cisalpine Gaul, where he held his regular assizes, and halted at Ravenna. He was resolved to invade Italy if force were used against the tribunes of the people who had vetoed the Senate's decree disbanding his army by a given date. Force was, in effect, used and the tribunes fled towards Cisalpine Gaul; which became Caesar's pretext for launching the Civil War. Additional motives are suspected, however: Pompey's comment was that, because Caesar had insufficient capital to carry out his grandiose schemes or give the people all that they had been encouraged to expect on his return, he chose to create an atmosphere of political confusion.

Another view is that he dreaded having to account for the irregularities of his first consulship, during which he had disregarded auspices and vetoes, and defied the Constitution; for Marcus Cato had often sworn to impeach him as soon as the legions were disbanded. Moreover, people said at the time, frankly enough, that should Caesar return from Gaul as a private citizen he would be tried in a court ringed around with armed men, as Titus Annius Milo had lately been at Pompey's orders. This sounds plausible enough, because Asinius Pollio records in his *History* that when Caesar, at the Battle of Pharsalus, saw his enemies forced to choose between massacre and flight, he said, in these very words: "They brought it on themselves. They would have condemned me to death regardless of all my victories—me, Gaius Caesar—had I not appealed to my army for help." It has also been suggested that constant exercise of power gave Caesar a love of it; and that, after weighing his enemies' strength against his own, he took this chance of fulfilling his youthful dreams by making a bid for the monarchy. Cicero seems to have come to a similar conclusion: in the third book of his *Essay on Duty*, he records that Caesar quoted the following lines from Euripides's *Phoenician Women* on several occasions:

Is crime consonant with nobility?
Then noblest is the crime of tyranny—
In all things else obey the laws of Heaven.

Accordingly, when news reached him that the tribunes' veto had been disallowed, and that they had fled the City, he at once sent a few battalions ahead with all secrecy, and disarmed suspicion by himself attending a theatrical performance, inspecting the plans of a school for gladiators which he proposed to build, and dining as usual among a crowd of guests. But at dusk he borrowed a pair of mules from a bakery near Headquarters, harnessed them to a gig, and set off quietly with a few of his staff. His lights went out, he lost his way, and the party wandered about aimlessly for some hours; but at dawn found a guide who led them on foot along narrow lanes, until they came to the right road. Caesar overtook his advanced guard at the river Rubicon, which formed the frontier between Gaul and Italy. Well aware how critical a decision confronted him, he turned to his staff, remarking: "We may still draw back but, once across that little bridge, we shall have to fight it out."

Suetonius, *Julius Caesar*, 30–31

When this was known Caesar addresses [*sic*] his troops. He relates all the wrongs that his enemies had ever done him, and complains that Pompeius had been led astray and corrupted by them through jealousy and a desire to detract from his credit, though he had himself always supported and aided his honour and dignity. He complains that a new precedent had been introduced into the state whereby the right of tribunicial intervention, which in earlier years had been restored by arms, was now being branded with ignominy and crushed by arms ... He exhorts them to defend from his enemies the reputation and dignity of the commander under whose guidance they have administered the state with unfailing good fortune for nine years, fought many successful battles, and pacified the whole of Gaul and Germany. Thereupon the men of the Thirteenth Legion, which was present ... exclaim that they are ready to repel the wrongs of their commander and of the tribunes.

Caesar, *Civil Wars*, 1.7

❋ ❋ ❋

Pompey never had this notion and least of all in the present cause. Absolute power is what he and Caesar have sought; their aim has not been to secure the happiness and honour of the community. Pompey has not abandoned Rome, because it was impossible to defend, nor Italy on forced compulsion; but it was his idea from the first to plunge the world into war, to stir up barbarous princes, to bring savage tribes into Italy under arms, and to gather a huge army. A sort of Sulla's reign has long been his object, and is the desire of many of his companions. Or do you think that no agreement, no compromise between him and Caesar was possible? Why, it is possible to-day: but neither of them looks to our happiness. Both want to be kings.

Cicero, *Atticus*, 8.11

❋ ❋ ❋

CIVIL WAR

The civil war lasted for three and a half years and was fought throughout the Roman Empire. As you read this brief outline of the major events follow the war on Figure 5.3.

49 BC

Pompey and his supporters sailed to the East, leaving Caesar in Italy. Caesar faced a hostile Senate but still made sound arrangements for the security of Italy. Before he left for Spain, Caesar had set up strong defensive points on both land and sea. He left Rome in April and sailed directly for Massilia. In Spain, his army was successful against some of the strongest Pompeian forces. He returned to Rome in September after detouring to Placentia in Cisalpine Gaul to put down a mutiny of his own soldiers. In other areas of the Empire, however, he did not achieve such success: in Africa, Curio and his troops were killed. Caesar remained in Rome for eleven days and was elected consul for 48 BC (having previously been appointed dictator) and worked on producing a solution to the debt problem.

48 BC

Caesar left Italy from Brundisium and sailed to the East, landing in Epirus. From here two major battles were fought: the first in April at Dyrrachium in which Pompey was successful and the second at Pharsalus where, according to Caesar, Pompey faced a great deal of internal squabbling. The Pompeian forces at Pharsalus outnumbered the Caesarian, but through tight

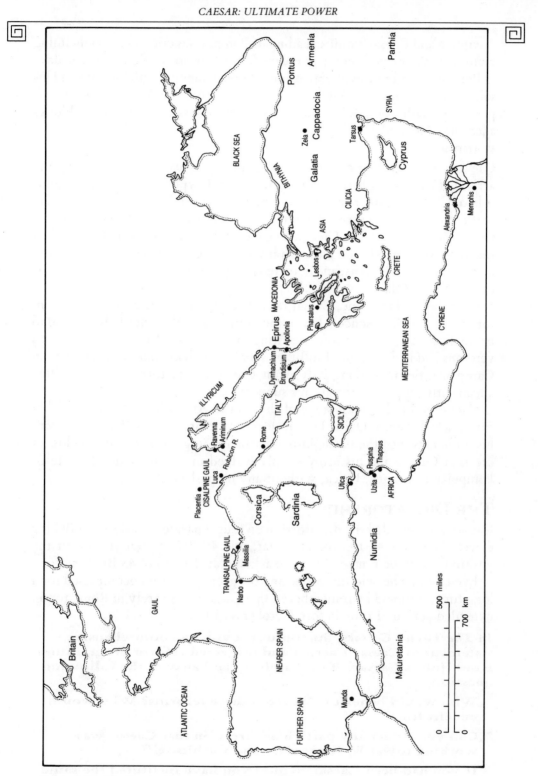

FIGURE 5.3   THE ROMAN EMPIRE DURING CAESAR'S TIME

discipline and Caesar's quick reading of Pompey's tactics an overwhelming victory was achieved. Pompey escaped, but was not to fight another day.

Pompey sailed to Egypt via Lesbos where he met up with his wife and his son, Sextus. Caesar followed and on his arrival in Alexandria he was presented with Pompey's head. Before long Caesar found himself block-aded into Alexandria.

47 AND 46 BC

Caesar met the young co-regent of Egypt, Cleopatra, while awaiting the arrival of a relieving force. During his stay in Egypt he confirmed the joint rule of Cleopatra and her brother-husband, but the latter was killed in the battle to rescue Caesar and his men. Alexandria finally surrendered to Caesar, and that summer Cleopatra gave birth to Caesar's son. Caesar then returned to Rome via the East. On his way he settled Syria and Tarsus and many other trouble spots, and defeated King Pharnaces of the Bosphorous at the Battle of Zela.

On his arrival in Rome, Caesar became dictator, an office granted to him for one year in his absence. He was met with chaos. Violence in Rome had to be quelled with armed force, resulting in great loss of life. Also, Caesar's veterans had had enough of military service and had gone on a rampage in Campania. Before leaving Italy again, Caesar had restored peace and filled vacant official positions with his supporters.

Caesar entered the last stage of this war in Africa. He was successful at Ruspina and again at Uzita, but the decisive victory came at Thapsus, where his soldiers turned the battle into a massacre. So great had been the loss of life that Caesar and his army simply walked in and took the last site of Pompeian resistance, Utica, without any bloodshed.

THE DICTATORSHIP

Caesar was awarded the dictatorship on four separate occasions: 49 BC for eleven days; late 48 BC for one year; mid 46 BC for ten years (but the position had to be renewed each year); and at the end of 45 BC for life.

Even though he held this office and the great power it encompassed for a long time, it should be remembered that Caesar was rarely in Rome for an extended period of time before October 45 BC.

In *The Twelve Caesars*, Suetonius provides a comprehensive statement of Caesar's actual and projected reform programmes. Read 'Julius Caesar' 40–44 carefully and answer the following questions.

Who would benefit most from these reforms? Who would benefit least?

Can you detect any particular direction that Caesar was working towards, for society and for himself?

If you had been Caesar, would you have instituted the same kind of reform package?

THE ASSASSINATION OF CAESAR

In 44 BC, Caesar was making preparations for another campaign, this time to settle the Parthian situation. He was dictator for life and had already nominated the officials who were to maintain the reins of government, both in Rome and the provinces, for the next two years. Caesar, however, was never to leave the shores of Italy again.

On 15 March, a date known to us as the Ides of March, he was brutally assassinated. The conspiracy was widespread, with some sixty people involved. Some of these had fought with Pompey during the civil war but had been accepted back into the governing circles of Rome; others had fought alongside Caesar. Most notable among their ranks were Marcus Brutus, Gaius Cassius, Decimus Brutus and Gaius Trebonius—men who held prominent positions in Rome.

Why would these people involve themselves in such an act of treachery? Read the following extracts from secondary sources to begin your consideration.

A perpetual dictator was frightful enough. It was strange that Caesar, for all his insight, did not trouble to discern that a perpetual dictator ruling by remote control was so frightful that he could not be endured. And as the period of remote control drew nearer, the plotting began and intensified.

Grant, *Julius Caesar*, 221

❋ ❋ ❋

But the leaders of the conspiracy were idealists, men who not only resented, as a personal thing, the imperial arrogance of Caesar, but who recognised that, with Caesar alive, autocracy would take a more and more stifling grip on Rome. They believed, in the nobility of their simple hearts, that republicanism could still be saved.

Balsdon, *Julius Caesar and Rome*, 167

❋ ❋ ❋

Although he had followers of lower rank, who served him with limitless admiration, and could count on his veterans, among his peers he found no allies who saw in him more than the furtherer of their own selfish ambitions, none who, convinced of the necessity of his political work, became willing pillars of his rule. Here we come to a point that should be carefully noted. Whereas Caesar during his earlier career and until well into the civil war explained and justified his policy by word and pen, he kept silent about his ultimate plans, so that these can only be inferred from actions and occasional utterances more or less well attested. Circumstances had so ordained that an answer was demanded of him to the question of how he conceived the future of the *res publica*, and this question in fact drove him into a corner, since it was posed with a particular expectation which he did not intend to fulfil. He wished to resolve the dilemma by leaving for the war against the Parthians. But already too much had happened which revealed his intentions. He had risen too high always to keep his self-control before the many signs of opposition. One also forms the impression that he eventually lost his patience and would not wait for the new order to grow to maturity.

Gelzer, *Caesar: Politician and Statesman*, 332

Caesar had certainly made staunch enemies. Several factors contributed to this:

- He had enlarged the Senate from six hundred to nine hundred and had brought into this institution many people from outside Rome.
- He had increased the numbers of praetors from six to sixteen, aediles from four to six, and quaestors from twenty to forty. This may appear to provide greater opportunities for those wishing to pursue a political career, but Caesar had been awarded the right to 'recommend' people to these positions. Hence he surrounded himself with supporters who owed their political existence to himself. And indeed many were promoted in preference to other more senior or supposedly more deserving nobles.
- All senators had to swear an oath of allegiance to Caesar personally.
- Coins minted for circulation in Rome had Caesar's head on them. This had broken with the tradition to commemorate only the dead in this manner.
- There were widespread rumours in Rome that Caesar intended to have himself declared king, an office viewed with total disgust since the abolition of the kingship centuries earlier.
- Caesar openly treated the ancient constitutional institutions with contempt.

The conspirators believed they were right and that they were acting for the good of Rome and the Empire. They believed that their action would not be viewed as a crime but as a means of saving the Republic.

What do you think? Had Caesar misused his power, or was he merely a realist who knew that Rome could only maintain the position it held by moving in a different direction?

CONCLUSION

The career of Gaius Julius Caesar was the turning point for Rome. The methods he employed to achieve his position of power, the skills he showed as a military leader, and the use he made of the power he finally wielded had completely changed the face of Rome.

In the last paragraph of *Caesar: Politician and Statesman*, Gelzer poses a rationale to explain Caesar to us. Read it and then make your own assessment of Caesar, the man and his power.

His ambition soared so high because he was conscious of his power to become the master of the Empire. He had never believed in the ideologies of the optimates and populares which he had encountered on his entry into political life. A born enemy of the optimates, he regarded demagogy as no more than the means to an end. On his way to power he did not meet men who could impress him. He only saw selfishness and envy, and eventually emerged from a life of continuous and bitter conflict as a cynic who assessed all relationships only according to their political value and, judging the others by himself, could not believe that their *res publica* could still be to them something other than 'a mere name without body and form'. This does not lessen the guilt of his murderers, but we can at least understand that things happened as they did.

LIST OF REFERENCES

ANCIENT SOURCES

Appian, *Appian's Roman History, Vol. 3, The Civil Wars*, Loeb Classical Library, 1972

Caesar, *The Civil Wars*, Loeb Classical Library, 1966

—— *The Gallic War*, Loeb Classical Library, 1979

Cicero, 'In Catilinam' in *Cicero in Twenty-eight Volumes*, Loeb Classical Library, 1968

—— *Letters to Atticus*, Loeb Classical Library, 1961

Cassius Dio, *Dio's Roman History*, Vol. 3, Loeb Classical Library, 1954

Plutarch, 'Caesar' and 'Pompey' in *Plutarch's Lives*, Vol. 5, Loeb Classical Library, 1961

Sallust, 'The War with Catiline' in *Sallust* Loeb Classical Library, 1971

Suetonius, 'Julius Caesar' in *The Twelve Caesars*, Penguin, 1979

Velleius Paterculus, *Compendium of Roman History*, Loeb Classical Library, 1967

SECONDARY SOURCES

Balsdon, J. P. V. D., *Julius Caesar and Rome*, English Universities Press Ltd, London, 1967

Gelzer, M., *Caesar: Politician and Statesman*, Basil Blackwell, Oxford, 1969

Grant, M., *Julius Caesar*, Chancellor Press, London, 1969

Gruen, E., 'P. Clodius, Instrument or Independent Agent?', *Phoenix*, No. 20, 1966

Sabben-Clare, J., *Caesar and Roman Politics 60–50 BC*, Oxford University Press, Great Britain, 1971

BIBLIOGRAPHY

SECONDARY SOURCES

Syme, R., *The Roman Revolution*, Oxford University Press, New York, 1939

CHAPTER SIX

THE TRIUMVIRATE STUDIES IN POWER

KATHRYN E. WELCH

44 BC	Mar	Caesar assassinated; compromise between senatorial Caesarians and conservatives
	Apr	Sextus Pompey in Spain; Octavian in Italy; Brutus and Cassius leave Rome
	May	Octavian quarrels with Antony
	June	Antony and Dolabella plan to take Cisalpine Gaul and Syria
	July	Octavian builds up support among the veterans; games held in Caesar's honour; veterans reconcile Antony and Octavian
	Aug	Brutus gathers a fleet; Brutus and Cassius leave Italy
	Sept	Antony uses armed force in the Senate; First Philippic given
	Oct	Antony attacks Brutus and Cassius in debate; troops mutiny when met by Antony in Brundisium
	Nov	Balbus, Oppius and Octavian court Cicero; Antony departs for Cisalpine Gaul; Octavian taked over two legions
	Dec	Second Philippic circulated as a pamphlet
43	Jan	Decimus under siege in Cisalpine Gaul; negotiations with Antony fail; Octavian's activities legalised by the Senate; Dolabella murders Trebonius in Syria
	Feb	Hirtius and Pansa gather troops to relieve Decimus at Mutina; Brutus seizes Macedonia
	Mar	Sextus Pompey makes agreement with the Senate at Massilia
	Apr	Antony defeated at Forum Gallorum and Mutina; Hirtius and Pansa killed
	May–July	Lepidus and Antony come to an agreement; Decimus murdered; Cassius defeats Dolabella in Syria

	Aug–Sept	Octavian gains consulship after marching on Rome; *Lex Pedia* condemns the assassins and Sextus Pompey
	Oct–Dec	Antony and Lepidus join up with Octavian; formation of the triumvirate (*triumviri rei publicae constituendae*); proscriptions; Cicero killed; Brutus and Cassius in the East; Sextus in Sicily
42		Julius Caesar deified; Battle of Philippi; Cassius and Brutus defeated. Republican forces regroup in Sicily
41		Antony remains in the East; he meets Cleopatra at Cilicia. Octavian in Italy; Perusine War; republicans control the sea
40		L. Antonius and Fulvia defeated at Perusia. Peace of Brundisium; marriage of Antony and Octavia
39		Treaty of Puteoli; Octavian marries Livia
38		Sardinia handed over to Octavian; Antony loses in Parthia
37		Agrippa moves against Sextus; Treaty of Tarentum
36		Battle of Naulochus; Lepidus defeated; Octavian awarded *tribunician sacrosanctity*; Antony suffers heavy losses in Parthia
35		Sextus killed in Asia; Octavian campaigns in Illyria
34		Antony occupies Armenia; holds triumph in Egypt; donations of Alexandria; Octavian defeats Dalmatians and Illyrians
33		Antony's third expedition to Armenia; Octavian undertakes building programme in Rome
32		Octavian sits between the consuls; seizure and reading of Antony's will; oath of allegiance taken by Italians
31		Battle of Actium
30		Deaths of Antony and Cleopatra

Julius Caesar's dictatorship had a profound effect on the Roman constitution. Free elections had last been held in 49 BC, which meant that all Roman magistrates, army commanders and officials since that time had been Caesar's approved candidates.

Although competition for Caesar's favour was strong, and his patronage opened the field to more 'new men', some *nobiles* managed to use him as a means of achieving high office. Two of the most prominent were M. Antonius (Antony) and M. Aemilius Lepidus. Both came from famous Roman families, but had been reared in uneasy circumstances. Antony's father had a disastrous command in the pirate war and had died a bankrupt. His step-father had been executed for involvement in the Catilinarian conspiracy. Lepidus's father had died in exile after being defeated by Pompey in 78 BC. They survived these setbacks to their political careers through good connections and, in Antony's case especially, useful service under Caesar in Gaul. In 49, Lepidus was urban praetor and Antony tribune, so they were of great use to Caesar when they sided with him at the outbreak of civil war. He rewarded them with office: Antony was *magister equitum* in 47; Lepidus was consul in 46, and *magister equitum* in 45 and 44. They continued to hold command in Caesar's army: Antony commanded the right wing at Pharsalus, and Lepidus was Governor of Spain in 48.

Antony had some problems in dealing with Caesar and was dropped from favour in 47 (due to incompetence) until his consulship in 44. There are some doubts about Antony's loyalty to Caesar in 44. He was invited by Gaius Trebonius to join the conspiracy against Caesar; although he was not involved, he failed to inform Caesar of the danger to his life. In fact, through 46 and 45, he and Lepidus were rivals for Caesar's friendship. Even among the earliest of Caesar's supporters, there were deep-seated difficulties caused by jealousy and resentment of Caesar and each other.

This ill-feeling, however, was felt more keenly by the ex-republicans, even those who had been honoured by Caesar after they changed sides. Both Marcus Junius Brutus and Gaius Cassius Longinus had fought on Pompey's side at Pharsalus, but they were among the first to join Caesar after this battle. Possibly through Brutus's mother (and Cassius' mother-in-law) Servilia, or perhaps through their Caesarean brothers-in-law, Lepidus and P. Servilius Isauricus, they were quickly given proconsulships. Both were named praetors for 44. Table 6.1 shows the relationships between these prominent figures.

Brutus and Cassius were perceived by their contemporaries as men of immense talent, but difficult to deal with. Cicero, who had also deserted the republican cause directly after the Battle of Pharsalus, influenced both towards republican ideals. He himself was 'forgiven' by Caesar, but never reconciled to the destruction of the republican system. His philosophical writings of the forties, many of which were dedicated to Brutus, are full of allusions to Brutus's legendary ancestor, the slayer of the last king of Rome, L. Junius Brutus. Cicero saw the future resting on Brutus and other similar *nobiles*, who could form a new *optimate* party.

While these men had different ideas on what the Republic was, they had similar backgrounds and values and understood the honour of the consulship. Brutus's father was killed in the same uprising as Lepidus's father, and both hated Pompey with a passion. It should not be surprising that for months after Caesar's assassination (brought about under the leadership of Brutus and Cassius) the 'staunch' followers of Caesar did not know whether to make a deal with them or the outsider, Octavian, who was Caesar's heir.

Cicero describes Antony's methods of government to his friend Atticus. (7 May 49)

Mind you don't let Antony's lions frighten you. He is really the most agreeable fellow. What do you think of the following act of statesmanship? He summoned by letter the Boards of Ten and Four from the towns. They arrived at his country house early in the morning. First, he slept till 9 o'clock. Then, being informed that the bodies from Naples and

TABLE 6.1   SERVILIA'S FAMILY

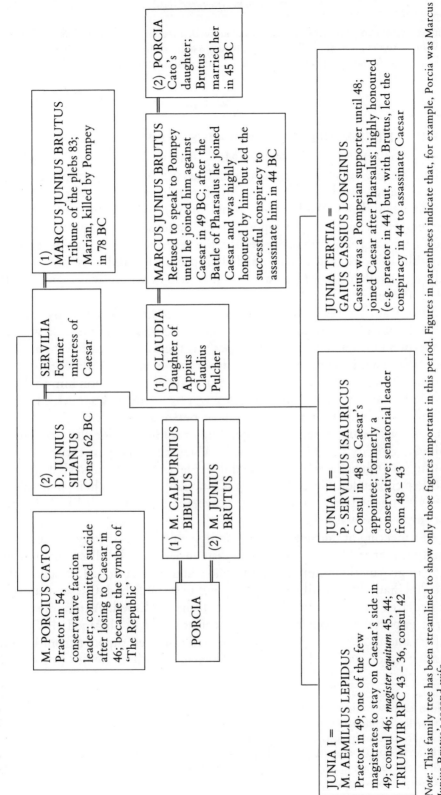

M. PORCIUS CATO
Praetor in 54, conservative faction leader; committed suicide after losing to Caesar in 46; became the symbol of 'The Republic'

(2) D. JUNIUS SILANUS Consul 62 BC

SERVILIA Former mistress of Caesar

(1) MARCUS JUNIUS BRUTUS Tribune of the plebs 83; Marian, killed by Pompey in 78 BC

PORCIA

(1) M. CALPURNIUS BIBULUS

(2) M. JUNIUS BRUTUS

(1) CLAUDIA Daughter of Appius Claudius Pulcher

MARCUS JUNIUS BRUTUS Refused to speak to Pompey until he joined him against Caesar in 49 BC; after the Battle of Pharsalus he joined Caesar and was highly honoured by him but led the successful conspiracy to assassinate him in 44 BC

(2) PORCIA Cato's daughter; Brutus married her in 45 BC

**JUNIA I =
M. AEMILIUS LEPIDUS**
Praetor in 49; one of the few magistrates to stay on Caesar's side in 49; consul 46; *magister equitum* 45, 44; TRIUMVIR RPC 43 – 36, consul 42

**JUNIA II =
P. SERVILIUS ISAURICUS**
Consul in 48 as Caesar's appointee; formerly a conservative; senatorial leader from 48 – 43

**JUNIA TERTIA =
GAIUS CASSIUS LONGINUS**
Cassius was a Pompeian supporter until 48; joined Caesar after Pharsalus; highly honoured (e.g. praetor in 44) but, with Brutus, led the conspiracy in 44 to assassinate Caesar

Note: This family tree has been streamlined to show only those figures important in this period. Figures in parentheses indicate that, for example, Porcia was Marcus Junius Brutus's second wife.

Cumae (with whom Caesar is annoyed) had arrived, he told them to come back next day, as he wanted to take a bath . . . This was yesterday's achievement. Today he has arranged to cross over to Aenaria to promise the exiles their recall. But enough of all this, and to our own concerns!

Cicero, Atticus, 10.13.1

❊   ❊   ❊

THE AFTERMATH OF CAESAR'S DEATH

Because he was consul in 44 BC, Mark Antony became Rome's political leader when Caesar was assassinated. The men who had conspired against Caesar proclaimed the restoration of traditional Roman government, which meant they looked to the consul, Antony, to be the head of state. This immediately placed him in a position of immense power, poised between the Caesarean following in the Senate, the veteran soldiers outside it and the 'republican' conspirators who needed his protection and assistance. Further help was available from his two brothers, one of whom was a praetor, the other a tribune.

After Caesar's assassination, Antony ensured his own safety by escaping from the Senate House disguised as a slave. He then had to decide whether to throw in his lot with the 'liberators' (as the assassins called themselves) and work with them to re-establish republican government, or lead Caesar's veterans against these men, as the army called upon him to do. He decided to play for time. His leadership was by no means guaranteed; he had fallen into it by luck, not by election or personal reputation. Lepidus was *magister equitum* and as such had command of soldiers inside the city. He had enjoyed a highly favoured place under Caesar for the past three years. C. Cornelius Dolabella, who became the second consul on Caesar's death, was another contender. Gaius Octavius (Octavian), Caesar's heir, had already been summoned from Greece by powerful men who disliked Antony. A compromise was necessary.

At a meeting of the Senate in the Temple of Tellus, Antony reminded the senators that if Caesar's acts were dismantled, nearly all of them would have to give up their 'appointments' and stand for election. The Senate then decided that while the liberators were not to be punished, Caesar was not to be declared a tyrant, nor were his acts to be abolished. Antony had taken three important actions before this meeting. He had obtained all Caesar's papers and money from Calpurnia; he had obtained support from Lepidus and the legion stationed in Rome; and he had consulted the 'leading men' of the state.

While Antony could hardly have been better placed to dominate Roman politics, there were still irreconcilable elements within the power bases. The army could not be brought to compromise with the assassins. Appian's account makes clear the problems Antony faced with the troops. Competition from Lepidus was already apparent. These two men did not wish to offend Caesar's supporters in the crowd, but were not ready to commit themselves to a policy of revenge.

While affairs [in the Senate meeting] were proceeding thus, Antony and Lepidus went out of the Senate, having been called for by a crowd that had been assembling for some time . . . To those who called for peace Antony said, "That is what we are striving for, that it may come and be permanent, but it is hard to get security for it when so many oaths and solemnities were of no avail in the case of Caesar." Then, turning to those who demanded vengeance, he praised them as more observant of the obligations of oaths and religion, and added, "I myself would join you and would be the first to call for vengeance if I were not the consul, who must care for what is said to be for the common good rather than for what is just. So these people who are inside tell us. So Caesar himself perhaps thought when, for the good of the country, he spared those citizens whom he captured in war, and was slain by them."

When Antony had . . . worked upon both parties in turn, those who wanted to have vengeance on the murderers asked Lepidus to [perform] it . . . when he had taken his place on the rostra he groaned and wept in plain sight for some time. Then recovering himself, he said " . . . Caesar, that truly sacred and revered man, has gone from us, but we hesitate to deprive the state of those who still remain. Our senators . . . are considering these matters and this is the opinion of the majority." They shouted again, "Avenge him yourself." "I should like to," he replied, "and my oath permits me to do it even alone, but it is not fitting that you and I alone should wish it or alone refuse it."

Appian, Civil Wars, 2.130–2

❊   ❊   ❊

THE DOUBTFUL TRUCE

Antony carefully staged Caesar's funeral in order to show the veterans and plebs of Rome that the compromise with the liberators did not mean he had forgotten his duty to Caesar. However, as it led to riots and arson, this action lost him considerable popularity with the opposing faction in the Senate who supported the assassins. The Senate at this time was a mixture of supporters of Caesar and those who resented the loss of republican liberty. Such was the confusion of the period that some men held both views: they had stood by Caesar, for example, but feared the violence unleashed at the funeral by Antony's actions.

Antony was given the opportunity to regain popularity with the conservative supporters of the assassins and the moderate group in the Senate by adopting two policies. He first proposed to recall Sextus Pompey, the son of Pompey the Great, who was rebuilding his army in Spain after his brother's defeat in the previous year. The second was to abolish the title of dictator. Antony then won approval from the most conservative senators by attacking and scattering the crowds intent on setting up an altar to Caesar. He was granted a bodyguard of 6 000 men who were allowed inside the city boundary. However, this time the veteran soldiers and civilians were outraged that a 'Caesarean' general could insult Caesar and attack the populace with an army. Balancing the need for senatorial approval and a personal army with the maintenance of his popularity among the soldiers was too difficult: he lost the trust of all groups.

OCTAVIAN'S ARRIVAL

Following the assassination, messengers quickly went to Octavian, to

TABLE 6.2 OCTAVIAN'S FAMILY

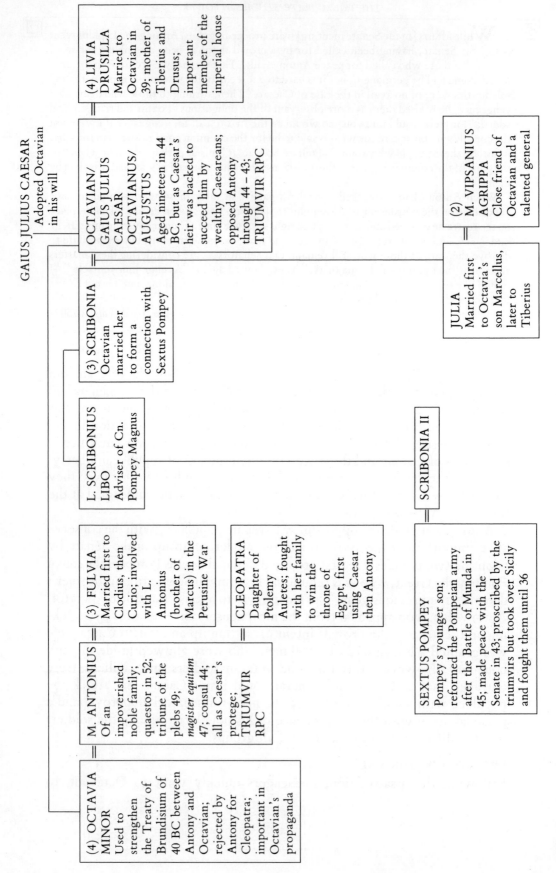

Note: This family tree has been streamlined to show only those figures important in this period. Figures in parentheses indicate that, for example, Fulvia was Antony's third wife, Octavia his fourth.

summon him away from his studies in Greece. Immediately on his arrival, he gained promises of support from L. Cornelius Balbus and C. Oppius, formerly Caesar's most trusted administrators, for whatever he might choose to do about his inheritance. They had the experience and the money necessary to stand behind the nineteen-year-old Octavian. On arriving in Rome, Octavian called on Antony, who was trying to balance the veteran soldiers against the various factions within the Senate. The two men immediately quarrelled. In view of Octavian's backing and potential support, Antony should have been more careful. Possibly, though, he believed he should have received more respect from such a very young man.

By the beginning of June, Antony's greatest worry was not Octavian, but the other consul, Dolabella. He and Antony had been rivals in politics before, and many of the conservatives looked upon Dolabella as an alternative leader to Antony in the return to a republican system. They would have preferred Brutus and Cassius, but these and other assassins had already been forced to leave Rome and dared not return. Dolabella was known as an unstable character, and Antony knew he could be bribed to desert the conservatives. However a Senate meeting at which he hoped to grant Syria to Dolabella and Cisalpine Gaul to himself was boycotted, so he then called a popular assembly and, in the presence of troops, had the necessary laws passed. This was a severe blow to the conservative factions, for two assassins were to be removed from these provinces by this law: Gaius Trebonius had already left for Syria and Decimus Brutus (a relative of Marcus Brutus) was in control of Cisalpine Gaul.

However, Antony could not stop his growing unpopularity with the moderate Caesarians and the veterans, who were being courted and won by Octavian's charming smile and the political possibilities he represented. Octavian had accepted the testamentary adoption offered in Caesar's will and began to call himself Caesar. The propaganda value of this name was immense: the veterans and plebs of Rome had already started to worship it. Octavian could count also on his family connections and friends to give him access to all the important figures of Roman politics. See Table 6.2

Antony's lack of popularity was due partly to the use he made of Caesar's notes. Antony interpreted the Senate's decision to let Caesar's acts stand to mean his proposed acts as well as those already passed. The proposed acts were all carefully written down in the notebooks, which Antony now possessed. The Senate soon realised that the notes were subject to Antony's interpretation. Antony's seizure of the money meant for Caesar's Parthian campaign further diminished his popularity, as did the tactlessness with which he went about instituting his policies.

An opposition 'Caesarean' party began to form around Octavian. Balbus and the consul-designate for 43, Aulus Hirtius, set about bringing him to the notice of their friends who had gathered at the Bay of Naples for the summer. They especially needed men of Cicero's status, and at one stage were calling on him daily. In these months, the idea that Caesar's heir could be used against Caesar's chosen consuls began to grow in Cicero's mind, perhaps planted there by these subtle friends of Octavian.

Cicero expresses to Atticus his dissatisfaction with the way in which the assassination was carried out, his fears of Antony and mistrust of Octavian. Assiduous attention from Octavian brought about a change in his attitude later in the year. (22 April 44)

Atticus, I fear the Ides of March have brought us nothing except joy and a satisfaction for our hatred and grief. The things I hear from Rome! And the things I see here! " 'Twas a fine deed, but half done"... Well, here is Antony posting up (in return for a massive bribe) a law allegedly carried by the Dictator in the Assembly under which the Sicilians become Roman citizens, a thing never mentioned in his lifetime!... Octavius is with me here— most respectful and friendly. His followers call him Caesar, but Philippus does not, so neither do I. My judgement is that he cannot be a good citizen. There are too many around him. They threaten death to our friends [the assassins] and call the present state of things intolerable.

Cicero, *Atticus*, 366 (14.12)

✳ ✳ ✳

SEXTUS POMPEY IN SPAIN

Antony also had to consider the situation concerning Sextus Pompey. Sextus's position was difficult. His father's clientele in Spain meant that he recovered in a year from the defeat inflicted by Caesar. By 44, he had raised six legions and it was feared that he would bring them into Italy. Moves to recall Sextus had begun in April, but proved to be nothing more than rhetoric. In July, Lepidus, at that time the proconsul of Spain, successfully persuaded him to hand over command of his army. Sextus, however, still failed to gain the right to return. The problems of compensating Sextus for the loss of his father's vast fortune, which had fallen into Antony's possession, and the possibility that the conservative faction would be strengthened meant that his cause was again shelved.

ANTONY AND THE 'LIBERATORS'

The men who still wanted to compromise with Antony were the liberators themselves, Brutus and Cassius. Having fled Rome during April, they spent the new few months in the country areas of Italy trying to build up support. In June, senators controlled by Antony offered them a minor commission. They were in an unenviable position: having 'liberated' their country they were now so out of favour with their liberated countrymen that even men of influence such as Cicero were unable to help them. Friendship with Antony and their brother-in-law, Lepidus, was in fact the best option.

As praetors, Brutus and Cassius publish an edict in which they attempt to bring Antony back to his compromising attitude of March 44. (May 44)

From Brutus and Cassius, Praetors, to M. Antonius, Consul.
Were we not convinced of your good faith and friendly intentions towards us, we should

not write you this letter, which, since you are in fact thus disposed, you will doubtless take in the best of part. We are informed by letters that a large number of veterans has already gathered in Rome, and that a larger number is expected before the Kalends of June. It would be out of character for us to entertain any doubt or apprehension concerning yourself. But having placed ourselves in your hands and dismissed our friends from the municipalities on your advice, having done that moreover not only by edict but in private letters, we surely deserve to share your confidence, particularly in a matter which concerns us.

Cicero, *Letters to his Friends* 329 (11.2)

The compromises of March were not possible in August. In view of the competition offered by Octavian, son of Caesar, Antony could not afford to appear to favour the assassins. Already, his young rival had the affection of Caesar's former soldiers. Octavian had organised games in Caesar's honour during which a comet appeared, which was taken as a sign that Caesar's spirit had risen to live with the gods. Octavian began to call himself *Divi Filius* (the son of a god). The name of the month *Quintilis* was changed to July. When more quarrels broke out between Antony and Octavian, the veterans ordered them to be reconciled. It was a sign of things to come that the large body of retired soldiers (who could be recruited again if necessary) could give orders to the Roman consul and his antagonist.

Brutus and his supporters were hoping that the popularity aroused by the Apollinarian games in July might restore his popularity and allow him to return to Rome. However, Octavian made sure that this plan failed.

The games were now approaching, which Gaius Antonius, the brother of Antony, was about to give on behalf of Brutus, the praetor, as he attended also to the other duties of the praetorship which [fell to] him in the latter's absence. Lavish expense was incurred in the preparations for them, in the hope that the people, gratified by the spectacle, would recall Brutus and Cassius. Octavian, on the other hand, trying to win the mob over to his own side, distributed the money derived from the sale of his property among the head men of the tribes by turns, to be divided by them among the first comers and went round to the places where his property was on sale and ordered the auctioneers to announce the lowest possible price for everything . . . all of which brought him both popularity and sympathy.

Appian, *Civil Wars*, 3.23

✳ ✳ ✳

ANTONY ATTACKED

Opposition to Antony was growing in the Senate. It had already awarded Brutus the province of Crete, and Cassius that of Cyrene, both in the East. At the beginning of August, L. Calpurnius Piso (formerly Caesar's father-in-law and a senior consular) began the month with a speech of condemnation in the Senate. Under mounting pressure from the senators as well as Octavian, a frustrated Antony attacked Cicero in a senatorial address. The next day Cicero retaliated, delivering the first of fifteen speeches, which he called the 'Philippics', attacking Antony. It was Cicero's first appearance in the Senate for many months.

Cicero wrote to Cassius to explain the situation in Rome. Note Cicero's care to avoid the charge of complicity in the conspiracy to murder Caesar. He was aware both of the legal implications and the hatred of the veteran soldiers for anyone involved in the assassination. (25 September 44)

From Cicero to Cassius, greetings.

I am very glad to find that my vote and speech meet with your approval. If I had been able to make such speeches often, the recovery of liberty and constitution would have been no problem. But a crazy desperado, far more wicked even than he whom you called the wickedest man ever killed, is looking for... a massacre. In charging me with having instigated Caesar's slaying, he has no other object than to incite the veterans against me (a risk which I am not afraid to take so long as he honours me with a share in the glory of your exploit). Accordingly, neither Piso, who was the first to make an (unsupported) attack on him, nor I, who followed Piso's example a month later, nor P. Servilius, who came after me, can enter the Senate in safety. The gladiator is looking for a massacre, and thought to make a start with me on 19 September. He came prepared for the occasion, having spent several days in Metellus' villa getting up a speech. How could that be done in an orgy of drink and debauchery?

Cicero, *Letters to his Friends*, 344 (12.2)

Antony was harried by various opposing groups, but as Roman consul he still controlled the state. He used armed force to conduct Senate meetings and loudly advertised his pro–Caesarean/anti–liberator image. During October, he attacked Brutus and Cassius in a public meeting and set up a statue to 'Caesar, Father and Benefactor'. He also accused Octavian of trying to kill him. Octavian successfully countered by accusing Antony of attempting to destroy his credit with the veterans. For Antony, it was a late start. Octavian had already offered bonus payments to the veterans in Campania. Then, when the Macedonian troops under Antony's command arrived in Brundisium, he found that they had already been influenced against him by Octavian's promises. Antony reacted to what he saw as mutiny by ordering the decimation of the troops. He was entitled to carry out these executions, but his decision to do so was not wise. It meant that the troops were far more inclined to turn to their alternative protector.

Antony Leaves Rome

During November, Balbus, Oppius, Hirtius and Octavian won the support of Cicero and some other conservatives by promising that Octavian would be willing to compromise with the assassins. Even if Cicero did not believe this, he decided that if he could first eliminate Antony, he could then deal with Octavian. The flaw in this was that Octavian had alternative courses of action, while Cicero knew that only Octavian could provide him with troops. Brutus and Cassius should have led the 'republican' army, but the only soldiers in Italy were Caesar's veterans, who hated the assassins as the murderers of their hero.

Now with Cicero's support, Octavian illegally encouraged the soldiers of the fourth legion to swear allegiance to him. They did so, but demonstrated their independence by refusing to fight Antony openly. They remembered that he was still a Caesarean general, even if his position as consul meant little to them. Once again, Antony reacted harshly. He attempted to have the Senate name Caesar's heir a public enemy. After all, Octavian was in open mutiny against the state. However, enough conservative and Caesarean senators were prepared to back Octavian's illegal actions, which included causing the mutiny of the Martian legion as well as the Fourth. Antony withdrew to his province (Cisalpine Gaul) with his loyal troops. Before leaving, he arranged for his brother Gaius to have the command of Macedonia.

On arriving in Cisalpine Gaul, Antony had to face the proconsul Decimus Brutus, who had been a ringleader in the conspiracy to murder Caesar. Decimus was a competent commander who would not be dislodged easily. While the position of strength Antony held at the beginning of the year had disintegrated, there were still some factors in his favour. Many of the soldiers supported him. Lepidus in Spain owed him favours; L. Munatius Plancus in Gaul always sided with the winner; C. Asinius Pollio in Further Spain was his close adherent. Also, he had left behind in Rome a small but strong band of supporters in the Senate led by Q. Fufius Calenus and including C. Vibius Pansa, the other designated consul for 43. Few wanted civil war, so he could depend on some to compromise. Antony was aware of all these factors, and that the alliance between Cicero and Octavian could be broken at any time.

＼Who were the faction leaders in Rome during 44 BC?

＼What were their sources of power?

＼Why was Antony constantly quarrelling with Octavian?

＼Why were Brutus and Cassius unable to take control of Rome?

CICERO, LEADER OF THE SENATE

At the beginning of January, the Senate met to decide its course of action for 43. The consuls were not united in their policy: Hirtius supported Octavian; Pansa (the son-in-law of Calenus who led the Antonian faction in the Senate) advocated a policy of compromise.

The Senate, led by Cicero, voted to legalise Octavian's actions of the year before, including causing the troops to refuse to follow Antony. Cicero's enmity with Antony was now fully fledged: during the winter, Cicero had circulated the pamphlet known as the 'Second Philippic', a vitriolic attack on Antony's morals, motives and general character. Calenus fought back for Antony with a vicious attack on Cicero delivered in the Senate (recorded by the historian Cassius Dio). However the Senate was not ready for open war. It would not proclaim Antony a public enemy, no matter how often Cicero pleaded for this. Instead, an embassy was sent to negotiate with Antony. Unfortunately, nothing was achieved.

Cicero was held in great respect by the Senate as the oldest consular and its best orator. Over the first months of 43, he convinced a majority of senators that Antony was the chief danger to the restoration of republican government. Cicero's energetic leadership brought Caesarean legions to fight Antony, whom they knew and liked, and a Caesarean Senate to declare war against him (which they finally did in March). However Antony was in more danger from the faction operating against him from *within* the Caesarean group than from conservatives such as Cicero. This faction did not want Antony, so they worked with Cicero against him; nor did they want to see the assassins of Caesar, of whom Decimus Brutus was the most hated, in control of Roman government.

Cicero concentrates for most of this speech on arguing against Antony's brilliant attempt to make Hirtius and Octavian see how much his and their best interests are identical. Antony's letter demonstrates how aware he had become of the realities of power in this period: who controlled the veterans controlled Rome, and the veterans worshipped Caesar. (Early April, 43)

Antonius to Hirtius and Caesar [Octavian]
When I heard of the death of Gaius Trebonius, my joy was not greater than my grief... That a criminal has paid the penalty to the ashes and bones of a most illustrious man, and that the power of the Gods has been revealed before the end of the year, the punishment for murder being either already inflicted or impending, is matter for rejoicing... the bitterest thing is that you, Aulus Hirtius, though you have been distinguished by Caesar's benefits, and left by him in a position in which you wonder at yourself—... And you, O boy... you who owe everything to a name... that you should strive to show that Dolabella was rightly condemned... and that this she-poisoner should be liberated from a siege... that you should strive that Cassius and Brutus may be as powerful as possible... you have had the vanquished Cicero for your general... you are fortifying Macedonia with garrisons... you have sent Cassius into Syria... you have taken away the veterans' colonies, though planted by law and by decree of the Senate... you supplied Brutus with the money of Apuleius... you have enlisted soldiers, either mine or veterans, on the plea that it was for the destruction of Caesar's murderers; and then these same soldiers you have set on unexpectedly to endanger him who had been their quaestor, or their general, or those who had been their own fellow-soldiers... What! is this the opinion of those veterans of yours to whom all courses are still open?... although you have set out to pervert them with flatteries and poisoned gifts... But you say you are bringing aid to the besieged soldiers. I do not mind their being safe, and going where they wish, provided only they suffer him to perish who has deserved it... [So you should] rather consider which is in better taste and more beneficial to your party, to avenge the death of Trebonius or that of Caesar; and whether it is more fitting that we should join battle so that the cause, so often slaughtered, of the Pompeians should more easily come to life, or should agree together, that we may not be a derision to our enemies... For whichever of us falls those enemies will profit... I am resolved to endure no insults to myself or to my friends, and not to desert the party Pompeius hated, nor to permit the veterans to be removed from their homes, nor to be dragged one by one to torture, nor to betray the pledged faith I have given to Dolabella... Finally, the sum of my decision tends to this: I can bear injuries inflicted by my friends if either they themselves are willing to forget the commission of them, or are ready with me to avenge Caesar's death.

Cicero, *Fifteen Philippics*, 13.22–46

* * *

The Siege of Mutina

During the winter, Antony trapped Decimus Brutus at Mutina in Cisalpine Gaul. Eventually Hirtius, Pansa and Octavian led their legions against Antony and defeated him, first at Forum Gallorum and then at Mutina. Cicero was jubilant when Antony was forced to flee to Spain. Decimus Brutus was freed and Antony was finally declared a public enemy. The fragile, unlikely alliance appeared to have worked.

The battle of Mutina has just been won. Cicero gives an account of it to Marcus Brutus. (21 April 43)

Our affairs are in better shape. I am sure your correspondents have informed you of what has occurred. The consuls have proved such as I have often described them to you. As for the boy Caesar, his natural worth and manliness is extraordinary. I only pray that I may succeed in guiding and holding him in the fullness of honours and favour as easily as I have done hitherto. That will be more difficult, it is true, but still I do not despair. The young man is persuaded (chiefly through me) that our survival is his work; and certain it is that if he had not turned Antony back from Rome, all would have been lost.

Cicero, *Letters to his Friends*, 7 (1.3)

＊ ＊ ＊

From Macedonia, Brutus wrote angrily to Atticus that there was more to fear from Octavian than Antony who was, after all, of proper status and background. Brutus was still not against compromising with Antony and when he had seized Macedonia, had taken Gaius Antonius prisoner but had not killed him. (June 43)

Our friend Cicero in his [toga] boasts to me that he has taken the brunt of Antony's war. What good is that to me if the price claimed for crushing Antony is to be succession to Antony's place, and if our champion against that evil has emerged in support of another evil, which is likely to be more firmly based and deeply rooted—if we allow it? His present activities make one begin to wonder whether it is despotism he is afraid of or a particular despot, Antony. For my part, I don't feel grateful to anybody who does not object to slavery as long as his master is not angry with him. Triumph, pay for his troops, encouragement in every decree not to let modesty deter him from coveting the position of a man whose name he has assumed—is that worthy of a Consular, of Cicero?

ibid., 25 (1.17)

In fact, after the victory over Antony in April, Cicero's alliance collapsed. Hirtius and Pansa both died during the fighting at Mutina; the consulship was vacant and the stability of the state was endangered. Antony escaped with his cavalry, and although Plancus in Transalpine Gaul, Lepidus in Nearer Spain and Pollio in Further Spain all promised to stand by the Senate, one by one they went over to Antony. Lepidus proclaimed that his troops would not fight a Caesarean general or his soldiers, their former comrades in arms. The refusal of the troops to fight was significant, but so too was the friendship between Antony and these three western proconsuls, friendships Cicero had tried desperately to overcome and Octavian and his followers had underestimated. While Cicero's power collapsed, Antony and Octavian made their own alliance.

Octavian was intent upon obtaining one of the consulships left vacant by the deaths of Hirtius and Pansa. With the help of his troops, he and his distant elderly relative Q. Pedius were made consuls in August 43 BC. Octavian was nineteen years old.

Cicero's final grasp at power had failed mainly because he did not control the army. He had attempted to marshall the military power of others, but could control neither Octavian nor the men behind him, and certainly not the rabidly Caesarean soldiers. The traditional channels of senatorial procedure and legislative activities were no longer enough. At the end of the year, his was one of the first names to appear on the proscription lists drawn up by Antony, Lepidus and Octavian. He died in December 43 BC.

∖**What were the difficulties faced by Cicero in 43? How did he overcome them?**

∖**Why was Cicero so deeply opposed to Antony? Did all the senators agree with him?**

∖**How did Antony recover after his defeat at Mutina in April 43?**

TRIUMVIRI REI PUBLICAE CONSTITUENDAE

Events moved rapidly towards the formation of a triumvirate. The new consul, Pedius, introduced the *Lex Pedia* under which all murderers of Caesar were tried and condemned in their absence. Sextus Pompey was also condemned under this law on the grounds that, had he been in Rome, he would have taken part in the conspiracy.

Towards the end of the year, Octavian moved north to meet Antony and Lepidus near Bononia (Bologna). They and their advisers formed the idea of a three-way dictatorship. This would confer 'legal' powers of consular *imperium* on them for five years (until January 38). Included in this shared *imperium* was the right to appoint magistrates and to divide up the western provinces between themselves. In November, P. Titius, a tribune of the plebs, passed a law which gave each of them the title *triumvir rei publicae constituendae* (one of a board of three men with powers to restore the state). One of their first actions was to deify Caesar.

FIRST DIVISION OF THE PROVINCES

In the division of the western provinces, all of Gaul except Narbonensis went to Antony; Narbonese Gaul and Nearer Spain went to Lepidus; Octavian gained Sicily, Sardinia and Africa. Octavian received a poor deal, as Sicily and Sardinia fell rapidly into Sextus's power. In the East, Cassius had won Syria from Dolabella, while Brutus held Macedonia and much of Asia Minor. Both the triumvirs and the 'liberators', as Brutus and Cassius called themselves, anticipated war in 42, and they set about raising money for the coming campaign: the liberators by plundering the cities of the East and the triumvirs by raising taxes and instituting massive proscriptions against rich senators and equestrians who were, or might become, enemies.

THE ELIMINATION OF THE LIBERATORS

After the institution of proscriptions and the death of Cicero, Brutus finally declared a personal war with Antony by executing his imprisoned brother, Gaius Antonius. After a discussion on strategy with Cassius at Smyrna, he moved into Lycia and continued to raise money and gather troops. By the middle of the year, Cassius and Brutus joined forces at Sardis; Antony and Octavian had transported their armies into Greece. Eventually the armies met at Philippi in the far north of Greece. In the first battle, Antony defeated Cassius, who then killed himself. Brutus successfully attacked the camp of Octavian, who was unaccountably absent at the time.

The loss of Cassius, who was by far the better military leader of the two, was disastrous for the republican cause. Brutus was defeated by Antony and also committed suicide.

While Plutarch sentimentally called Brutus the 'noblest Roman' and Cassius 'the last of the Romans', Cicero's letters contain evidence that they were difficult men to work with. They also contain evidence of unrepublican behaviour: Brutus produced coins which bore his portrait, a regal action for which Caesar had been criticised. The eastern provinces, especially Rhodes, suffered greatly from Brutus and Cassius' extortionate demands. These actions indicate that even had they won the battles of Philippi, they would have behaved little better than the victors.

THE NEW 'REPUBLICAN' FORCES

In the propaganda of the period, the 'Republic' was still a useful rallying cry. The survivors of the Battle of Philippi regarded themselves as the true defenders of the state, but factions broke out among them. Just as the triumvirs had spent most of 43 trying to prove that each was the best Caesarean, so now each of the republican leaders attempted to show that he had more right to command than the others. The three men who thought they qualified were Sextus Pompey, who had been named prefect of the seas and coasts in 43; L. Staius Murcus, Cassius' fleet commander; and Cn. Domitius Ahenobarbus, Brutus' legate. Murcus and Ahenobarbus had recently achieved a decisive victory over the triumviral navy and so had a large and useful fleet. Murcus's policy was to join Sextus, who had used his father's clientele to sieze Sicily and Sardinia. Ahenobarbus, however, saw Sextus as the son of the man who had betrayed his father at Corfinium in 49. He assumed command of half the fleet and set up an independent command in the Adriatic. Both groups caused major hardship to Octavian, as Sextus controlled the western coasts of Italy, while Ahenobarbus could blockade the eastern coasts.

DISTRIBUTION OF THE PROVINCES

A new distribution of the provinces took place after the triumvirs' conquest of the East. This formed the basis of all future agreements. Already Lepidus was being overlooked. He had remained as consul in Rome with Plancus and therefore was not present when the victors redivided the Roman world. Antony gained jurisdiction of the East and Gaul; Octavian received everything else. Lepidus was to be given Africa if his loyalty, which had been called into question, was confirmed. Even when he gained this province, he controlled far less than the other triumvirs.

THE PERUSINE WAR

Octavian now entered upon the most crucial five-year period of his life. During 41, Antony was in the East, but his wife Fulvia and his brother Lucius, the consul in that year, took up the cause of the landowners in the north of Italy who were about to be dispossessed by Octavian. Land was to be confiscated from eighteen cities in order to settle the veterans of Philippi. Lucius, proclaiming that he wished to see the Republic restored, called upon Octavian to give up his triumviral powers and promised that Antony would do the same. He tried to gain the support of the Antonian generals, Pollio, Calenus and Plancus as well as Octavian's general Q. Salvidienus Rufus.

Velleius Paterculus wrote during the reign of Tiberius. His prejudices are not difficult to find. Notice in this account of the battle of Perusia, how nothing is Octavian's fault, but everything can be blamed on Fulvia.

Caesar [Octavian] returned to Italy, which he found in a much more troubled condition than he had expected. Lucius Antonius, the consul, who shared the faults of his brother but possessed none of the virtues which he occasionally showed, by making charges against Caesar before the veterans at one moment, and at the next, inciting to arms those who had lost their farms when the division of lands was ordered and colonists assigned, had collected a large army. In another quarter, Fulvia, the wife of Antony, who had nothing of the woman in her except her sex, was creating general confusion by armed violence. She had taken Praeneste as her base of operations; Antonius, beaten on all sides by the forces of Caesar, had taken refuge in Perusia; Plancus, who abetted the faction of Antony, offered the hope of assistance, rather than gave actual help. Thanks to his own valour and his usual good fortune, Caesar succeeded in storming Perusia. He released Antonius unharmed; and the cruel treatment of the people of Perusia was due rather to the fury of the soldiers than to the wish of their commander.

Velleius Paterculus, *Roman History*, 2.74.2–4

Mark Antony's attitude to the uprising remains unclear. It was supposed to be in his interests, yet he did nothing openly to help or hinder it. Plutarch was in no doubt as to the reason.

• • • now as a crowning evil, [Antony's] love for Cleopatra supervened, roused and drove to frenzy many of the passions that were still hidden . . . in him, and . . . destroyed whatever good and saving qualities still offered resistance . . . judging by the proofs which she had had before this of the effect of her beauty upon Gaius Caesar and Gnaeus the son of Pompey, [Cleopatra] had hopes that she would more easily bring Antony to her feet. For Caesar and Pompey had known her when she was still a girl and inexperienced in affairs, but she was going to visit Antony at the very time when women have most brilliant beauty and are at the [height] of intellectual power. Accordingly, she made such [a prize] of

Coin depicting Mark Antony on the obverse, Cleopatra
on the reverse (Australian Coin Review)

Antony that, while Fulvia his wife was carrying on war at Rome with Caesar in defence of
her husband's interests, and while a Parthian army was hovering about Mesopotamia . . . he
[allowed] her to hurry him off to Alexandria.

Plutarch, *Antony*, 25, 28

Fulvia died in Greece a short time later, apparently heartbroken. Lucius
Antonius simply disappeared from history. Octavian not only put down the
uprising but siezed the province of Cisalpine Gaul on the death of Antony's
friend Calenus.

Perusia was reclaimed, but Octavian still had to face Sextus, whose army
and navy had been reinforced by many who fled the proscriptions, the
defeat of Philippi and now the Perusine war. With these forces, Sextus had
defeated three fleets sent against him from 42 to 40.

THE PACT OF BRUNDISIUM

After Perusia, Sextus and Ahenobarbus had expected that Antony would
desert Octavian and form a new alliance against him. When Antony was
shut out of Brundisium by Octavian, both men began to attack Italy,
believing that the alliance between Antony and Octavian was over and that
Antony would support them. However, too many men had a vested interest
in the triumvirate, including the majority of the soldiers. Negotiations
between Antony and Octavian began and were successful. Although
Ahenobarbus was able to turn his alliance with Antony into a permanent
arrangement, Sextus was ignored and returned to Italy. Antony and
Octavian organised a new division of provinces. Lepidus kept only Africa;
Antony kept control of all the eastern provinces; the western provinces,
including Gaul, went to Octavian. Antony agreed to marry Octavia Minor,
Octavian's sister, and promised to assist Octavian to defeat Sextus. Possibly
at this stage he was not quite as besotted with Cleopatra as Plutarch
believed.

Caesar [Octavian] was exceedingly fond of his sister, who was, as the saying goes, a wonder of a woman. Her husband, Gaius Marcellus, had died a short time before and she was a widow. Antony, too, now that Fulvia was [dead], was held to be a widower, although he did not deny his relations with Cleopatra; he would not admit, however, that she was his wife, and in this matter, his reason was still battling with his love for the Egyptian. Everybody tried to bring about this marriage. For they hoped that Octavia, who besides her great beauty, had intelligence and dignity, when united to Antony and beloved by him, as such a woman naturally must be, would restore harmony and be their complete salvation. Accordingly, when both men were agreed, they went up to Rome and celebrated Octavia's marriage.

Plutarch, *Antony*, 31

* * *

THE TREATY OF PUTEOLI

The threat to the triumvirate from Sextus, who controlled Sicily, Sardinia and Corsica, continued in 39. Sextus' various attempts to negotiate with the individual triumvirs (especially Antony) had failed, but his control of the sea had cut off grain supplies to Italy. Octavian, in the capital, was particularly affected by this, for food shortages caused frequent riots. He decided to marry Scribonia, Sextus' wife's aunt, in an attempt to form some kind of alliance, but the blockade continued.

During 39, there was growing dissatisfaction among Sextus's camp. Octavian was enticing many of the exiles from the proscriptions, Perusia and Philippi back to Rome with promises of restoration and some compensation. In response to factional strife, Sextus put Murcus to death, which deepened the divisions within the republican base. Eventually, Sextus was forced to negotiate. He, Antony and Octavian met near the Bay of Misenum and the following terms were agreed to:

- Sextus was to allow grain to proceed to Rome and all his garrisons were to be removed from Italy;
- Sextus's governorship of Sicily, Sardinia and Corsica was recognised and the Peloponnese was added to his sphere;
- all exiles could return to Rome unless they had helped to assassinate Caesar;
- Sextus was to be consul in 33 and L. Scribonius Libo (his father-in-law and chief adviser) was to be consul in 34;
- compensation for the loss of Pompey the Great's property was to be paid;
- Sextus was to become an augur.

This treaty relieved the problem for Octavian and the exiles but it terminally weakened Sextus's position. While his original strength was the patronage available to him as the only surviving son of Pompey the Great, his real power was in his position of refuge for all those with a grievance against the triumvirs. Sextus was no longer an alternative to the triumvirs; he was one of them. Before the end of the year, Octavian had divorced Scribonia and found an excuse to resume hostilities. After the Treaty of Puteoli, Sextus fought for his own survival, not that of the Roman exiles.

Coin depicting Augustus. The legend
states that Augustus is the son of the
divine imperator Caesar and has been
hailed imperator twenty times by his
army. (Macquarie University, NSW)

Coin depicting M. Agrippa.
The legend states that Agrippa
has been consul three times
(Macquarie University, NSW)

Octavian was committed to the destruction of Sextus. As the only man
who could rival Octavian's own base for power, Sextus could not be a
lasting ally. Sextus's opportunities to draw upon his father's clientele and
power, still enormous after the many defeats which the Pompeians had
suffered, meant that he was independent of Caesar and his veterans, as
Antony, Lepidus, and the other noble Caesarean generals could not be.
Therefore, Sextus was of far more potential danger to Octavian than was
Antony. While Sextus might have been satisfied with returning to Rome
and a quiet life, Octavian focused all his military activity for the next three
years against him.

THE TREATY OF TARENTUM

The powers of the triumvirate officially lapsed at the end of 38. Neither
Antony nor Octavian was ready to do without the other: Octavian had still
not defeated Sextus, and Antony faced a Parthian campaign. Although
problems between the two had occurred, Octavia organised a meeting at
Tarentum in 37. Under the terms of this new agreement, the legal power of
the triumvirate was renewed for five years and the division of provinces
maintained. Octavia persuaded Octavian to accept 120 ships from Antony
for the war against Sextus; in return he would assign to Antony 20 000
soldiers for the Parthian expedition. Sextus was dropped from the list of
projected consuls and his augurate was taken away. Antony then returned
to the East. The negotiations again failed to include Lepidus.

Octavian threw all resources into the military campaign against Sextus,
who had defeated him several times and had renewed the grain blockade.
Octavian's best general, Agrippa, had returned to Italy from Gaul. Agrippa,
who had given up his voted triumph rather than embarrass Octavian, spent a

year constructing and equipping a new fleet in the south of Italy. By 36 they were ready to attack Sicily. Lepidus was requested to bring a land army over from Africa and attack from the south. Octavian, bolstered by his new fleet, and a new weapon, the *harpax* (a grapnel shot from a catapault), attacked from the sea. Eventually, Sextus was forced into a sea battle at Naulochus, in which he was defeated by Agrippa and Octavian. He fled to the East and was put to death in 35 by order of Antony.

The victory was of utmost importance for Octavian's rise to power. With the freeing of the seas and the famine over, his former unpopularity was completely reversed. As well, his military reputation began to approach that of Antony. In 36, Octavian, his wife Livia and his sister Octavia were granted *tribunician sacrosanctity*, which set aside his family as sacred. It was the beginning both of Octavian's unique standing in Rome and of a royal house.

Characteristically, Octavian played down the significance of this turning point. *Res Gestae* (25.1) says only that he freed the sea of pirates and gave back the captive slaves. The name of Pompey was completely excluded.

Lepidus Loses His *Imperium*

Almost as an addendum to the campaign against Sextus was Octavian's elimination of Lepidus. Lepidus had come from Africa to fight Sextus and had successfully moved through the south of Sicily to Messana, while Octavian and Agrippa attacked the north-eastern coast. It was Lepidus who took charge of Sextus's land army, but then used his force of twenty-two legions to order Octavian to leave. Octavian appealed to the troops, and his popularity with them proved greater than their respect for Lepidus's right to command. Lepidus was stripped of his triumviral powers and exiled. Octavian took this action without any consultation with Antony. Although the triumvirate became in effect a duumvirate (board of two men), the original title was maintained.

> **Why was it necessary for Antony and Octavian to campaign against the 'liberators'?**
>
> **Why did the Perusine War break out?**
>
> **What was the role of Octavia in the period 40 – 32 BC?**
>
> **What dangers did the triumvirs face from Sextus Pompey? How did they manage to overcome them?**
>
> **Why was it so easy for Octavian to eliminate Lepidus?**

ANTONY IN THE EAST

After the victory at Philippi, Antony had assumed control of the eastern provinces of the Roman world. He spent very little time in Rome, except for visits in 40 and 39. His first expeditions entailed raising money from the already drained eastern provinces. In 41 he met Cleopatra in Cilicia, but although a romantic relationship began at this time, his other concerns kept him away from Egypt for four years.

THE PARTHIANS

Since Crassus' defeat at Carrhae in 53, the Parthian kingdoms had received great attention from military commanders in Rome. It had been suggested that Pompey and Caesar should have been fighting them rather than each other at the time that civil war broke out. Caesar had been on the point of beginning a massive expedition against Parthia when he was assassinated. Once in control of the East, Antony began to involve himself in Parthian affairs. In the years 41 and 40, he faced an invasion by Parthians led by Quintus Labienus, the son of a republican military leader who had made his home there and now called himself '*Parthicus Imperator*'.

In 39, Antony's forces under P. Ventidius successfully attacked the Parthians in Armenia. During 39 – 38, while Antony was busy with affairs in Rome, his generals continued their success, clearing Syria of Parthians and killing Pacorus, their king. In 37, however, when Antony himself invaded Parthia, he committed several major military errors (such as becoming separated from his siege train), and after sustaining heavy losses was forced to retreat under gruelling conditions. Later Augustan and Antonian writers blamed Antony's failure in Parthia on Cleopatra, for whom he had deserted Octavia.

Cleopatra and Octavia had both offered cash and reinforcements for the Parthian campaigns, but although Antony badly needed help, he refused Octavia's assistance and accepted only Cleopatra's. The 'Great Romance' of Antony and Cleopatra had begun.

It is possible that the relationship was based on pragmatism as well as romance. Antony had become aware that he needed a separate power base from Octavian and the Caesarean veterans of the west. He had spent time building up this base, imitating Pompey's methods of placing his own clients, who owed nothing to Caesar or his heir, in positions of influence. Cleopatra was therefore of far greater importance to him than Octavia.

In 34, Antony gained a minor success when he occupied Armenia and captured its king, but instead of advertising this in Rome, where Octavian was gaining popularity, he celebrated a splendid triumph in Alexandria. During the festivities, Antony and Cleopatra sat on high thrones along with their children, Alexander Helios and Cleopatra Selene (twins conceived in 39 BC), Ptolemy Philadelphus (born in 36), and Cleopatra's elder son, Caesarion. The latter was proclaimed the legitimate son of Julius Caesar and called 'king of kings'; he and Cleopatra were proclaimed joint rulers of Egypt and Cyprus. Alexander Helios was to govern Armenia, Parthia and Media; Ptolemy Philadelphus, Syria and Cilicia; Cleopatra Selene, Cyrenaica and Libya. All this was done under Antony's triumviral authority.

The combination of the insult to the people of Rome in staging the triumph in Alexandria, and the insult to Octavia, a noble and faithful Roman wife, gave Octavian great ammunition for a propaganda campaign against Antony. Octavian ensured that these events received as much bad publicity as possible in Rome, while other honourable settlements (many of which Octavian later approved) were not mentioned.

OCTAVIAN VERSUS ANTONY AND CLEOPATRA

From 34, events moved steadily towards an open confrontation between the two remaining triumvirs. Despite Antony's desertion, Octavia continued her attempts to reconcile them but this proved to be an impossible task.

Antony's aims in this period were tied up with Cleopatra's. With Caesar's help, Cleopatra had already ruthlessly fought her family for the Egyptian throne. She probably did not want to rule Rome, as Octavian's propaganda was informing the Italian population, but had her heart set on Syria and the Levant. Through Antony, she gained control of many of these areas. Herod, another of Antony's protégés, feared that she would grasp his possessions in Judaea. However, Antony did not allow Cleopatra to rule him to that extent. He handed over Jericho as a gift to Cleopatra, but Herod kept his kingdom.

Antony and Cleopatra were well aware that a clash with Octavian was becoming inevitable and that they needed each other to fight him. Both sides minted vast amounts of coins for payment of the troops; both attempted to justify their positions. Octavian in Italy had the upper hand in the field of public relations. With the help of his friend Maecenas, Octavian pictured Antony as the 'depraved and drunken Roman', now a slave to the 'deadly monster'. He pointed out what would happen to Italy if he, Caesar, could not hold back the alien hordes: strange animal-headed gods on the Capitol; Rome under the power of a woman; Italy overrun by 'ethnics' from the East. He appealed to every Roman prejudice. Antony retaliated by casting slurs on Octavian's parentage, sexual preferences and courage— where was Octavian during the battle of Philippi?

Suetonius provides an example of Antony's propaganda against Octavian.

But Antonius again, trying to disparage the maternal ancestors of [Octavian] as well, [taunts] him with having a great-grandfather of African birth, who kept first a perfumery shop and then a bakery at Aricia. Cassius of Parma also taunts [Octavian] with being the grandson both of a baker and of a money-changer, saying in one of his letters: "Your mother's meal came from a vulgar bakeshop of Aricia; this a money-changer from Nerulum kneaded into shape with hands stained with filthy lucre".

Suetonius, *Augustus*, 4.2

At the end of 33 the triumviral powers officially came to an end. Antony continued to use the title, but Octavian dropped it, although both continued to act as if they held *imperium*. Ahenobarbus, the former republican leader, and C. Sosius, supporters of Antony, were consuls in 32. They protected

Antony's interests by refusing to read to the Senate his dispatches when they arrived from Egypt. (Because they were so eastern centred, these would have given more ammunition to Octavian for propaganda attacks.) To overcome the power of the two Antonian consuls, Octavian seated himself between them in Senate meetings, thus claiming to share the presidency with them. When Sosius reprimanded him, his motion was vetoed by a tribune. A second attempt to call Octavian to order failed. The consuls and over three hundred members of the Senate left Rome to join Antony in the East.

Once such open enmity had been declared, Antony formally divorced Octavia. Octavian reacted by producing Antony's will, which had been placed in the care of the Vestal Virgins. Octavian learned of its presence from Plancus and M. Titius, two men who had deserted Antony. He committed the illegal and sacrilegious act of seizing the will and reading it in the Senate. The terms were all that Octavian had hoped for, so much so that he was accused of writing them himself. In the will, Antony acknowledged his children by Cleopatra and stated that Caesarion was truly the son of Caesar; he wished to be buried not in Rome, but alongside Cleopatra in Egypt.

Antony's friends and supporters in Rome preferred to say that the will was a forgery, even if they thought it was not, because its sentiments contravened Roman custom so badly. The Roman upper class was extremely xenophobic: its literature expressed hatred for Greeks and eastern peoples. Antony was not so rigid in his views. His acceptance of Greek, Alexandrian and eastern custom disgusted his countrymen, but brought him the affection and loyalty of the peoples of these areas. Because his own attitudes were so relaxed, he underestimated the effect of his actions on his own supporters. They did not want to follow Octavian, nor did they like Antony's alliance with Cleopatra.

Antony had little choice but to maintain this alliance. Octavian controlled the armies of the West. Antony needed the East, especially Egypt, where the resources not only included vast wealth, manpower and food supplies, but also Caesarion, who claimed to be the son of Julius Caesar. Caesarion's prominence in the festival at Alexandria and his inclusion in Antony's will signified that Antony and Cleopatra planned to use the boy to undermine Octavian's position as Caesar's heir.

The plan was good, but Antony had wasted too much time putting it into effect. Octavian's stranglehold on Roman politics increased with each victory. He defeated the Illyrians and Dalmatians in 35 – 33, thus securing the north-west border of Italy and clearing piracy from the area. He celebrated a 'proper' Roman triumph and, along with Agrippa and his other generals, began a programme of providing new buildings, water supplies and cheap food. This programme, as well as the anti-Antonian propaganda, was winning over the civilian and military population. Eventually he organised an oath of loyalty to be made by all the cities of Italy. His claims that this was spontaneous were probably not quite true. In 32, many senators supported Antony, though Octavian had formally deprived him of his triumviral powers. The cities within their patronage would not have sworn such an oath without qualms. Bononia (Bologna), for example, actually refused, because of its long association with the Antonii. Octavian later confiscated much of its territory.

However, Octavian did not declare war on Antony, but rather on Cleopatra of Egypt. In this way, he isolated Antony, who was committed to Cleopatra, from his Roman followers. For financial, political and personal reasons, Antony could not desert Cleopatra, nor the power base which was his only hope against his enemy, even though his fellow senators urged him to. Many left his camp, including the former 'republican' Ahenobarbus, whose son had married Antony's daughter. He claimed that Cleopatra's continued presence was the reason for his desertion.

THE CAMPAIGN OF ACTIUM

During late 31, both armies moved into Greece. Octavian left his trusted friend Maecenas in charge of Rome but, as a counter to the senators present in Antony's camp, took most of the remaining senators with him. Agrippa was once more commander of the fleet.

In the battle that followed, Antony failed to defeat Octavian's land army and was trapped and defeated in a naval battle at Actium. When Antony's left wing began to fail, Cleopatra's flagship (and the war treasury) was endangered and he signalled her to retreat, then escaped with forty ships. However, he was forced to abandon both his fleet and land army, which later surrendered to Octavian. What might have really been a badly organised retreat was seized upon by Octavian as proof that Antony had degenerated into a coward who would desert his loyal Roman troops to follow a foreign mistress.

Octavian still had to defeat Cleopatra and Antony in Egypt. In 30, Alexandria fell to him. Antony, on hearing an untrue rumour that Cleopatra was dead, committed suicide. Cleopatra, knowing that if she lived she would be led as a prisoner in Octavian's triumph, organised her own suicide by smuggling an asp into her room and letting it bite her.

⟍**Why was it necessary for Octavian and Antony to fight a war of propaganda?**

⟍**By what means did Octavian destroy Antony's credibility?**

⟍**How did Antony build up a separate power base from Octavian?**

CONCLUSION

In 43, Antony had called Octavian a boy who owed everything to his name. This was very true. Because of his name, Caesar's friends Balbus, Oppius and Hirtius sponsored Octavian to heights which no nineteen-year-old

Sard intaglio showing Augustus as Neptune.
This gem celebrates the victory of Augustus over Antony at Actium.
(Francis Bartlett Donation. Courtesy Museum of Fine Arts, Boston)

Roman youth should have aimed for. Because he was 'Caesar', troops were ready to desert the consul and fight a civil war for him. The army's devotion to Julius Caesar was something which Cicero and the assassins could do nothing about. Cicero failed because Octavian maintained their alliance only while it suited him. After all, the troops were under his control, not Cicero's. Lepidus and Antony could maintain powerful positions in the state because the army saw them as Caesarean generals, but Lepidus's power lasted only as long as he did not challenge the position of the Caesarean heir. Antony saw that he could not defeat Octavian with an Italian army. When Octavian deposed Lepidus so easily, Antony worked hard to strengthen his alternative eastern power base.

The power and independence of the veteran soldiers cannot be underestimated in the triumviral period. Their fanatical devotion to Caesar was matched only by their determination to protect their own interests. The backing of these men gave Lepidus, the weakest member of the triumvirate, strength to compete with Antony and Octavian in 43 BC. Antony's policy throughout 44 and 43 twisted and turned as he tried to maintain their support. He attempted to overcome the problem by means of his eastern resources, but in doing so, gave Octavian the opportunity to portray him as a deserter of Italy to a people who hated foreigners.

Octavian was always visible to the army and people as the heir of Caesar and, therefore, their protector and leader. Once in a position to do so, he made sure that the army knew that his first priorities were the avenging of Caesar's murder and their own welfare. The first temple he had built was dedicated to Mars the Avenger, as a public demonstration of this policy. The campaigns against Brutus and Cassius, even though his own role in them was less than glorious, were of the utmost importance to him. After their defeat, he could ensure that the army was devoted not only to 'Caesar's heir' but to the new Caesar.

Octavian learned quickly that his presentation of the facts was all-important. His understanding of the Italian mentality, what appealed to it and what could be expected to disgust it, developed as he went on to rule the Roman world for the following forty years. Thus Sextus, Lepidus, Antony and Cleopatra all suffered not only defeat but also loss of reputation because Octavian made sure his reasons for fighting them and his subsequent victories were portrayed as he wanted them to be. Poets and historians of the Augustan age naturally sang the praises of the victor, and, for the most part, happily adopted his presentation of the vanquished.

Horace's famous ode celebrates the victory at Actium and a Rome saved by Caesar from the monstrous Cleopatra. Note the absence of Antony in the poem.

Now is the time to drain the flowing bowl, now with unfettered foot to beat the ground with dancing, now with Salian feast to deck the couches of the gods, my comrades. Before this day it had been wrong to bring our [wine] forth from ancient bins, while yet a frenzied queen was plotting ruin against the Capitol and destruction to the empire, with her polluted crew of creatures foul with lust—a woman mad enough to nurse the wildest hopes, and drunk with Fortune's favours. But the escape of scarce a single galley from the flames sobered her fury, and Caesar changed the wild delusions bred by Mareotic wine to the stern reality of terror, chasing her with his galleys, as she sped away from Italy, even as the hawk pursues the gentle dove, or the swift hunter follows the hare over the plains of snow-clad Thessaly, with [his] purpose fixed to put in chains the accursed monster. Yet she, seeking to die a nobler death, showed for the dagger's point no woman's fear, nor sought to win with her swift fleet some secret shores; he even dared to gaze with face serene upon her fallen palace; courageous, too, to handle poisonous asps, that she might draw black venom to her heart, waxing bolder as she resolved to die; scorning, in sooth, the thought of being borne, a queen no longer, on hostile galleys to grace a glorious triumph— no craven woman she!

Horace, *Odes*, 1.37

* * *

LIST OF REFERENCES

ANCIENT SOURCES

Appian, *Appian's Roman History, Vol. 3, The Civil Wars*, Loeb Classical Library, 1979

Cicero, *Cicero's Letters to Atticus*, Penguin, 1978

—— 'M. Brutus and Cassius to Antony', 'Cicero to M. Brutus' and 'Cicero to Cassius' in *Cicero's Letters to his Friends*, Vol. 2, Penguin, 1978

—— *Cicero: Fifteen Philippics*, Loeb Classical Library, 1969

Horace, *Odes and Epodes*, Loeb Classical Library, 1964
Plutarch, 'Life of Antony' in *Makers of Rome*, Penguin, 1968
Suetonius, 'Life of Augustus' in *Works*, Loeb Classical Library, 1920
Velleius Paterculus, *Compendium of Roman History*, Loeb Classical Library, 1967

AUGUSTUS SAVIOUR OF ROME

JANE AND BRUCE DENNETT

Gods of our fathers . . . do not prevent this young man from the rescue of an age.
—Virgil

63 BC	Augustus born Gaius Octavius
29	Augustus, still known as Octavian, rules Rome following a period of civil war Begins to create the Augustan system of government known as the Principate
27	He is given the title Augustus, and continues to extend the power of the Principate at the expense of the Senate
	Augustus begins major public works in Rome
23	Augustus becomes *maius imperium proconsulare* and *tribunicia potestas*. These two offices increased his personal power in both Rome and the provinces
19 – 18	Augustus takes control over selecting his own successor
12	Augustus becomes *pontifex maximus*, increasing his prestige and influence in matters of religion
AD 6	Augustus establishes *aerarium militare*
9	Varian disaster—loss of three legions under Varus in the Teutoburg forest
14	Death of Augustus; Tiberius becomes Emperor

Keep in mind the following questions as you read this chapter:

Was Augustus the architect of the Roman Empire? How important were his administrative and provincial reforms?

How capable a politician was Augustus?

Augustus was born Gaius Octavius into the senatorial class in 63 BC. He became known as Gaius Julius Caesar Octavianus (Octavian) when he became heir to the political power of his great-uncle Julius Caesar. In 27 BC, at thirty-six years of age, he became Caesar Augustus. From this time until his death in AD 14 he was generally accepted as being Emperor of Rome.

Statue of Augustus (Vatican Museum, Rome.
Courtesy Mansell Collection)

While the previous chapter covers the life of Augustus (Octavian) from the death of Julius Caesar to the deaths of Antony and Cleopatra, this chapter is concerned with the later part of Augustus's eventful life. Augustus has been hailed as one of the great figures of history. His greatness lay in his ability to seize power, his capacity to retain and consolidate it, and, most importantly, his application of that power. Augustus was responsible for one of the most significant transformations in the history of Rome.

His reforms touched every aspect of Roman and provincial life: laws and constitution, administration, the economy and finance, Roman society, the Empire and the physical face of the city of Rome itself. These achievements included:

- creating the office of Principate, and associated with this a special position for himself as holder of supreme power in Rome;
- providing stable government and rescuing Rome from years of civil war;
- reforming the administration of Rome and the provinces, including establishing an urban praefecture (local government) that endured for centuries;
- uniting many separate regions of the Empire under a common Roman rule of law—the genuine beginnings of a homogeneous *imperium Romanum*;
- rebuilding Rome as a centre worthy of being the 'first city' of the ancient world;
- providing an environment that encouraged both economic prosperity and a flourishing of literature and the arts.

Augustus was not cast in the classic heroic mould. He was neither dashing nor dramatic in manner or appearance. His reputation as a soldier is not exceptional. His mind appears to have been systematic and thorough rather than brilliant. Augustus was not a theoretical or academic thinker; rather, he had a persistent and practical approach. He appears to have been a man ready to learn from his mistakes, ready to compromise, and a man not easily deterred by mishaps or failures.

Some observers have found this apparent inconsistency between his monumental achievements and less than heroic personal style disconcerting. As a result, they have often sought to highlight the role of others in Augustus's career, in particular, M. Vipsanius Agrippa in Augustus's seizure of power, and his third and last wife Livia in the retention of that power. However attempts to minimise the personal domination of Augustus fail to ring true. His individual authority held almost total sway, and the 'Augustan touch' was fundamental to the prosperity and stability of the time. This is clearly borne out by the turmoil faced by many of his successors in their attempts to function within the system created by Augustus.

While Augustus was undoubtedly exceptional, there were some unfortunate legacies of his period in power:

- He failed to make substantial changes in Rome's social classes. This meant that Rome's increasing economic prosperity continued to be shared among a narrow elite.
- The Principate and the Emperor's right to rule established by Augustus became firmly based on military power. This meant that force rather than legality would often decide who ruled Rome in future.
- He created a system of government that was open to abuses of power and privilege. Some of the heirs to Augustus's office, Caligula and Nero in particular, were among the most cruel and violent in Rome's history.

Despite these weaknesses, apparent to us in hindsight, Augustus remains by any test a giant among leaders.

EVIDENCE

The duration and achievements of Augustus's reign have left a significant amount of archaeological evidence, including remains of his public works throughout Rome and the Empire, as well as coins and inscriptions. These pieces of archaeological evidence are valuable to the historian, but the bulk of our information about Augustus comes from written evidence.

THE *RES GESTAE*

There is a strong link between the archaeological and the written evidence in the form of the *Res Gestae*. This inscribed monument, built in Rome and other places throughout the Empire, was Augustus's account of his achievements. He saw the *Res Gestae* as his final monument. In the *Res Gestae*, Augustus provides a list of his achievements. Since they were for public display, they most likely are historically reliable because they could easily have been challenged at the time.

While the facts presented in the *Res Gestae* tell us what happened, they provide little insight into the reasons why events happened. However, what the *Res Gestae* doesn't say provides a useful clue to Augustus's thoughts. For example, it gives only fleeting reference to Rome's civil wars and makes no mention of any of Augustus's political opponents. There is no reference to any serious military reverses, such as the massacre of Varus's legions in AD 9. Nor does it mention all the aspects of Augustus's significant personal power, such as the provinces placed under his individual control in 27 BC.

CASSIUS DIO

Cassius Dio is perhaps the most significant of the ancient writers. He provides the only full-length account of Augustus's reign, giving excellent insights into the growth and workings of the Augustan system of government. His material on the political settlements of 23 BC and 19 BC is vital in understanding the creation of the Principate. Cassius Dio, however, should be read with care, as he was sympathetic to the imperial system created by Augustus. He produced his work two centuries after the events recorded and did not fully appreciate the gradual pace of growth of the Augustan system.

SUETONIUS

Although popular, Suetonius is now regarded as more of a gossip-columnist than a historian. Suetonius's work includes some reliable factual details, but he is more concerned with personal weaknesses and the tendency of power to corrupt than he is with historical accuracy.

TACITUS

Tacitus does not deal specifically with Augustus. He devotes his attention to Augustus's successors and in doing so makes some harsh judgements about the Augustan system. Tacitus reflects suspicion of the imperial system and should be read with this fact in mind.

MODERN SCHOLARS

A comparison of recent and ancient works reveals a change in perceptions about this period. The German historian T. Mommsen describes Augustus's Principate as a sharing of power between the Emperor (or *Princeps*) and the Senate. Mommsen calls this system of government a *dyarchy*. (Scullard, 219) More recent historians have been critical of this view, suggesting that it over-emphasises the Senate's power and ignores the remarkable domination of state affairs by Augustus. The fairest picture of the Augustan Principate presented by modern scholars appears to be that approach supported by E. T. Salmon, among others. Salmon accepts the dominance of Augustus's political power over the Senate but points to the fact that the Senate still retained considerable prestige and was a crucial part of the Principate's constitutional right to rule.

THE CREATION OF THE PRINCIPATE

The creation of the office of 'Principate' and the structure for the adminis-tration of the Empire laid out by Augustus were his greatest achievements. He created a very personal constitutional system. Originally the Principate took its name from the title *Princeps Senatus*—the equivalent of first citizen—bestowed upon Augustus in 29 BC when he was still known as Octavian. From the time of Augustus's successor, Tiberius, the office of Principate became synonymous with the title of Emperor.

The Principate was, in theory, meant to be a sharing of power between the *Princeps* and the Senate. In practice, the power of Princeps grew to that of a monarch at the expense of the Senate. This happened in an evolutionary rather than revolutionary fashion, a fact that Cassius Dio fails to acknowl-edge in *Roman History*. The office of Principate gained power gradually over the years as a result of a series of political arrangements or 'settlements' made between Augustus and the Senate. The most important settlements defining and extending his powers took place in 27, 23 and 19 BC.

UNCHALLENGED LEADER

By 29 BC, Augustus (then still known as Octavian) had defeated the last of his political opponents in the civil war that followed Julius Caesar's assassination. Following these conflicts Augustus stood unchallenged, his opposition vanquished. His first task was to consolidate his power and return Roman society, ravaged by years of civil strife, to normal. This task required considerable political skill and discretion, as he had to balance centralised control against the risk of being seen as a tyrant. Strong central government was needed to protect Rome from foreign enemies and the risk of renewed internal strife. Charges of dictatorship or tyranny would have made it difficult for Augustus to unite the various factions in Rome under his leadership.

Augustus began by introducing a public works programme in Rome: he provided shows and gladiatorial contests for the populace; he restored public finances; and he demobilised half the army, providing them with generous pensions. These troops were resettled throughout Italy and the Empire. After being proclaimed *Princeps Senatus*, Augustus reduced the number of senators, which was to his own advantage as it reduced the number of senators who could remember the days of the old Republic.

THE FIRST SETTLEMENT

In January 27 BC, Augustus (Octavian) offered to renounce all power. This was a carefully calculated move—he had shrewdly judged the mood of the Senate. The offer appears to have been designed to deflect the charges of those who sought to label him a tyrant. Almost certainly Augustus knew that the Senate feared a return to civil strife more than it feared him. The Senate not only refused the offer but gave him the title Augustus (meaning 'revered one'), the name he was to use and make famous from that time on. As well, they granted him direct and personal control over the provinces of Spain, Gaul and Syria. An important step had been taken in granting to Augustus more constitutional power than had been held by any other Roman.

His regime, however, was not without opponents. When he returned from a tour of the western provinces of Spain and Gaul in 24 BC, he was confronted with a conspiracy led by Fannius Caepio, a staunch republican. The conspiracy failed, because Augustus retained firm control of the army.

THE SECOND SETTLEMENT

In 23 BC the Senate made Augustus *maius imperium proconsulare*, which meant he had extensive power, not only in his own provinces but also in the provinces still controlled by members of the Senate. Augustus, in this capacity, could give orders directly to the Roman military in any province and, in doing so, over-ride the wishes of the senatorial administration. Such power dramatically changed Rome's constitutional history. However, Augustus applied this added power with such diplomacy that it aroused little opposition.

In 23 BC he also received *tribunicia potestas*, which meant he gained increased direct power in Rome, including the power to veto the Senate in matters of administration; bring matters of public importance directly before the people; and summon the Senate at will and propose the first item of business.

The powers granted to him by both *maius imperium proconsulare* and *tribunicia potestas* provided Augustus with the legal basis for his authority throughout both Rome and the Empire.

THE THIRD SETTLEMENT

During 19 and 18 BC a number of other settlements were made which increased the power and prestige of Augustus's position at the expense of the Senate. The most notable of these concerned the right of succession. It should have been the responsibility of the Senate (the only body with the legal power to do so) to name Augustus's replacement. Nevertheless, in 18 BC, Augustus named his own successor, Agrippa. Such an action, once accepted, clearly indicated that the Principate had become institutionalised.

The powers entrusted to Augustus by these settlements were augmented in 12 BC when he was appointed *pontifex maximus*. This office added prestige to his growing personal power. It is important to note that Augustus never actually demanded power from the Senate. His growing list of duties and honours were granted to him.

Cassius Dio, on the settlements:

And because of this the senate voted that Augustus should be tribune for life and gave him the privilege of bringing before the senate at each meeting any one matter at whatever time he liked, even if he were not consul at the time; they also permitted him to hold once for all and for life the office of proconsul, so that he had neither to lay it down upon entering the pomerium nor to have it renewed again, and they gave him in the subject territory authority superior to that of the governor in each instance. As a result both he and the emperors after him gained a certain legal right to use the tribunician power as well as their other powers...

Cassius Dio, *Roman History*, 53.32.5–6

➤ **List the powers granted to Augustus that Cassius Dio refers to here.**

➤ **What do you think was the real significance of Augustus being allowed to bring business before the Senate whenever he chose?**

ANALYSIS OF THE OFFICE OF PRINCEPS

Augustus did not plan the office of the Princeps and its power. Rather, it evolved from his attempts to cope with individual administrative difficulties. The legal division of power is the basis for Mommsen's concept of the *dyarchy*. In theory, many powers were shared between Augustus and the Senate. These included:

- administration of various provinces, even though after 23 BC Augustus held supreme military power in all provinces;
- finance and the power to mint coins;
- the power to call trials and sit in judgement, although Augustus acted more like a high court of appeal;
- the municipal administration of Rome, although Augustus became

unhappy with what he regarded as inefficiency in this area and made a number of direct changes, minimising the Senate's influence.

One problem Augustus faced was that he could not find enough people from the senatorial class to fill positions in provincial administration and the public service. As a result he turned to the equestrian class, members of which had been denied a role in government during the days of the Republic and were glad of the opportunity to participate in state administration. As well as drawing upon the talents of both the Senate and the equestrian class, Augustus employed a large personal staff who were officially part of his household but fulfilled important administrative and clerical tasks to assist him in running the state. Many members of this private entourage were former slaves. This demonstrates how Augustus was able to attract the support of various factions and classes within Roman society and unify them under his leadership.

While there were areas of shared authority, the real prestige and power rested with Augustus. The Senate may have had legal and constitutional power to bestow the title of Princeps, and all the honours and offices which went with it, but Augustus controlled the army. The reality of force, therefore, rather than the facade of constitutional authority, was the true basis of power in Rome. However, as with so much of Augustus's reign, his authority was legitimised by his sensible use of power, his quiet lifestyle, his lack of ostentation and, most important of all, his willingness to grant the Senate the prestige due to that office. He may have held the power, but he treated the institution of the Senate, individual senators and the memory of the Republic with respect.

> The Principate was not formally a monarchy, but rather a "dyarchy", as German writers have called it; the Princeps and the senate together ruled the state. But the fellowship was an unequal one, for the Emperor, as supreme commander of the armies, had the actual power. The dyarchy is a transparent fiction. The chief feature of the constitutional history of the first three centuries of the Empire is the decline of the authority of the senate and the corresponding growth of the powers of the Princeps, until finally he becomes an absolute monarch. When this comes to pass, the Empire can no longer be described as the Principate.
>
> Bury, *A History of the Roman Empire*, 15

↘ **Define the concept of 'dyarchy' referred to above.**

↘ **Draw up a table to compare the work of the Senate and Augustus under the Principate.**

THE IMPACT OF AUGUSTUS'S REIGN

SOCIETY AND THE ECONOMY

Between 27 BC and AD 14, Augustus, as Princeps (or Emperor), presided over the beginnings of Rome as we generally imagine it: imperial power, a vast empire, wealth, impressive public buildings and a flowering of art and culture.

Augustus laid the foundations for such a society by providing sound and stable government. He created an atmosphere in which the Roman economy flourished. His system of civil administration, taxation and financial management, while not perfect, was essentially conducive to economic growth. The only major shortcoming of Augustus's management of the growing economic prosperity was his reluctance to provide the kinds of social reforms that would have shared it more widely. This is not surprising, however, as Augustus was conservative on social issues.

Augustus valued Roman tradition. He encouraged men to continue wearing the toga and the women of his own household to produce clothes from homespun yarn (which he wore himself). He does not seem to have favoured change for change's sake; most of his political reforms or financial changes were in response to obvious inefficiencies. Shortcomings in the traditional social fabric, however, were far less obvious; hence he saw little need to change them. He did, however, pass strict laws designed to hasten the repopulation of war-torn Italy. Laws were passed to encourage marriage, remarriage and procreation, although even the mighty Augustus found it difficult to enforce laws directed at the bedrooms of Rome. His reform of the criminal code proved far more successful.

LITERATURE

Some of the greatest names in Roman literature are associated with Augustus's reign. Among them are the great historian Livy and the poets Ovid and Horace. It is interesting to note that Horace writes of Augustus subjugating Britain. The reality is that even though Augustus planned on three occasions to annex Britain, each attempt had to be postponed due to problems elsewhere in the Empire. This is clearly an instance of poetic licence; Horace is attempting to flatter his Emperor.

RELIGION

Augustus displayed a keen interest in Rome's religion and in many of its antiquarian ceremonies. He appears to have believed that all the traditions and beliefs which comprised Roman religion were an essential ingredient in Rome's greatness, and he sought to preserve them.

In his role as *pontifex maximus* he played a key part in the worship of the goddess Vesta. Vesta was the Roman hearth-goddess, linked to family life and in turn to the power and security of Rome. It was Augustus's duty to choose the Vestal Virgins. These young women, the children of noble households, served the goddess for as many as thirty years, remaining celibate. Augustus extended their privileges.

Augustus also favoured the deities of Apollo and Diana and in 17 BC ordered a celebration of games, the *Ludi Saeculares*, in their honour. He also renewed the worship of *Lares Compitales*, a religion about which there is some uncertainty. Theories about the religion ranged from the *Lares* being ghosts, to them being deities of the farmland. Whatever theory he believed,

Bronze *Lares* (Louvre, Paris. Courtesy Giraudon)

the revival of this religion by Augustus is another clue to his values. Respect paid to ghosts or family ancestors was honouring the past and a family's heritage; deities of the countryside took metropolitan Romans back to their roots. Augustus was a great believer in the role traditional values had played in Rome's rise to greatness and often urged others not to forget them.

Emperor worship—the deification of Augustus in his own lifetime—was a more vexed question. Such adulation was not likely to find personal favour with Augustus. This does not mean that he disdained honours and praise; rather, he was always very careful about which honours he accepted and when. Emperor worship arose spontaneously in the eastern parts of the Empire, where it was common for individuals to be so acclaimed. Augustus had brought considerable benefits through peace and good government to these regions, hence they offered their respect in a manner appropriate to local custom.

What was typical and appropriate in the East, however, might not fit in elsewhere, especially in Rome. Augustus acted with caution, arranging a compromise. Many eastern cities worshipped the goddess Roma as the symbol of Rome. They added to this the worship of Augustus. The cult thus became *Roma et Augustus*. Augustus found this acceptable; he felt that it was worship of his part in the greatness of Rome, not of him alone. His motives in allowing the cult were political, since there was evidence that it unified people within provinces and bonded them to Rome. With these objectives in mind, he extended this kind of worship to the West, specifically Gaul. However, he actively discouraged the cult in Rome. In the provinces it was useful; amongst the Romans it could have been counter-productive, since Augustus was trying to revive old cults, not become the focus of a new one. Within Rome he preferred to be seen as another citizen, a much honoured leader, but nevertheless a man.

Such a realistic response to the problem of Emperor worship was typical of Augustus. His attitude provided a stark contrast to the behaviour of his successors: Caligula and Nero in particular were carried away by their own divinity. Augustus appears to have kept his feet firmly on the ground.

FINANCIAL MANAGEMENT

Augustus was a talented and practical 'money manager'. Unlike many of his successors, Augustus carefully considered the cost of each new venture. He was not mean, but he was interested in 'balancing the books' or making a profit. Would a new enterprise earn money for Rome's coffers? Was another aqueduct, building, bridge or road worth the cost? Should it perhaps be abandoned or postponed? This was one of the reasons why he began to impose limits upon the size of the Empire.

The reforms Augustus made to the financial system were realistic and gradual. The central agency controlling Rome's finances was the *aerarium* or treasury, to which Augustus made few changes. Those he made were:

- to replace its officials, the financial quaestors (a position created by the old Republic in 447 BC, including members of the plebeian class) with officials of praetorian rank. Augustus felt these were better qualified;
- to add an *aerarium militare* in AD 6. This treasury administered the pensions of former soldiers.

Augustus left behind a treasury in better health than the one he found at the commencement of his reign.

The Senate was responsible for supervising the *aerarium*, which should have meant that, as in republican days, they, not Augustus, controlled the purse strings. This arrangement, however, is another example of the gap between theory and practice in the Augustan Principate. While Augustus did not disturb the *aerarium* or the Senate's supervision, the *fisci* (funds controlled personally by the Emperor) became the backbone of Rome's finances. The *fisci* were made up of:

- the Emperor's private fortune and property;
- revenues from the imperial provinces;
- public funds controlled by the Emperor.

It is likely that the bulk of provincial taxes (imperial and senatorial) went to the Emperor's *fisci* rather than the *aerarium*. With personal control of most of Rome's finances, Augustus was effectively treasurer of the Empire.

ADDITIONAL REVENUE

To finance the rising cost of imperial administration, extra taxes had to be imposed. These took the form of indirect taxes on sales and inheritances. Another valuable windfall came from the treasures of Egypt gained from Augustus's victory over Antony and the fall of Cleopatra in 31 BC.

THE CITY OF ROME

It was one of Augustus's proudest boasts that he had presided over the rebuilding of the city of Rome, making it a worthy capital for the world's greatest empire. In 27 BC, Rome was essentially an unplanned city; a growing but rambling metropolis with inadequate public buildings, narrow streets, substandard water supply in some areas and poor municipal administration.

Augustus's public buildings changed the face of Rome. According to Augustus himself in the *Res Gestae*, he restored at least eighty-two temples and built many others. He encouraged construction in fine materials, especially the white marble from the Carrara quarries. According to Suetonius, Augustus claimed that he found a city of brick and left one of marble. In addition, he built warehouses, granaries, public baths, libraries and theatres. He introduced controls over the size of streets and buildings in the poorer parts of Rome.

The municipal administration of Rome was poorly organised. At the beginning of Augustus's reign, for example, the methods of combating one of the city's greatest dangers, fire, were uncoordinated and voluntary. Augustus redesigned the municipal administration with effective, co-ordinated fire fighting units (the *vigiles*). He also created within Rome a special board to supervise the water supply. Steps were taken to control the annual flooding of the Tiber.

AUGUSTUS AND ITALY

As Rome prospered under Augustus's rule, so too did Italy. Augustus

Bridge of Augustus, Rimini, Italy (Alinari)

provided the first real opportunities for all eligible Italians to share in the government of Rome. Men from all over Italy who were part of the municipal system of administration were admitted to the senatorial and equestrian classes of Rome.

Augustus also began to spend public funds on projects throughout Italy. Repairs to roads were a priority. Not only were good roads essential to Rome's defence network; they also brought obvious benefits to the trade and commerce of local towns. A permanent body, the *curatores viarum*, was set up to supervise the roads. In addition, the rural areas of Italy were patrolled by a special imperial corps to reduce the activities of highwaymen and brigands.

THE EMPIRE

Augustus's greatness rests more on his success as an administrator than as one who extended the boundaries of Empire. He seems to have decided that there were certain natural frontiers to the Roman Empire beyond which it was better not to venture. He was prepared for some extension of Roman authority into neighbouring provinces only when such an advance would either increase Rome's security or bring tangible benefits in terms of trade. In Egypt, for example, the Empire was meant to halt at the first cataract of the Nile, the boundary between the rich fertile region and the desert beyond. He seems to have regarded the Rhine region and the Danube River as suitable points at which to halt Rome's expansion in the north.

Augustus appears to have been concerned that Rome should not over-stretch its resources by attempting to rule too much, particularly when, in the case of the German tribes, the people to be subjugated proved trouble-some. In retrospect, however, this approach seems to have been a mistake. It has been argued that had Rome's dominion been extended a little further north, then the life of the Roman Empire may have been prolonged, because this is the region that spawned Rome's most persistent enemies. Such a move, it is argued, would have suppressed some of the violent tribes who took part in the eventual destruction of Rome. All these arguments, however, remain speculative.

Augustus decided that wars of conquest taken too far would produce greater debt than profit. The disaster that befell the army of the Roman Governor of Germany, Quinctilius Varus, in the German Teutoburg Forest in AD 9 confirmed Augustus's fears about overextending the Empire. He did, however, consolidate a Roman Empire that dominated the Mediterranean coastline, securing Rome's economic and imperial future for generations to come.

While consolidating the Empire, Augustus introduced a number of important reforms within the army, improving both its organisation and the conditions of the troops. It was Augustus who founded the famous 'Praetorian Guard'. This group later played a key role in determining who ruled in

Rome. Its political role did not become clear, however, until the reign of Tiberius. Augustus also recognised the need for Rome to have an efficient navy, and introduced the reforms necessary to create such a force.

AUGUSTUS'S IMPERIAL VENTURES

Between 26 BC and 19 BC, Augustus subjugated the people of north-western Spain, the *Cantabri* and *Astures* tribes. In 25 BC he ordered his forces to advance into Judaea and part of Arabia in a move designed to produce a profit by providing Roman traders in Alexandria with a share of the Arab dominated eastern trade.

In the East, Augustus did not want to give up the Roman claims to Parthia and Armenia. They were, however, troublesome areas and he was reluctant to launch a full-scale military campaign. His policy became one of compromise designed simply to guarantee the safety of the Empire's frontier at the smallest possible cost.

In Gaul, Augustus consolidated the gains made by Julius Caesar, improving administration of the region and establishing many new Roman-style towns.

MANAGEMENT OF THE PROVINCES

The population of Augustus's Empire numbered in the millions; most of these people were in the provinces. By AD 14 there were nearly twenty-five separate provinces within the Empire. These had been gained by:
- conquest, perhaps the most common method since Rome's growth from a village on the Tiber;
- administrative change, where new provinces were created by subdividing old ones that were too large for effective management;
- annexation of dependent kingdoms. (Where possible Augustus preferred to leave these states under their native rulers but converted them into provinces if the boundaries of Empire were threatened or the local rulers failed to maintain order.)

The best example of a dependent state ruled by a native dynasty was Judaea, ruled by King Herod and his sons.

Augustus improved the efficiency of provincial administration. Even Tacitus, who was not a supporter of the imperial system, conceded that the management of the provinces improved under the Augustan system. Augustus personally undertook numerous tours of inspection. He selected provincial governors with care, and provided them with a vastly improved clerical and administrative staff. This was a considerable advance over the days of the Republic, when selection of governors was less formal and the quality of support staff was poor.

Augustus revised the system of salaries for provincial governors. Under the Republic, governors simply received an allowance, and exploitation by Roman governors of their provinces to supplement this allowance was common. Augustus changed this. He provided governors with a generous fixed income, and removed one of the major causes of corruption.

Augustus also reformed the provincial tax system, making it more equitable and efficient. Provinces were not expected to contribute to Rome beyond their means, but they did contribute local taxes for the provision of services within the province and direct and indirect taxes to Rome. Direct taxes included those on land such as the *tributum soli* and indirect taxes included the *portoria*, a kind of duty paid on goods crossing frontiers.

Research

> ╲Make notes on Augustus's policy towards Germany. What were the main campaigns in this area?

> ╲Make a list of the 'trouble spots' (scenes of rebellion) in the Roman Empire in Augustus's time.

AUGUSTUS THE MAN

As with any outstanding political figure, Augustus's personality defies a simple label or description. He was a very complex individual. A simple family man at home, he presided over the most dramatic constitutional change in Rome's history.

THE FAMILY AND THE SEARCH FOR A SUCCESSOR

Like many Roman men of noble birth, he had more than one wife. His first wife was Mark Antony's stepdaughter Claudia, his second was Scribonia. His third marriage, to Livia Drusilla, was long and successful. She appears to have been an active partner in the decision-making process during the greatest years of Augustus's rule.

There were rumours that Livia continually conspired to ensure that her son Tiberius, by a previous marriage, became Augustus's successor. Herein lay the most blatant flaw in the Augustan system, the succession. The Principate was the product of one man and one personality. It was idiosyncratic, a unique product of Augustus's mind and gifts. His successors generally proved far less capable of administering that system.

Augustus was acutely aware of the problem of providing a suitable successor. At various times throughout his rule he attempted to select and groom his replacement. The first of these was his nephew Marcus Marcellus; next was Agrippa, a friend who married into Augustus's family. The deaths of these early candidates in 23 BC and 12 BC respectively saw Augustus's attention directed towards Tiberius. When Tiberius fell from favour, Augustus's grandsons Gaius and Lucius Caesar were seen as likely candidates for the office and adopted as Augustus's own sons. The early deaths of these two boys (Lucius in AD 2, Gaius in AD 4) saw Tiberius returned to favour (he ultimately succeeded Augustus as Princeps). This apparent vacillation must have caused considerable strain within the family, as each candidate rose and fell in Augustus's estimation. Augustus's decision to pre-empt the role of the Senate in choosing his successor and the fact that a close relationship with Augustus's family was essential, indicates the extent to which the Principate had begun to resemble a monarchy.

| Coin depicting head of Tiberius (Macquarie University, NSW) | Coin depicting Gaius and Lucius Caesar (Macquarie University, NSW) |

A POSITION OF PRE-EMINENCE

In theory, Augustus's successor should have been selected by the Senate from any member of Rome's noble families who displayed outstanding merit. The fact that such a process was not seriously considered by the Senate is evidence of both the fear they held of conflict arising and a possible return to civil war, and the pre-eminent position that Augustus held. This position was clearly based on a number of factors.

- Augustus had proved to be an administrator and politician of rare skill.
- There was a view at the time that strong, decisive central leadership was vital to Rome's prosperity.
- Augustus retained the consistent and loyal support of the army. In the event of a crisis, he possessed an overwhelming advantage in force.
- His personality and manner appear to have won Augustus respect from all sections of Roman society.
- Even though he had the backing of the army, Augustus remained conscious of the need to carry with him the legitimising approval of the Senate.

Augustus's ascendancy was based upon his skills as an individual, the support of the military and the constitution of Rome. If necessary he could have dispensed with the last of these, but such an action was not compatible with his desire for compromise, consensus and legitimate government. Unfortunately, Augustus's successors lacked his political gifts but outstripped him in vanity and lust for personal power. Some of them relied on force far more than on the Roman constitution. Augustus created a system to match his talents, but even as a Roman god he couldn't control those who came after him!

Augustus had not indeed fashioned [the Principate] suddenly or overnight. He had preferred the evolutionary method, largely because as a *circumspectissimus et prudentissimus princeps* he was disposed to take steps only when they were needed. In part, too, he may have avoided haste out of a desire to accommodate to his new system the practices and traditions of the old for which he had so genuine a regard: not for nothing does he insist that he acted *maiorum nostrorum exemplo*. And yet another factor making for gradualness was possibly his habit of consultation with others; for, as Crook has recently remarked, "the Romans had an immemorial tradition that men in positions of responsibility should not take decisions alone", and we may be sure that in his scrupulous respect for other traditions, Augustus did not ride roughshod over this one. Dio's famous picture of him seeking the advice of Agrippa and Maecenas is no doubt fictitious, but the state of affairs which it implies surely must be accepted as fact. We know, indeed, that Augustus consulted with Agrippa on matters military, and there are good grounds for believing that he sought his counsel, and that of others as well, on other matters too. The summit, however, is a lonely place. In the last analysis the responsibility for fashioning the new form of government must have rested with him and not with his aides. As he proudly remarks, he surpassed all in *auctoritas*; surely he then was the *auctor* of the *optimi status*, of the system we call the Principate.

Salmon, *The Evolution of Augustus' Principate*, 477–8

Why does Salmon claim that the creation of the Principate was evolutionary?

From whom does he claim Augustus sought advice?

What is Salmon's assessment of the role of advisers or helpers such as Agrippa in fashioning the Augustan system?

Does this assessment agree with the facts as you know them?

What qualities would Augustus's successors need to continue the Principate as shaped by him?

CONCLUSION

Augustus was responsible for massive achievements. The city of Rome and the Empire benefited materially from his rule. He was a man of considerable political skill. Augustus was not a man dominated by theories; he was essentially practical. The political system he created, and the reforms he introduced, were all designed to solve specific problems. His ability to gain and retain support from a wide range of interest groups in Rome was the key to his success.

Critics tend to focus upon his part in the demise of the Republic. In fairness, fear of civil war arising from the political struggles linked to republicanism, not Augustus himself, killed the Republic. Its administrative system had been stretched to breaking point by the growing size and complexity of the Empire. Augustus created a government to meet the needs of the day.

Further criticism is often levelled at Augustus because of the abuses of the Principate's powers by his successors. Augustus, however, can hardly be held responsible for the shortcomings of those who came after him. He did everything in his power to leave Rome a better place than he found it.

In my sixth and seventh consulships, after I had extinguished civil wars, and at a time when with universal consent I was in complete control of affairs, I transferred the republic from my power to the dominion of the senate and people of Rome. For this service of mine I was named Augustus by decree of the senate, and the door-posts of my house were publicly wreathed with bay leaves and a civic crown was fixed over my door and a golden shield was set in the Curia Julia, which, as attested by the inscription thereon, was given me by the senate and people of Rome on account of my courage, clemency, justice and piety. After this time I excelled all in influence, although I possessed no more official power than others who were my colleagues in the several magistracies...

Augustus, Res Gestae, 34.1–3

How does Augustus claim to have gained supreme power?

After reviewing the creation of the Principate and Augustus's role in the Empire, do you think that Augustus's summary of his political career is completely accurate?

Research

What acts of Augustus support the inscription on the golden shield which recognised his 'valour, clemency, justice and devotion'.

LIST OF REFERENCES

ANCIENT SOURCES

Augustus, *Res Gestae*, Oxford University Press, Oxford, 1981
Cassius Dio, *Dio's Roman History*, Vol. 6, Loeb Classical Library, 1968
Suetonius, 'Augustus' in *The Twelve Caesars*, Penguin, 1981
Tacitus, *The Annals of Imperial Rome*, Penguin, 1977

SECONDARY SOURCES

Bury, J. B., *A History of the Roman Empire from its Foundation to the Death of Marcus Aurelius (27 BC – 180 AD)*, John Murray, London, 1922
Salmon, E. T., *A History of the Roman World 30 BC to AD 138*, Methuen, London, 1985
—— *The Evolution of Augustus' Principate*, Historia 6, Franz Steiner Verlag, Wiesbaden, 1956
Scullard, H. H., *From the Gracchi to Nero: A History of Rome from 133 BC to AD 68*, Methuen, London, 1985

BIBLIOGRAPHY

SECONDARY SOURCES

Jones, A. H. M., *Ancient Culture and Society: Augustus*, Chatto and Windus, London, 1977
Kagan, D., *Problems in Ancient History Volume Two: The Roman World*, Macmillan, New York, 1975

CHAPTER EIGHT

TIBERIUS IN THE SHADOW OF AUGUSTUS

KATE CAMERON

42 BC	Tiberius born to Tiberius Claudius Nero and Livia Drusilla. His parents later divorce
38	Augustus divorces Scribonia, and marries Livia Drusilla (who is also divorced)
37	Birth of Drusus, Tiberius's brother
33	Death of Tiberius Claudius Nero. Nine-year-old Tiberius delivers his father's funeral oration
	Augustus betroths Tiberius to Vipsania, daughter of Marcus Agrippa, his closest friend
29	Augustus celebrates his triumph; Tiberius given second place of honour in the procession
27	Tiberius assumes his *toga virilis* at the age of fifteen
26	Tiberius goes to Spain as military tribune
25	Marriage of fourteen-year-old Julia (Augustus's daughter) to Marcellus
24	Tiberius makes speech to Senate requesting remission of tribute for provincials who had suffered an earthquake
23	Tiberius becomes quaestor at the age of nineteen
	Death of Marcellus
22	Tiberius acts successfully as prosecutor in treason trial
21	Marriage of Julia and Agrippa
20	Tiberius successful in military campaign in Armenia; retrieves from the Parthians the Roman standards lost at Carrhae
19	Marriage of Tiberius and Vipsania

17	Augustus adopts Julia's sons, Gaius and Lucius
16	Tiberius becomes praetor in Gaul
15	Tiberius wages successful campaigns against the Raetians and the Vindelicians
	Tiberius received into the college of priests
14	Birth of Drusus, son of Tiberius and Vipsania
13	Tiberius becomes consul at the age of twenty-nine
12	Death of Julia's husband, Agrippa
	Augustus forces Tiberius to divorce his pregnant wife Vipsania and betroths him to Julia
	Tiberius, Governor of Illyria, wins the Pannonian War
	Senate awards Tiberius a triumph but Augustus reduces it to the lesser 'insignia of a triumph'
11	Tiberius and his brother Drusus receive *proconsular imperium*
	Tiberius subdues rebellious Dalmations and Pannonians
	Tiberius's soldiers salute him as imperator, a title Augustus has forbidden him to use
	Marriage of Tiberius and Julia
10	Tiberius on campaign in Illyricum
	A son is born to Tiberius and Julia (he dies soon after birth)
	Tiberius wins ovation for his successes in Pannonia
9	Death of Drusus; Tiberius accompanies his brother's body to Rome and delivers the funeral oration
8	Tiberius wins victories in Germany and is hailed imperator
7	Tiberius is consul for the second time
	Tiberius celebrates his triumph then returns to Germany
6	At the age of thirty-six, Tiberius receives tribunician power for five years
	Tiberius pacifies Armenia
	Augustus offers Tiberius a diplomatic position in the East
	Tiberius refuses and instead retires from public life on the island of Rhodes
2	Divorce of Tiberius and Julia
	Augustus exiles Julia
AD 2	Death of Lucius ⎫ Heirs of Augustus
4	Death of Gaius ⎭
	Augustus adopts Tiberius and also Agrippa Postumus (Julia's son)
	Augustus forces Tiberius to adopt Germanicus, his brother Drusus's son
	Tiberius returns to the wars in Germany
5	Military campaign in Germany continues
6	Tiberius hailed imperator by his troops in Germany

7	Military campaigns in Illyricum led by Tiberius
9	Tiberius twice more hailed imperator
	Tiberius's triumph postponed because of continued fighting in Germany
11	Campaigns continue in Germany
12	Tiberius again hailed imperator; finally celebrates triumph
13	Tiberius's *imperium* made equal with that of Augustus; this gives him equal power over the provinces and the armies
	Tiberius's tribunician power renewed
14	Tiberius conducts census
	He returns to campaign in Illyricum
	Tiberius hailed imperator
	Death of Augustus
	Tiberius becomes Emperor at the age of fifty-five

Augustus was a hard act to follow. He had ruled Rome for over forty years, most of the time enjoying great popularity. The circumstances under which he had come to power had been forgotten, overshadowed by the grand achievements of his rule. Augustus was remembered for restoring order and discipline after a long period of bitter civil war. He was an excellent administrator who brought peace, security and general prosperity to the people of Rome.

As founder of the Principate, Augustus had adapted republican institutions to suit his own personal system of government. While on the surface traditional republican practices continued, Augustus actually exercised great personal power through his control of finances and of military and administrative appointments. He appointed the senators and officials who shared government with him. They, in turn, conferred honour and power on Augustus; *pontifex maximus*, consul, imperator, permanent tribune of the people and *pater patriae* were just a few of the titles he was awarded and used.

No other Roman had enjoyed such prestige; no other Roman had exercised such power. After his death he was given the ultimate honour, he was made a god—the 'Divine Augustus'.

TIBERIUS AS SUCCESSOR

During his Principate, Augustus had tried to find a successor from within his own family, using his only child, Julia, as the pawn in his plans. He first married her to his nephew, Marcellus, who died when Julia was sixteen. They had not produced an heir. Augustus then maried her to his old friend Agrippa. Julia had five children to Agrippa before he, too, died. Augustus adopted two of Julia's boys as his own sons. The succession of another Julian seemed assured. How then did the aged Tiberius, who was not a Julian by birth, become the next Emperor?

Bust of Tiberius (Mansell Collection)

In *The Annals of Imperial Rome*, Tacitus, our main primary source on these events, suggests that Tiberius 'wormed his way in' and that the intrigues of his mother, Livia, gained him the succession. Suetonius, in *The Twelve Caesars*, offers another explanation. He claims that Augustus adopted Tiberius as his heir in the national interest, because he was the only general capable of defending Rome against her enemies.

Head of Livia (Classics Department Museum, Australian National University, Canberra. Photo Professor J. R. Green, University of Sydney)

Read the timeline of Tiberius's career at the start of this chapter. Was Tiberius a suitable candidate for the position of Emperor? Consider the following issues.

- How extensive was his political experience? How closely had he followed the *cursus honorum*?
- What military experience did he have?
- How was he regarded by his troops?
- In what ways did Augustus advance Tiberius's career?
- How and why did Tiberius's position change within Augustus's family?
- Why might Tiberius feel resentment against Augustus?
- Why might Augustus feel hostility towards Tiberius?
- Were there any other candidates who could have succeeded Augustus?

THE IMAGE OF TIBERIUS

Tiberius became Emperor at the age of fifty-five after a long and successful military career. What was he like as an Emperor? What was he like as a person? It is not easy to gain a clear picture of the character and rule of

Tiberius from the primary sources, because most of them are so clearly biased against him.

Tacitus writes his history with a moral purpose, to record the virtue or wickedness of the Emperors. He despises the Principate in general and Tiberius in particular. While he gives Tiberius credit for some virtues in the early part of his reign, the overwhelming impression he creates is of a hypocrite and a cruel and sinister tyrant.

> While he was a private citizen or holding commands under Augustus, his life was blameless; and so was his reputation. While Germanicus and Drusus still lived, he concealed his real self, cunningly affecting virtuous qualities. However, until his mother died there was good in Tiberius as well as evil. Again, as long as he favoured (or feared) Sejanus, the cruelty of Tiberius was detested, but his perversions unrevealed. Then fear vanished, and with it shame. Thereafter he expressed only his own personality—by unrestrained crime and infamy.
>
> Tacitus, *Annals*, 6.50

Suetonius's view of Tiberius is not much better. He, too, admits that there were some good aspects of Tiberius's early rule, but he seems far more interested in Tiberius's vicious passions and the monstrous vices he is supposed to have indulged on the island of Capri. The lasting impression conveyed by Suetonius is of Tiberius as a miserly and despised old man.

> The first news of his death caused such joy at Rome that people ran about yelling: "To the Tiber with Tiberius!" and others offered prayers to Mother Earth and the Infernal Gods to give him no home below except among the damned.
>
> Suetonius, *Tiberius*, 75

Cassius Dio, who wrote about two hundred years after Tiberius's death, follows a similar pattern. He describes Tiberius's nature as peculiar, but does acknowledge that he was a capable ruler until the death of Germanicus, after which:

> He changed his course in many respects. Perhaps he had been at heart from the first what he later showed himself to be, and had been merely shamming while Germanicus was alive, because he saw his rival lying in wait for the sovereignty...
>
> Cassius Dio, *Roman History*, 57

There is one ancient writer who gives a favourable account of Tiberius. Velleius Paterculus published his brief history in AD 30 when Tiberius was still in power, and gives a very enthusiastic account of his Principate. He celebrates Tiberius's military achievements and applauds the virtues and talents Tiberius displays as a ruler.

> Credit has been restored in the forum, strife has been banished from the forum, canvassing for office from the Campus Martius, discord from the senate-house; justice, equity and industry, long buried in oblivion, have been restored to the state; the magistrates have regained their authority, the senate its majesty, the courts their dignity...
>
> Velleius Paterculus, *Roman History*, 2.126.2

While Tacitus saw the Principate as disguised despotism, Velleius saw it as a genuine restoration of the Republic. Unlike Tacitus, Velleius has no *stated* aim in writing his history, but the loyal service shown by the Velleii to both Augustus and Tiberius, and the advancements the family achieved under the Principate, should be considered. Could these factors have influenced Velleius's glowing portrait of Tiberius?

ASSESSING THE SOURCES ON TIBERIUS

Faced with such biased and sometimes conflicting accounts, how is it possible to gain a reliable picture of Tiberius and his rule?

Firstly, we need to acknowledge that history is not just fact but also interpretation. Historians are influenced by all sorts of things—their social and political position, their attitude to their subject, their reason for writing, their intended audience. All these considerations affect the way they perceive and interpret events.

Secondly, there is the question of sources. What material was available to the historian? Did the historian witness the events described, or merely rely on hearsay or a story passed down through generations? Did the historian have access to primary source material such as personal or public documents? Has the historian uncritically used the material of earlier writers?

Once the sources are collected, the historian has to decide what is most useful. The selection and arrangement of material is one of the most important aspects of writing history. When we consider Tacitus's picture of Tiberius, for example, we need to be aware that Tacitus was able to select from the wide variety of sources available to him and to arrange this material in a way that illustrated his theme. In this way he is able to magnify the importance of the treason trials and overlook more praiseworthy aspects of Tiberius's rule. The evidence he presents then 'proves' his case— that Tiberius was a tyrant.

Read Figure 8.1. Carefully evaluate each of the sources in this chapter using the techniques described.

CIRCUMSTANCES OF TIBERIUS'S ACCESSION

Yet a long time elapsed before he assumed the title of Emperor. When his friends urged him to accept it he went through the farce of scolding them for the suggestion, saying that they did not realize what a monstrous beast the monarchy was; and kept the Senate guessing by his carefully evasive answers and hesitations, even when they threw themselves at his feet imploring him to change his mind.

Suetonius, *Tiberius*, 24

❋ ❋ ❋

The senate now wallowed in the most abject appeals. Tiberius remarked incidentally that, although he did not feel himself capable of the whole burden of government, he was nevertheless prepared to take on any branch of it that might be entrusted to him. "Then I must ask, Caesar," called out Gaius Asinius Gallus, "which branch you desire to have

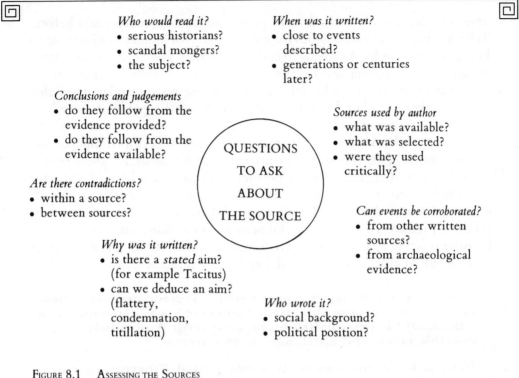

Who would read it?
- serious historians?
- scandal mongers?
- the subject?

When was it written?
- close to events described?
- generations or centuries later?

Conclusions and judgements
- do they follow from the evidence provided?
- do they follow from the evidence available?

QUESTIONS
TO ASK
ABOUT
THE SOURCE

Sources used by author
- what was available?
- what was selected?
- were they used critically?

Are there contradictions?
- within a source?
- between sources?

Can events be corroborated?
- from other written sources?
- from archaeological evidence?

Why was it written?
- is there a *stated* aim? (for example Tacitus)
- can we deduce an aim? (flattery, condemnation, titillation)

Who wrote it?
- social background?
- political position?

FIGURE 8.1   ASSESSING THE SOURCES

handed over to you." This unexpected question threw Tiberius off his stride. For some moments he said nothing. Then, recovering his balance, he replied that, since he would prefer to be excused from the responsibility altogether, he felt much too diffident to choose or reject this or that part of it.

Tacitus, Annals, 1.1

Both Suetonius and Tacitus record Tiberius's reluctance to become Emperor, but they do not accept his explanation. Instead, they interpret his actions as farcical and hypocritical.

Tiberius claims that the position of Emperor would force him to become a miserable and overworked slave. This claim seems reasonable, given his own experience. Throughout his career, he had conscientiously carried out the duties of his political appointments and for the last few years of Augustus's reign, Tiberius had in effect been governing the Empire. In AD 6 he was made Augustus's partner in tribunician power. This position, as well as his proconsular authority, involved Tiberius greatly in the administration of the Empire. In AD 13 his tribunician power was renewed and he was also given consular *imperium* as colleague of Augustus—it was in this position that he carried out the census in AD 14. As virtual co-ruler, Tiberius knew what the job involved.

His reluctance to become Emperor could be justified on other grounds. He was fifty-five years old and he was clearly the greatest general of his time. He had already retired from public life some twenty years before, living in virtual exile on Rhodes for eight years. Not long after returning to Rome he was sent by Augustus to conduct the long and arduous campaigns in Germany, Pannonia and Illyricum, where he was victorious and three times hailed imperator by his troops. Considering his age and unparalleled service, Tiberius's claim that he did not feel himself capable of the whole burden of government sounds reasonable.

Perhaps another reason for Tiberius's reluctance to become Emperor was his resentment of the way he had been treated by Augustus. He knew he was not Augustus's first choice for the position of Emperor. In his will Augustus indicated his reluctant choice of Tiberius: 'Since fate has cruelly carried off my sons Gaius and Lucius, Tiberius must inherit two-thirds of my property . . . ' (Suetonius, *Tiberius*, 23) Tiberius had been humiliated many times by Augustus, yet apart from his self-imposed exile in Rhodes he had always carried out Augustus's wishes with loyalty and diligence.

➤ **Can you think of other reasons why Tiberius may have been reluctant to become Emperor? Consider his background as a Claudian; his personality (compared with Augustus); possible rivals and challenges to the throne.**

➤ **Why have the ancient writers interpreted Tiberius's actions as insincere?**

➤ **Considering his reluctance to become Emperor, why did Tiberius accept the position?**

TIBERIUS'S ADMINISTRATION

While Tacitus, Suetonius and Cassius Dio disagree on the point at which Tiberius finally revealed himself as a cruel tyrant, they all acknowledge that in the early years of his rule Tiberius was a most capable administrator of Rome and the Empire. They differ slightly in emphasis and interpretation, but agree on the main aspects of his beneficial rule. Other written sources and also archaeological evidence support this view.

➤ **The following extracts from the main sources relate to three aspects of the early years of Tiberius's rule: law and order, finances and the provinces. Read them carefully then make your own judgements about his efforts. If you have access to the sources, compile your own sets of extracts illustrating the way other aspects of Tiberius's administration have been recorded and interpreted. It would be useful to look at his frontier policy, his attitude towards religion and his treatment of the army.**

LAW AND ORDER

Right is now honoured, evil is punished; the humble man respects the great but does not fear him, the great has precedence over the lowly but does not despise him . . . Honour ever awaits the worthy; for the wicked punishment is slow but sure; fair play has now precedence over influence, and merit over ambition . . .

Velleius Paterculcus, Roman History, 2.126.3–4

❋ ❋ ❋

. . . beatings and confiscations did not exist. His estates in Italy were few, his slaves unobtrusive, his household limited to a few ex-slaves. Any disputes that he had with private citizens were settled in the law courts.

Tacitus, Annals, 4.6

❋ ❋ ❋

Tiberius safeguarded the country against banditry and local revolts by decreasing the distance between police posts; and at Rome provided the Praetorian Guards, who had hitherto been billeted in scattered City lodging houses, with regular barracks and a fortified camp. He also discountenanced City riots, and if any broke out, crushed them without mercy.

Suetonius, Tiberius, 37

❋ ❋ ❋

He held court himself, as I have stated, but he also attended the courts presided over by the magistrates, not alone when invited by them, but also when not invited. He would allow them to sit in their regular places, while he himself took his seat on the bench facing them and as an assessor made any remarks that seemed good to him.

Cassius Dio, Roman History, 57.7

❋ ❋ ❋

THE PROVINCES

. . . when Aemilius Rectus once sent him from Egypt, which he was governing, more money than was stipulated, he [Tiberius] sent back to him the message: "I want my sheep shorn, not shaven".

ibid., 57.10

❋ ❋ ❋

He remained fully occupied with public business—legal cases concerning citizens, and petitions from the provinces. On his initiative, the senate decreed three years' remission of tribute to two cities ruined by earthquakes, Cibyra and Aegium. A governor of Farther Spain . . . was convicted of violence and deported as a bad character to the island of Amorgos.

Tacitus, Annals, 4.12

❋ ❋ ❋

The cities of Asia have been restored, the provinces have been freed from the oppression of their magistrates

Velleius Paterculus, Roman History, 2.126.4

❋ ❋ ❋

Even the emperor's agent in Asia, Lucilius Capito, had to defend himself before it [the Senate] when the people of the province prosecuted him . . . The case was tried, and Capito condemned. For this act of justice, and the punishment of Gaius Junius Silanus in the previous year, the cities of Asia decreed a temple to Tiberius, his mother, and the senate.

Tacitus, Annals, 4.14

Arch of Tiberius, Orange, France

* * *

The only free money grant any province got from him was when an earthquake destroyed some cities in Asia Minor.

Suetonius, *Tiberius*, 48

(Compare this with the accounts of Tacitus and Cassius Dio.)

* * *

FINANCES

Levies of grain, indirect taxation, and the other revenues belonging to the State were managed by associations of Roman knights. But the imperial property was entrusted by the emperor to carefully selected agents... The public suffered, it is true, from oppressive food prices. But that was not the emperor's fault. Indeed, he spared neither money nor labour in combating bad harvests and stormy seas.

Tacitus, *Annals*, 4.6

* * *

With what generosity at the time of the recent fire on the Caelian Hill, as well as on other occasions, did he use his private fortune to make good the losses of people of all ranks in life!

Velleius Paterculus, Roman History, 2.130.2

✦ ✦ ✦

While expending extremely little for himself, he laid out very large sums for the common good, either rebuilding or adorning practically all the public works and also generously assisting both cities and private individuals.

Cassius Dio, Roman History, 57.10

✦ ✦ ✦

Tiberius cut down the expenses of public entertainments by lowering the pay of actors and setting a limit to the number of gladiatorial combats on any given festival.

Suetonius, Tiberius, 34

✦ ✦ ✦

Tiberius was close-fisted to the point of miserliness, never paying his staff a salary when on a foreign mission, but merely providing their keep.

ibid., 46

✦ ✦ ✦

No magnificent public works marked his reign: his only two undertakings, the erection of Augustus's Temple and the restoration of Pompey's Theatre, still remained uncompleted at the end of all those years.

ibid., 47

✦ ✦ ✦

. . . when completing the buildings which Augustus had begun without finishing them he [Tiberius] inscribed upon them the other's name . . . This principle of inscribing the original builder's name he carried out not only in the case of the buildings erected by Augustus, but in the case of all alike that needed any repairs . . .

Cassius Dio, Roman History, 57.10

✦ ✦ ✦

TIBERIUS AND THE SENATE

Tacitus and Cassius Dio were senators and Suetonius an imperial official, so they had access to the archives which held the *Acta* (proceedings of the Senate). Consequently, their accounts of this aspect of Tiberius's rule should be reliable. They all acknowledge that there was co-operation between Tiberius and the Senate and that he showed the Senate respect and even deference. Yet they are inclined to interpret this relationship as hypocrisy on the part of Tiberius and fearful servility on the part of the Senate. At one level, their interpretation of events is coloured by the image they are trying to promote of Tiberius as a tyrant, but at another level this apparent contradiction reflects something that was inherent in the relationship which existed between Tiberius and the Senate.

When Tiberius became Princeps he was faced with a Senate which had been under the control of Augustus. Augustus had determined its composition and regulated its proceedings; under his personal rule the Senate's role was strictly circumscribed. The modern historian, Syme, claims that the Senate had been corrupted and debased by Augustus and had become subservient. (Syme, 427) If this was the case, then their suspicion of Tiberius can be appreciated—here was a man who had virtually inherited the position of Emperor, yet he espoused republican principles. He disdained the subservience and flattery of the Senate and instead expected them to carry out a role for which most had had very little experience. For his part, Tiberius must have felt the conflict between his duty to carry out the instructions and policies of Augustus and his genuine desire to foster republican ideals. There were elements of frustration and suspicion on both sides.

Despite their negative interpretations of these difficulties, the ancient writers agree on a broad range of incidents which help to illustrate Tiberius's relationship with the Senate. Tiberius showed personal modesty and respect for the Senate by:

- refusing some titles of honour offered him by the Senate;
- declining offers of divine honours for himself and his mother;
- observing traditional behaviour in the Senate House, such as entering unescorted and rising to greet the consuls;
- assuming the consulship only three times after becoming Princeps, each time to give honour to one of his colleagues (Germanicus, Drusus and Sejanus);
- approaching the Senate when he felt Drusus should be given *tribunicia potestas* and Germanicus *proconsular imperium*;
- commending Germanicus's sons Drusus and Nero to the care of the Senate after the death of their father.

Tiberius encouraged the Senate's participation in government by:

- transferring elections of magistrates from the *comitia* to the Senate, a policy begun by Augustus;
- enlarging the judicial functions of the Senate to conduct important state trials, trials of provincial officials and prosecutions of *maiestas*.
- delegating decision making to the Senate, (e.g. allocation of the African command);
- including senators on any important commission or board of enquiry;
- helping deserving senators who were in financial difficulty so that they could retain their rank;
- encouraging freedom of expression and decision making. (There are many instances recorded where the Senate voted against Tiberius.)

There were also instances where Tiberius acted against the Senate. He did this by:

- transferring some senatorial provinces to imperial control;
- intervening in debates and trials (generally on the side of reason);
- nominating four of the twelve candidates for praetorships (Velleius Paterculus was one of his nominations);
- influencing the nomination of candidates for the consulship.

Despite such interference, Tacitus was able to acknowledge:

The consuls and praetors maintained their prestige. The lesser offices, too, each exercised their proper authority. Moreover, the treason court excepted, the laws were duly enforced.

Tacitus, *Annals*, 4.6

Tiberius had high, perhaps unrealistic, expectations of the Senate and he was often disappointed by their performance, hence his comment that they were 'men fit to be slaves'. He did, however, establish a good working relationship with the Senate which is acknowledged by the ancient writers. This relationship had its weaknesses, including the Senate's inexperience or reluctance to play the role expected of them and Tiberius's own personality and manner. The situation was undermined by the ambition and power of Sejanus and further weakened by Tiberius's prolonged absences from Rome.

THE TREASON TRIALS

This aspect of Tiberius's rule has been grossly misrepresented by the ancient writers. They create an impression of Tiberius as a sinister and bloodthirsty tyrant who used the treason law to kill off all who opposed or offended him.

Among other ways in which his rule became cruel, he pushed to the bitter end the trials for *maiestas*, in cases where complaint was made against anyone for committing any improper act, or uttering any improper speech, not only against Augustus, but also against Tiberius himself and against his mother.

Cassius Dio, *Roman History*, 57.19

❋ ❋ ❋

Not a day, however holy, passed without an execution; he even desecrated New Year's Day. Many of his men victims were accused and punished with their children— some actually by their children . . . An informer's word was always believed. Every crime became a capital one, even the utterance of a few careless words.

Suetonius, *Tiberius*, 61

❋ ❋ ❋

Frenzied with bloodshed, the emperor now ordered the execution of all those arrested for complicity with Sejanus. It was a massacre. Without discrimination of sex or age, eminence or obscurity, there they lay, strewn about—or in heaps.

Tacitus, *Annals*, 6.19

Such graphic language creates a powerful impression, but to what extent can the impression be substantiated by the facts?

Tiberius was not responsible for initiating the treason law. It first appeared in Rome in 103 BC when the tribune Saturninus created the crime of *maiestas populi Romani imminuta* (derogation to the majesty of Rome). From its inception the *maiestas* charge was vaguely defined and was often misused to bring unpopular people into court.

Under the Republic, treason was an action committed against the state— those whom the people had empowered to govern. Under the Empire, the

Princeps was the embodiment of the state and treason came to be interpreted as treachery or insult against the Princeps.

Augustus included treason laws in his Julian Laws of 18 BC, but he seldom
invoked them. When Tiberius became Princeps he inherited this law, *Lex
Julia de maiestate*, and was faced with the problem of interpretation and
application. The situation was made worse by the fact that the charge of
maiestas could be initiated by private citizens who would be given one-
quarter of their victim's property if a prosecution succeeded.

Considering the vagueness of the definition of the law of *maiestas* and the
rewards of a successful conviction, it is not surprising that many unscrupulous people attempted to lay charges. Naturally this generated fear and
unrest.

Many of the early trials were probably test cases to determine how the
law should be interpreted. Tiberius dismissed or acquitted all except two of
the *maiestas* charges laid in the first five years of his rule. Far from using the
law for his own ends, Tiberius moderated its application. He did not accept
that derogatory remarks made about him or his mother were grounds for
punishment, and he dismissed with contempt many such charges. When
people brought charges of *maiestas* tacked on to other charges, Tiberius
would insist that the charges be heard separately. He often intervened to
pardon those accused or to mitigate sentences handed down by the Senate,
before whom most of these trials were conducted, and in AD 21 he decreed
that where a conviction was made, there should be a ten-day interval
between sentence and execution.

The most serious accusations against Tiberius's use of the *maiestas* law
refer to the period of panic after the execution of Sejanus, whose conspiracy
created a personal and political crisis for Tiberius. It is not surprising that he
would be determined to punish the conspirators and their supporters, but
even so, Tiberius did not condone indiscriminate charges and five cases
from this period were dismissed without trial, three due to his direct
intervention.

What basis is there then for the impression created by the ancient
writers? Tacitus, in particular, magnifies the significance of the treason
trials so that they appear to be a permanent and important feature of
Tiberius's rule. The modern historian Walker has tabulated all the *maiestas*
trials mentioned by Tacitus and the facts provide quite a different picture.

Of the eighty-six *maiestas* proceedings under Tiberius, there were:
• nineteen acquittals (five due to Tiberius's intervention);
• twelve dismissals (seven due to Tiberius's intervention);
• four sentences cancelled or mitigated (two due to Tiberius);
• twenty-one sentences other than death (usually banishment); and
• eighteen executions, only five on Tiberius's personal order.
Considering that the crime of *maiestas* encompassed charges such as murder,
insurrection, extortion, misgovernment, slander and seditious propaganda,

then eighty-six cases (or fifty-two as suggested by Salmon) over twenty-three years in a city of over one million people is not quite as sensational as the ancient writers would have us believe.

> **Early in his Principate, Tiberius was asked whether cases under the treason law were to receive attention. He replied, 'the laws must take their course'. (Tacitus, *Annals*, 1.72) Why do you think Tiberius persisted with such a troublesome law? Why didn't he just ban it?**

> **In what ways could Tiberius have modified either the Roman legal system or the *maiestas* law to make it less open to abuse?**

Research

> **Try to discover why Tacitus exaggerates the importance of the treason trials under Tiberius.**

TIBERIUS AND THE PEOPLE

Tiberius was the least sensational of the Julio-Claudian Emperors. No great wars of conquest, massive public works, extravagant games or festivals distinguished his twenty-three-year rule. Unlike his predecessor, Augustus, he did not encourage adulation from the Senate, nor did he court popularity with the people.

As a general, Tiberius had always taken great care to avoid needless losses. He favoured diplomatic rather than military solutions where possible, because he was more interested in saving his men than in pursuing personal glory on the battlefield. Look back to the timeline and see how many times he was hailed imperator by his grateful troops. As Emperor he retained the same attitude, which fitted well his desire to follow Augustus's policy of non-aggression. Apart from Germanicus's hot-headed exploits in Germany and minor wars in Africa, Gaul and Thrace, Tiberius's reign was a relatively peaceful one throughout the Empire. The *pax Romana* (Roman peace) really began under Tiberius.

Tiberius did not seek popularity or personal glory through public works. He did not have much of an opportunity, as Augustus had extensively built or rebuilt Rome—remember his proud boast that he had 'found Rome brick and left it marble'. Tiberius attended to the completion or restoration of buildings in a most unassuming way. He did not add his own name to them, and always acknowledged the original builder. Among those buildings he did erect were the temple to Augustus and the barracks for the Praetorian Guard and the urban cohorts (city troops). In the provinces, Tiberius supervised the construction of utilitarian projects such as roads, bridges and aqueducts.

Tiberius's military training had given him a concern for order and discipline which, as Emperor, he saw as the basis of good government. He had a personal dislike of games and gladiatorial shows. He found them undignified and a dreadful waste of money, and deplored the disorder they often produced. There had been riots at games in Rome in which spectators had been killed, as had some of the soldiers sent to restore order. Tiberius introduced regulations to limit the size and number of the games. This did not endear him to the people, who flocked to games outside Rome whenever the opportunity arose. At one venue a wooden theatre collapsed and, according to Tacitus, 50 000 people were badly injured or crushed to death.

Tiberius was careful with finances in his own household and in government. The ancient writers suggest he was thrifty to the point of miserliness, although they all cite examples of his generosity. Tiberius continued the type of hand-outs which had become the custom under Augustus, although he did try to limit them. He showed his genuine concern for the people in less spectacular ways.

The corn supply was always a major concern in Rome, and Tiberius surpassed Augustus in the amount of corn he brought to Rome. In AD 19, when there was a shortage of corn and a consequent price rise, he fixed the price at a level the people could afford, and made up the difference to the corn merchants.

Tiberius lowered the unpopular one percent sales tax to half a percent, following the incorporation of Cappadocia as a province. When faced with a financial crisis in AD 33, he increased the circulation of money by lending the treasury one hundred million sesterces, interest free, for three years. Tiberius helped his people financially, in Rome and in the provinces, by providing aid for the victims of major disasters, including the collapsed amphitheatre at Fidenae, the Tiber floods, the disastrous fire on the Aventine and earthquakes in the provinces.

Perhaps Tiberius's greatest contribution to the welfare of the people was his maintenance of law and order. This applied in Rome, Italy and the provinces. He carefully supervised the *curatores* who were responsible for the provision of essential services in Rome. He appointed the City Prefect who, with the aid of the urban cohorts, was responsible for keeping law and order in the city. Tiberius maintained Augustus's special police for the suppression of brigandage in Italy and Sardinia and their activities were most successful. Tiberius closely watched the administration of the provinces to ensure efficient government and fair taxation.

The average citizens living under the rule of Tiberius were not pampered by frequent gifts of bread and circuses, the spectacle of a triumph or a share in the spoils of war. They could, however, travel in safety throughout Italy and the provinces and live securely under the rule of law.

TIBERIUS'S POPULARITY

Tiberius received gestures of appreciation from the provinces for his protection from extortionate governors and for his help in times of natural disaster. In Rome, however, it seems he did not enjoy great popularity.

> From the reading you have done, try to work out why Tiberius was so unpopular. Put yourself in the sandals of a Roman citizen, either a pleb or a patrician; a provincial; a senator; and a soldier. Draw up a chart listing the benefits and disadvantages of Tiberius's rule to you in each of these roles.

CONCLUSION

There are many more fascinating aspects of Tiberius's personality and rule which will help you to draw your own conclusions about Tiberius. Investigate the following topics, ideally through primary sources.

> Investigate Tiberius's behaviour and attitude toward his mother, Livia; wives, Vipsania and Julia; son, Drusus; stepson, Germanicus; stepson's wife, Agrippina.

> Why did Tiberius befriend and promote Sejanus? What powers was Sejanus given and how did he use and abuse these powers? What was Sejanus's ambition? How did Tiberius deal with Sejanus's betrayal? What effect did the whole affair have on Tiberius?

> When and why did Tiberius go to Capri? What did he do while he was there? (There are extraordinary contradictions in the primary sources.) How did Tiberius's withdrawal to Capri affect both the Senate and the administration of the Empire?

LIST OF REFERENCES

ANCIENT SOURCES

Cassius Dio, *Dio's Roman History*, Vol. 7, Loeb Classical Library, 1981

Suetonius, 'Tiberius' in *The Twelves Caesars*, Penguin, 1973

Tacitus, *The Annals of Imperial Rome*, Penguin, 1985

Velleius Paterculus, *Compendium of Roman History*, Loeb Classical Library, 1979

SECONDARY SOURCES

Salmon, E.T., *A History of the Roman World 30 BC to AD 138*, University Paperbacks, London, 1968

Syme, Ronald, *Tacitus*, Clarendon Press, Oxford, 1958

Walker, Betty, *The Annals of Tacitus*, Manchester University Press, 1952

BIBLIOGRAPHY

SECONDARY SOURCES

Garzetti, Albino, *From Tiberius to the Antonines*, Methuen & Co Ltd, London, 1974

Seager, Robin, *Tiberius*, Eyre Methuen, London, 1972

CALIGULA
MADMAN OR MADMAN?

JANE AND BRUCE DENNETT

Let them hate me, so long as they fear me
Accius

AD 12	Birth of Gaius Julius Caesar Germanicus (Caligula) at Antium
19	Death of his father, Germanicus, in Syria
31	Caligula becomes pontifex
32 – 37	Caligula joins Tiberius on Capri
33	Caligula becomes quaestor Death of Agrippina the Elder
35	Caligula marries Junia Claudilla
37	Death of Tiberius Caligula enters Rome as Princeps Caligula's illness
38	The 'four suicides': Tiberius Gemellus, Junius Silanus, Macro and Ennia Caligula marries Lollia Paulina
39	Caligula divorces Lollia and marries Milonia Caesonia Birth of Drusilla, Caligula's daughter
39 – 40	Expedition to Germany and Gaul
41	Death of Caligula

As you read this chapter, keep in mind the following questions:

\ What impact did Caligula's rule have on Rome and the Empire?

\ Caligula has an evil reputation. Is this justified?

Although he ruled Rome and the Empire for only four years (AD 37 – 41), Caligula is one of the most famous (or infamous) Emperors in history. His real name was Gaius Julius Caesar Germanicus, son of Germanicus and Agrippina the Elder. The nickname Caligula, meaning 'little boots' or 'bootlet', was a term of affection bestowed upon him as a small boy by his father's troops. Such an endearing title appears misplaced in the light of Caligula's adult behaviour.

Caligula is a well-known and controversial figure even today, two thousand years after his death. He is the subject of historical study, modern psychological analysis and the focal character in the R-rated film *Caligula*. This chapter will attempt to discover the real Caligula and to make a valid historical judgement of the man, the Emperor and his impact on the Roman Empire established by Augustus.

EVIDENCE

While the archaeological evidence for this period is not as useful or as plentiful as written evidence, some archaeological evidence is available. Milestones in Spain show that a road-building programme established by Augustus was continued by Caligula. The city of Rhegium, a port built by Caligula to facilitate corn shipments, was regarded by ancient writers as his only enduring achievement. Written sources include Suetonius, Cassius Dio, Philo, Josephus and Caligula's successor, Claudius.

All these writers, while providing important insights, must be read with care; each includes an element of bias that prevents complete objectivity. Claudius is very harsh in his judgement of Caligula, but this is typical of the writings of many Roman Emperors, for whom it was the custom to enhance their own reputation by criticising that of their predecessor. Claudius's writings did not survive, but they did influence other writers of the period. Suetonius, we must remember, had strong views about the tendency of power and luxury to corrupt.

The universal condemnation of Caligula by the ancient writers aroused doubts among some modern historians, who suspected collusion and bias. The result has been a number of 'revisionist' interpretations, which seek to explain Caligula's actions more fairly. The end result, however, remains the same—four stormy years of eccentric, inefficient and despotic rule endured by the Roman Empire which was, fortunately, securely anchored to the foundations laid by Augustus and Tiberius.

BACKGROUND AND ACCESSION

Caligula was born at Antium in AD 12, a member of the Julian family. He spent his early years in Germany, where his father, Germanicus, was commander of the legions of the Rhine. As a small child, Caligula was dressed in a miniature uniform (hence his nickname) and paraded as a mascot for the troops. Perhaps this was Caligula's first experience of political intrigue! Germanicus most likely used Caligula in this way as part of a programme to win back the support of mutinous troops in Germany

Coin depicting head of Caligula
(Macquarie University, NSW)

Coin depicting head of Germanicus
(Macquarie University, NSW)

in AD 14. (Although 'Caligula' was the name by which he was most commonly known, Caligula himself disliked the appellation, finding it undignified, and coins and inscriptions that survive from this period bear the name Gaius.)

After the death of Germanicus in AD 19, Caligula went to Rome, living firstly with his mother and then with his great-grandmother Julia Augusta (Livia) until her death in 29. He then spent three years living with his grandmother Antonia. In AD 31 Caligula was elected pontifex, and in 32 he joined his great-uncle Tiberius on Capri. He did not assume the *toga virilis* (worn upon reaching manhood) until that year. In 33 Caligula was named quaestor.

Tiberius died in AD 37. At the Senate's first meeting following his death, Tiberius's will was read by Macro. It included legacies for the citizens of Rome and the Roman army, as well as his wishes as to his successor. The will gave no clear direction, designating Caligula (his brother's grandson) and Tiberius Gemellus (his own grandson) joint heirs. At Macro's urging, the Senate declared the will null and void, setting it aside and proclaiming Caligula 'Princeps'.

Research

One of the leading figures in Caligula's rise to power was Quintus Naevius Cordus Sutorius Macro, prefect of the Praetorian Guard. Find out about this man's life and his influence on Roman affairs during this period.

Following these events, Caligula's accession to the Principate was straightforward and undisputed. Even though he had limited experience in public affairs, Caligula had three main claims to the Principate—he was popular with the army, he was of Julian blood, and there were no other suitable candidates (Tiberius Gemellus being too young). Caligula's arrival in Rome, orchestrated by the Praetorian prefect Macro, was greeted enthusiastically by the populace. Hopes ran high for the new order among those who saw Tiberius's rule as the 'dark days'. Nevertheless, some members of the nobility in the Senate were prepared to oppose him, due to his youth and inexperience, and because of the lack of Julian supporters in the Senate at this time.

It is evident that different groups in Rome at this time viewed Caligula's accession differently.

Every one looked forward to the succession of the young Gaius, because every one expected to find in him a pliable character and a ruler after his own heart. The populace—and they came nearest to the truth—looked forward to the son of Germanicus, to an affable purveyor of liberal entertainment; Macro looked forward to 'the best of slaves'; the Senate, a body to whom experience never succeeded in teaching wisdom, rather than copy the pessimism of L. Arruntius and admit that where age, capability, and experience had failed, youth and inexperience were not likely to succeed, preferred to hope pathetically for an increase in its own powers. Already, perhaps, some of its members thought of Gaius, as one of their most eminent predecessors had thought of another youth, as of a person to be praised, honoured—and then dispensed with.

Balsdon, *The Emperor Gaius (Caligula)*, 22–3

＼**What did the populace, or ordinary people, hope to gain from the new Emperor?**

＼**What do you think is meant by Macro's expectation of 'the best of slaves'?**

＼**What is your impression of the attitudes to power and politics in Rome that the young Emperor now entered?**

Research

＼**Why would the Roman people be pleased at the prospect of being ruled by the son of Germanicus?**

THE EARLY MONTHS

Upon his accesssion, Caligula took a number of steps to consolidate his power and influence. He:

- reduced taxes and distributed largess to the populace;
- provided entertainment such as races and gladiatorial contests for the populace;
- halted treason trials, curbed the activities of paid informers or *delatores* and freed many who had been imprisoned as a result of *maiestas*;
- ended censorship of many historical works;
- pledged to the Senate a policy of co-operation;
- doubled the sum bequeathed by Tiberius to the Praetorian Guard.

As well, Caligula made his uncle Claudius his fellow consul. This move gave rise to speculation. What was Caligula's real intention?

- Was this evidence of an inexperienced young man seeking support?

- Was it the clever politician attempting to bring in the support of the Claudian family?
- Was Caligula trying to convince the Senate that he was not greedy for personal power?
- Was he simply attempting to use his uncle, whom he regarded as an idiot, to mislead his political opponents?

Whatever the true reason behind the joint-consulship, Caligula and Claudius waited until July 37, when the existing consulship expired, before taking up the post. The delay appears to be an attempt by Caligula to convince the Senate of his desire for co-operation.

CALIGULA'S ILLNESS

In October 37, Caligula fell seriously ill. The causes of this bout of ill-health are the subject of considerable speculation. Some ancient writers refer to it as 'brain fever'. Modern scholars have likened it to a severe nervous breakdown or 'delirium tremens'—the result of too much alcohol. Caligula certainly showed evidence of being a sickly young man, suffering from epilepsy (referred to by the ancients as the 'falling sickness') and bouts of insomnia. There were also references to violent mood swings and instability prior to his illness.

It has been widely accepted that this illness coincided with a transformation in Caligula's personality and behaviour. Robert Graves, author of the historical novel *I, Claudius*, suggests that Caligula emerged from his sickbed claiming to have been transformed into a god. While the remaining disastrous years of Caligula's rule could be attributed to this claim, such a colourful explanation would oversimplify the reality. Even prior to his illness, Caligula displayed dark moods and occasional vindictiveness. Although many cite as proof of his madness his repeated claims to divinity, such claims were not uncommon in the ancient world, especially in the eastern part of the Roman Empire.

The fate of two Romans who made pledges to the gods for Caligula's recovery provides an insight into Caligula's state of mind on his recovery. The first man promised to forfeit his own life should Caligula recover; the second offered to become a gladiator and fight in the arena if the Emperor was spared. Their motives are subject to conjecture: perhaps they were simply pious men; perhaps ambitious men seeking rewards for their loyalty. Whatever their motives, Caligula was unimpressed by this gesture. Upon his recovery, he took pleasure in insisting that each man honour his promise. The first was thrown from the Tarpeian rock; the second was compelled to fight for his life for an amused Emperor.

ABUSES OF POWER

Caligula emerged from his illness with a personality more unbalanced than previously. The winter of 37 – 38 saw the forced suicide of four people and ushered in Caligula's reign of terror.

Bust of Caligula (Gliptoteca, Copenhagen..
Courtesy Mansell Collection)

The first suicide was that of Tiberius Gemellus, the grandson of the late Emperor, Tiberius. Gemellus had been included with Caligula in his grandfather's will as joint heir and had been adopted by Caligula and made *Princeps Iuventutis*. Caligula decided, however, that he had to be removed.

The abuses continued. The second suicide ordered was that of Caligula's father-in-law, M. Junius Silanus. While Suetonius tended to exaggerate, his account of the incident does indicate paranoia on the part of Caligula. According to Suetonius, when Silanus delayed following the Emperor's ship to sea, Caligula took this as a sign that Silanus hoped that the Emperor's vessel would be lost, enabling Silanus to seize power for himself. So Caligula decided that his father-in-law must die.

The third and fourth suicides were those of Macro and his wife, Ennia. Macro may have seen himself in Caligula's early years as a king-maker, the power behind the throne. In this capacity he continued to offer advice and attempted to influence the young Emperor. Caligula's action in ordering the suicide demonstrated that he would not tolerate the advice of common men or mere mortals.

The fact that an Emperor could simply order one of his subjects to die by his own hand demonstrated the political, social and religious power that Caligula held. The weakness of the office created by Augustus was that it could fall into the hands of a flawed personality.

Caligula's behaviour became increasingly bizarre. The worst stories depict a bloodthirsty monster, a sexual deviant and an unbridled egotist. Suetonius and Cassius Dio accused him of enjoying the sight of cruel and unusual punishments. He ordered that the hands of a thief be cut off and hung about his neck; other victims were tortured for meal-time entertainment. One hapless victim was beaten about the head, neck and back with a chain at regular intervals for days on end. His suffering was ended only when Caligula found the smell of the victim's rotting brain unpleasant.

A crowd bursting into the Theatre about midnight to secure free seats angered him so much that he had them driven away with clubs; more than a score of knights, as many married women, and numerous others were crushed to death in the ensuing panic. Caligula liked to stir up trouble in the Theatre by scattering gift vouchers before the seats were occupied, thus tempting commoners to invade the rows reserved for knights. During gladiatorial shows he would have the canopies removed at the hottest time of the day and forbid anyone to leave; or cancel the regular programme, and pit feeble old fighters against decrepit criminals; or stage comic duels between respectable householders who happened to be physically disabled in some way or other. More than once he closed down the granaries and let the people go hungry.

The following instances will illustrate his bloody-mindedness. Having collected wild animals for one of his shows, he found butcher's meat too expensive and decided to feed them with criminals instead. He paid no attention to the charge-sheets, but simply stood in the middle of a colonnade, glanced at the prisoners lined up before him, and gave the order: "Kill every man between that bald head and the other one over there!" . . . Many men of decent family were branded at his command, and sent down the mines, or put to work on the roads, or thrown to the wild beasts. Others were confined in narrow cages, where they had to crouch on all fours like animals; or were sawn in half—and not necessarily for major offences, but merely for criticizing his shows, failing to swear by his Genius, and so forth.

Caligula made parents attend their sons' executions, and when one father excused himself on the ground of ill-health, provided a litter for him. Having invited another father to dinner just after the son's execution, he overflowed with good-fellowship in an attempt to make him laugh and joke . . .

Once Caligula asked a returned exile how he had been spending his time. To flatter him the man answered: "I prayed continuously to the gods for Tiberius's death, and your accession; and my prayer was granted." Caligula therefore concluded that the new batch of exiles must be praying for his own death; so he sent agents from island to island and had them all killed. Being anxious that one particular senator should be torn in pieces he persuaded some of his colleagues to challenge him as a public enemy when he entered the House, stab him with their pens, and then hand him over for lynching to the rest of the Senate; and was not satisfied until the victim's limbs, organs, and guts had been dragged through the streets and heaped up at his feet.

Suetonius, *Gaius Caligula*, 26–8

> ◥Which of all these acts do you regard as the most cruel and callous? Why?
>
> ◥Can we believe everything Suetonius says? Give a reason for your answer.

Caligula's sexual preferences have provided substance for much rumour and literary licence, ranging from the charges of homosexuality and incest levelled by Suetonius and Cassius Dio to the debauchery depicted in the film *Caligula*.

ADMINISTRATION

Caligula's administration of Rome was inefficient and erratic. It was not always possible to identify a consistent administrative policy, since this could vary with his whims and moods. His style of administration was heavily influenced by the personal characteristics of despotism and extravagance.

INTERNAL ADMINISTRATION

As his enthusiasm for despotic personal rule grew, he frequently attempted to undermine and belittle the authority of the Senate, while extending the authority and altering the nature of the office he had inherited. A classic example of such behaviour was Caligula's desire to have his horse, Incitatus, made a member of the Senate. He appears to have been attempting to imitate the style of an eastern monarch, answerable to no-one.

Caligula's dictatorial behaviour was matched by his unbridled extravagance. Parties, displays and games drained the treasury, gradually undermining the sound financial footing secured for the Empire by Augustus and Tiberius. An example of his extravagance is his ship building. Caligula was not content to build ordinary ships; to be worthy of him, galleys had their sterns encrusted with jewels, and for his refreshment, each ship carried fruit trees.

Even Caligula, however, did not have unlimited wealth. As his funds and those of the treasury dwindled, he was compelled to seek new sources of revenue. Old taxes were increased and new ones introduced. This, with a resumption of treason trials (designed to place at Caligula's disposal the confiscated land and wealth of those found guilty) replenished his finances but made him universally unpopular. It is generally accepted that his despotism and extravagance hastened Caligula's removal from office.

There is some debate among historians as to how successful Caligula's fund-raising drive was. Some argue that his successor, Claudius, inherited an Empire in financial crisis. Such an idea fits the popular notion of these Emperors: the wanton extravagance of Caligula followed by the unassuming efficiency of Claudius's early years. This view, however, ignores one significant historical fact—if Caligula had not maintained the finances available to the Princeps personally, then Claudius would have been unable to make the generous donatives he made at his accession.

In *Roman History*, Cassius Dio argues that Caligula's excursion into imperial matters outside Rome, in particular the military expedition north to Germany and Gaul in 39 – 40, was an attempt to bring back booty to further ease the domestic financial situation. Whether or not Cassius Dio can be relied upon, the fact remains that a successful military operation of this kind would have enhanced Caligula's reputation and diverted attention from the weakness of his administration's performance in Rome.

IMPERIAL ADMINISTRATION

Fortunately, Augustus and Tiberius had created an imperial framework solid enough to withstand at least four years of Caligula. At his passing, the Empire was little worse for his period in office than it had been at the outset. It was, however, changed by three distinctive policy decisions.

EXPANSION OF THE EMPIRE

Caligula pursued an energetic military policy in Germany and planned to reoccupy Britain, which had first been claimed for Rome by Julius Caesar. His motives for such actions were probably a combination of financial needs and a desire to divert attention from his administrative performance in Rome. Ancient writers such as Suetonius are very harsh in their judgements of Caligula's leadership of this military expedition. They delight in ridiculing him because his army halted on the coast of Gaul and refused to cross the Channel. They make much of Caligula reading a proclamation claiming Britain without actually having set foot on the island, and then, as Suetonius tells it, ordering his troops to collect *musculi* (sea-shells) in their helmets as part of his prize as conqueror.

This could be an example of the desire of Suetonius and others to use any means to discredit an Emperor they loathed. Roman engineers, who were a key part of Caligula's army, had huts also referred to as *musculi* due to their shell-like shape. Caligula may simply have been ordering these dismantled or collected as part of breaking camp prior to the army's return to Rome. The criticism ignores the possibility that Caligula's lack of military success may have been due to his fear of treachery in Rome during his absence, requiring his speedy return. Caligula simply did not have the time to convince his troops of the necessity of crossing the Channel. On a similar venture to Britain in 43, Caligula's successor, Claudius, was also confronted with troops unwilling to risk a voyage across the Channel. Unlike Caligula, his position in Rome was reasonably secure. With the luxury of time, he waited and persuaded his troops that the crossing was safe and workable.

THE APPOINTMENT OF KINGS

Caligula adopted a policy of appointing vassal kings to administer parts of the Empire on his behalf. Two views can be taken on this policy. One is that this step simply appealed to Caligula's megalomania, his delusions of grandeur; that he saw himself as the ruler of monarchs, an earthly king of kings. The other view presents a Caligula far saner and more calculating. By appointing vassal kings who owed their position and loyalty to him alone, Caligula further undermined and side-stepped the authority of the Senate, since it would be normal practice to appoint a member of the Senate as provincial governor. Caligula must have been aware of the fact that such provinces had often been the seat of rebellion in the past.

ALIENATING THE JEWS

Caligula's relationship with the Jews could have led to a large-scale uprising; this was probably only prevented by his death in 41. Caligula was apparently incapable of resolving disputes between the Jewish and Greek populations in Alexandria. Furthermore, he insisted on having his statue in the image of a god placed in the synagogue at Jerusalem. The bad feeling created by Caligula's treatment of the Jews was to be the basis for a subsequent rebellion.

CALIGULA'S DEATH

It is generally accepted that the pattern of Caligula's life determined the cause and nature of its ending. As he became more tyrannical, the Roman political system that had worked so well under Augustus proved incapable of finding the legal means of removing a tyrant. The only solution was assassination of a dictator, known to the ancients as 'tyrannicide'. Caligula seems to have prompted this action by his constant personal abuse of Cassius Chaerea, a tribune of the Praetorian Guard. Caligula and his wife and daughter were murdered in January 41. Caligula was stabbed more than thirty times, such was the fury that he aroused, and many of the wounds were clearly inflicted after he was dead. The populace greeted his death with relief and rejoicing. They praised Cassius Chaerea for his action, but the complex nature of the Romans' allegiance to their rulers (many of whom were thought to become gods in death) meant that the unfortunate Chaerea was executed for treason.

CONCLUSION

Caligula's evil reputation was well-earned and deserved. By modern standards his behaviour was clearly monstrous, bordering on the insane. It is not, however, valid for historians to judge ancients by the morals and standards of contemporary society. While Caligula may have been a deviant, many of his actions and beliefs were moulded by the world into which he was born. He was surrounded from birth by extravagance and repeatedly told of his superiority. It is important, therefore, that we consider these facts and read the judgements of the ancients with care.

The impact of Caligula's four years in power was essentially fleeting. He altered the veneer and appearance, but failed to damage the structure itself. The Empire remained strong, and weathered the storms of Caligula's whims.

The two most enduring aspects of Caligula's reign according to the ancients were, firstly, his reputation for malice and depravity, and secondly, his more subtle impact upon the office created by Augustus, drawing to it more personal power than had been the case previously. Even after his death, and after the concessions made to the Senate by his successor, Claudius, the office of Princeps continued to hold more power than it had under Augustus.

LIST OF REFERENCES

ANCIENT SOURCES

Cassius Dio, *Dio's Roman History*, Vol. 7, Loeb Classical Library, 1968
Suetonius, 'Gaius Caligula', *The Twelve Caesars*, Penguin, 1975

SECONDARY SOURCES

Balsdon, J. P. V. D., *The Emperor Gaius (Caligula)*, Greenwood Press, Westport, Connecticut, 1977
Graves, Robert, *I, Claudius*, Penguin, Harmondsworth, 1977

BIBLIOGRAPHY

SECONDARY SOURCES

A. Garzetti, *From Tiberius to the Antonines: A History of the Roman Empire AD 14 – 192*, Methuen, London, 1974
E. T. Salmon, *A History of the Roman World 30 BC to AD 138*, Methuen, London, 1985
H. H. Scullard, *From the Gracchi to Nero: A History of Rome from 133 BC to AD 68*, Methuen, London, 1985

CLAUDIUS LOW-POTENTIAL HIGH-ACHIEVER

Jane And Bruce Dennett

Emperor . . . by an extraordinary accident
—Suetonius

10 BC	Birth of Tiberius Claudius Nero Germanicus at Lugundum, Gaul
AD 37	Claudius and Caligula consuls
41	Death of Caligula Claudius acclaimed Emperor
43	Invasion of Britain
44	Claudius returned the provinces of Achaea and Macedonia to the Senate
46	Thrace added to the Empire
48	Death of Messalina Claudius marries Agrippina
50	Claudius adopts Nero
54	Death of Claudius

Was Claudius a fool or an administrative genius? Bear this question in mind as you read the chapter.

Born in 10 BC in Gaul, Tiberius Claudius Nero Germanicus was the younger son of Drusus and Antonia. Some historians have described him as a fool, a weakling and a tyrant; others have praised him as an administrative genius, a humane and caring ruler and the best of the Julio-Claudian Emperors. This chapter will attempt to determine the truth.

The facts of history tend to support the more generous view of Claudius, although he was not a man without flaws. He inherited a government in turmoil following the death of Caligula, and was able to:
• restore calm and establish stable government;
• expand the civil service;
• re-establish the finances of the Empire;

- expand the boundaries of the Empire;
- assimilate the conquered peoples into the populace of the Empire;
- increase the power of the Principate.

EVIDENCE

Archaeological evidence, while useful, is not as important as written evidence during this period. In general, archaeological evidence is used to check the validity of claims made by ancient writers. Nevertheless, there are a number of areas where archaeological evidence can play a role in the evaluation of Claudius's Principate. Coins and inscriptions issued by both the Emperor and the Senate are plentiful, as are the remains of Claudius's significant public works. The most notable of these are the impressive harbour at Ostia, aqueducts in Italy, and the Roman towns built in Britain as a result of Claudius's military expedition.

The variety of written evidence relating to Claudius highlights the task of the historian, who has to weigh the evidence and sit in judgement. Your view of Claudius will vary according to which of the ancient writers you read. Cassius Dio and Suetonius present Claudius as a weakling, easily manipulated, and as a man with the capacity for cruelty. L. Annaeus Seneca mocks him as a fool (see Ball, *The Satire of Seneca*). Letters written by Augustus describing Claudius in his youth complete the picture of an incompetent individual. However, the limited remains of Claudius's own works, such as a speech delivered in AD 48 to new members of the Senate, give the image of a capable and thoughtful man. Rather than see this as a contradiction, we should be alerted to the dangers of assessing a person on the basis of their youth. (No modern historian would dare judge a twentieth century figure such as Sir Winston Churchill on the basis of his school reports.)

Coin depicting head of Claudius.
The legend indicates the honours and
powers awarded the Emperor.
(Macquarie University, NSW)

Researching Claudius is like putting together a jigsaw puzzle which has pieces missing. The first six years of Tacitus's account of Claudius's rule is missing, as are most of Claudius's own works. (It is widely accepted that he was a prolific writer of Roman history.) The missing pieces in the puzzle give rise to speculation. Were his works lost purely by chance? Were they a fiction to begin with? (Surely the works of an Emperor would have been prized and preserved.) Were they deliberately destroyed by Claudius's wife, Agrippina, who was charged with his murder, in order to deprive her dead husband of credit due? These questions remain unresolved.

Modern scholars have viewed with suspicion the apparent inconsistency between Claudius's significant achievements and the evaluation of him by the ancients. Since the discovery in the early 1920s of a letter written by Claudius to the citizens of Alexandria, the modern reappraisal of Claudius has continued to depict him more favourably. The most generous view of Claudius is to be found in Robert Graves' historical novels *I, Claudius* and *Claudius The God* and the television series, *I, Claudius* based on these works. A balanced review of the evidence reveals a capable ruler but a man not as exceptional as Graves' view would lead us to believe.

The Emperor Claudius is one of the most perplexing problems in Roman history. His own utterances which have been transmitted to us in stone, bronze or papyrus, few though they are, show that he possessed sound practical judgment and no little political wisdom. His administration was enlightened in domestic affairs. In the foreign field he solved with dignity the main problems inherited from his predecessors. He endowed the Principate with those policies which, continued by Vespasian, Trajan, and Hadrian, made it more efficient and at the same time more humane. Despite these facts the cumulative judgment of antiquity agrees in portraying him as a fool and a baneful influence on the development of the Empire.

We are well acquainted with the personality of Augustus and with the passions and programs of the generation of Romans which he profoundly modified and by which he was in turn affected. We know a great deal about Tiberius, who felt that a rigidly conservative policy was the best means of consolidating the Augustan Principate. But from the death of Augustus in AD 14 to the accession of Claudius in AD 41 new stresses, new conflicts, and new needs had developed.

The purpose of this study, then, is not primarily to unearth new data on Claudius's reign but to seek new light on the motives and principles that actuated his administration.

Scramuzza, *The Emperor Claudius*, 3–4

↘ **Why does Scramuzza describe Claudius as a 'perplexing problem'?**

↘ **According to Scramuzza, what were the changed conditions facing Claudius?**

↘ **What is the purpose of modern studies (such as Scramuzza's) of Claudius?**

BACKGROUND AND ACCESSION

A careful examination of Claudius's background reveals an education and upbringing that would make him well-qualified to rule in Rome. This fact was often ignored by observers who dwelt upon his ungainly appearance. Claudius suffered from a childhood illness, a kind of palsy that may have slowed but did not stunt his intellectual development. It certainly left him with an uncontrollable stammer, a tendency to dribble unchecked and a constant twitch of the head. His body was not in proportion; he had a large head, a pot belly and spindly legs, and he walked with an awkward shuffle.

Claudius was related to two of the most distinguished families in ancient Rome—the Claudians and, more distantly, the Julians. He was widely read in Roman history and tradition, and although often mocked in public, still had access to the world of power and influence through a range of high offices. He was a member of the equestrian order and became consul in AD 37. While Claudius did not exercise any real power until he became Emperor, he had an ideal opportunity to observe the workings of government at first hand.

An unseemly appearance and lack of grace may have been burdens for the child and young man, but they almost certainly saved his life. During Caligula's reign of terror the fact that Claudius was not too closely linked to the Julian family and the conviction of many that he was a fool, meant that he was not perceived as a genuine threat either by Caligula or the republican elements in the Senate.

Caligula's assassination in January 41 saw the office of the Principate fall to the fifty-year-old Claudius. In *The Twelve Caesars*, Suetonius tells the story that on the night of Caligula's death, Claudius was found hiding behind a curtain in the palace, trembling and fearful for his own life. He was discovered when his feet were seen projecting beneath the fabric. Claudius was proclaimed Emperor quite unconstitutionally by the Praetorian Guard, since they were not legally empowered to do so. The Senate, whose responsibility it was to elect an Emperor, was still debating whether to return to the Republic or choose a successor for Caligula. They were compelled, reluctantly, to accept the military's nomination because they did not have sufficient power to resist.

Claudius must have been aware that he was chosen by the Praetorian Guard in the hope that he would be pliable and would sanction Caligula's assassination. He must also have been aware of the ill-feeling against him in the Senate, given that he had been imposed on them by the military. This was a position of exceptional delicacy, requiring a skilled politician who could navigate the treacherous political waters in the early days of the new administration. Contrary to the charges of the ancients, it seems unlikely that either a weakling or a fool could have succeeded.

THE EARLY MONTHS

Claudius had to build support carefully and cautiously in the early months of his reign. He did this in a number of ways.

- He sought the allegiance of the Julians by publicly praising Augustus and proclaiming him as his model. He also took the name 'Caesar'.
- He decided to execute Caligula's assassin, Cassius Chaerea. This was a difficult decision, clearly based more on political expediency than justice. No one wept for Caligula, but his murderers had to be dealt with to ensure that the principle of removing the Emperor by violent means was not sanctioned. While the execution of Cassius Chaerea would win him support from the Julians, it could antagonise the Praetorian Guard. Claudius attempted to soften the blow to the Praetorian Guard by awarding them one of the most generous bonuses in the history of Rome. Each received a donative of either 15 000 or 20 000 sesterces. Although it bought their loyalty, and served Claudius's ends well in the short term, it established a dangerous precedent.
- The nobility in the Senate were a constant danger to Claudius, since it was they who rightly should have sanctioned his rule. His fear of them was evident in his refusal to enter the Senate House itself for the first thirty days of his Principate. He took steps to win their support by immediately abolishing treason trials and the new taxes imposed by Caligula. He also minimised the trappings of his office and deferred to the Senate in recognition of their importance.

Despite these steps, Claudius was confronted at various stages during his fourteen-year Principate with conspiracies hatched in the Senate and occasional attempted rebellions in the provinces. Each of these, when detected, was dealt with ruthlessly. These incidents may have given rise to his reputation as a bloodthirsty tryant.

ADMINISTRATION OF THE EMPIRE

Like so much of Claudius's career, his administration of the Empire has inspired both positive and negative judgements. Some regard his creation of an efficient and expanded civil service, open to commoners of talent, as one of his greatest achievements. They see it as a logical extension of the secretariats that emerged under Tiberius and essential to the proper administration of an Empire growing in size and complexity. This adminis-trative network, however, has also prompted less flattering claims, namely that Claudius was nothing more than a figure-head for the real rulers of Rome—the bureaucrats within this new civil service.

The truth appears to lie somewhere between these two claims. While Claudius must receive credit for an important contribution to the future efficient government of the Empire, there is evidence to suggest that his supervision of the administration was sometimes slipshod, opening the way to bribery and corruption. Claudius at times failed to appreciate that not all men possessed his personal integrity. He can also be fairly charged with some instances of favouritism in the selection of his new civil service.

INTERNAL ADMINISTRATION

There is general agreement that Claudius achieved substantial reforms in the internal administration of Rome.

BUREAUCRATIC REFORM

Claudius created new offices of state, including secretary-general (to supervise all official correspondence); financial secretary; legal secretary; and librarian. These officials, most of them imperial freedmen, centralised and streamlined government business, increasing its efficiency. The expansion of the bureaucracy gave Claudius greater access than the Senate to information about the affairs of state, which increased the power and prestige of the office of the Principate. Extended executive powers enabled the enlarged bureaucracy to act decisively, which undermined the authority of the Senate. The status of the senatorial nobility was further diminished by the fact that Claudius's bureaucracy, his instruments of power, were freedmen, not members of the old aristocracy.

Under Claudius's Principate, public finances were rationalised. Inefficient separate *fisci* (treasuries) were combined to form a single centralised public treasury. This placed most aspects of the Empire's finances firmly in the Emperor's hands.

Those historians who see Claudius emerging as a tyrant point to these reforms as a deliberate attempt to destroy the authority of the Senate. While we must accept that a weakening of the Senate's position was a logical consequence of these steps, it is unfair to claim that it was Claudius's motive. It is far more likely that he simply sought to improve the efficiency of government.

Although these reforms were major, they were undertaken gradually and with considerable political acumen, so as to lessen the apparent affront to the Senate and to avoid alarming the populace. This appears to negate, once again, claims that Claudius was little more than a fool.

Clearly, Claudius's study of history produced a mind immersed in tradition and the affairs of state. Few in Rome knew their history better than Claudius, and he was able to apply the lessons and stratagems of the past to contemporary problems. The best example of this was Claudius's habit of justifying to the Senate his reforms and gradual changes in the light of past tradition and precedent. It is unlikely that Caligula or Tiberius could have achieved these reforms as smoothly.

SOCIAL AND ECONOMIC REFORM

The streamlined administration opened the way for significant social and economic reform, distinguishing Claudius as a progressive and energetic ruler. His achievements included:

- subsidising ship owners and builders to ensure that sufficient corn could be imported to feed Rome's growing population, particularly in the event of famine;
- rebuilding Rome's port at Ostia;

Roman ruins at Ostia, Italy (Mansell Collection)

- renewing Rome's water supply;
- introducing more humane laws for the treatment of slaves;
- continuing his study of history and his writing (although unfortunately none of these histories survives).

Cassius Dio on the building of the port at Ostia:

On the occasion of a severe famine he considered the problem of providing an abundant food-supply, not only for that particular crisis but for all future time. For practically all the grain used by the Romans was imported, and yet the region near the mouth of the Tiber had no safe landing-places or suitable harbours, so that their mastery of the sea was rendered useless to them. Except for the cargoes brought in during the summer season and stored in warehouses, they had no supplies for the winter; for if any one ever risked a voyage at that season, he was sure to meet with disaster. In view of this situation, Claudius undertook to construct a harbour, and would not be deterred even when the architects, upon his enquiring how great the cost would be, answered, "You don't want to do it!" so confident were they that the huge expenditures necessary would shake him from his purpose, if he should learn the cost beforehand. He, however, conceived an undertaking worthy of the dignity and greatness of Rome, and he brought it to accomplishment. In the first place, he excavated a very considerable tract of land, built retaining walls on every side of the excavation, and then let the sea into it; secondly, in the sea itself he constructed huge moles on both sides of the entrance and thus enclosed a large body of water, in the midst of which he reared an island and placed on it a tower with a beacon light.

Cassius Dio, *Roman History*, 60.11

What skills does Claudius show in the decisions recounted in this source?

In the light of opinions of Claudius, comment on his actions as documented here.

How does this account influence your opinion of Claudius? Does it reflect a capable ruler or a fool? Why?

SHORTCOMINGS OF CLAUDIUS'S ADMINISTRATION

The weakness that became apparent in Claudius's administration was that through preoccupation or deliberate neglect, he permitted too much power to fall into the hands of his wives, particularly Messalina and Agrippina. Both these women utilised and sometimes abused the privileges associated with Claudius's office. While Claudius often discouraged undue ceremony, his wives appeared to delight in the trappings of office. His home became increasingly like a royal palace, complete with courtiers, and his family began to accept as their due the prestige and deference bestowed on royalty.

According to the available archaeological evidence, Agrippina began to appear on Roman coins during Claudius's reign. This was a privilege and status not normally associated with the wife of the Princeps. Claudius's third wife, Valeria Messalina, was a very controversial figure. She was only sixteen, over thirty years Claudius's junior, when he succeeded Caligula (who had arranged the marriage). Messalina bore Claudius two children: a daughter, Octavia, and a son, Britannicus. She developed a reputation for sexual depravity and cruelty that aroused comment even in a society where erotic and sadistic excesses were not uncommon. The extent of Messalina's political influence over her husband is not clear, although there is evidence to suggest that she often incited his fears of conspiracy and encouraged him to remove people she did not like.

Messalina had affairs with many men, to which Claudius turned a blind eye. In 48, however, she actually went through the forms of marriage to consul-elect Gaius Silius. Suetonius infers that this bigamous marriage was the prelude to a take-over by Messalina and Silius, and there is strong evidence to justify such a charge. Apparently Silius had arranged for support from the prefect of *vigiles* and the head of the imperial gladiatorial school. The plot failed and both Messalina and Silius were put to death. There is uncertainty about who made this decision; some claim that Claudius ordered their deaths, while other sources assert that Claudius's chief secretary, Narcissus, gave the orders in Claudius's name. If true, this would indicate that vast power had fallen into the hands of Claudius's civil service secretaries.

Claudius can also be charged with occasional spells of absent-mindedness and a failure to follow through the detail of each government decision. This paved the way for abuses of power by some of his senior civil servants. These freedmen, some of whom were less principled than Claudius, were permitted great power, especially in the final years of Claudius's reign.

But his firmest devotion was reserved for Narcissus, his secretary, and Pallas, his treasurer, whom he encouraged the Senate to honour with large gifts of money and the insignia of quaestors and praetors as well. They were able to acquire such riches, by legitimate and illegitimate means, that when one day Claudius complained how little cash was left in the Privy Purse, someone answered neatly that he would have heaps of pocket money if only his two freedmen took him into partnership.

As I mention above, Claudius fell so deeply under the influence of these freedmen and wives that he seemed to be their servant rather than their emperor; and distributed titles, army commands, indulgences or punishments according to their wishes, however capricious, seldom even aware of what he was about.

Suetonius, *Claudius*, 28–29

⟍**How does this document influence our view of Claudius?**

⟍**Does Suetonius's bias become a factor to consider? If so, why? If not, why not?**

THE ANNEXATION OF BRITAIN

Claudius wanted to be remembered for his role in expanding Rome's empire. He did have some success in this area, adding five provinces to the Empire: Britain, Lydia, Thrace and two provinces in Mauretania. The most successful imperial expedition resulted in the annexation of Britain. Begun in AD 42, the campaign against Britain continued for twelve years under a series of leaders carefully selected and appointed by Claudius until, by 54, most of south-eastern Britain was securely part of the Roman Empire.

THE BATTLE

Before beginning his military campaign against Britain, Claudius had to wait until two of his generals, Suetonius Paulinus and Hosidius Geta, had subdued a rebellion in Mauretania. Once this task was complete, the Roman army, comprising four legions and auxiliary troops totalling forty to fifty thousand men, headed toward Britain. A formidable force, they were commanded by Aulus Plautius and their ranks included a future Emperor of

Head of Claudius (Courtesy of the Trustees of the British Museum)

Rome, Titus Flavius Vespasian. Vespasian, who was part of the Second Legion, distinguished himself in the campaign.

In 42, the troops paused before crossing the English Channel. As with Caligula's earlier abortive invasion, the troops appear to have been hesitant about facing the perils of a sea voyage. Unlike Caligula, however, Claudius, with a little time and diplomacy, overcame their reluctance. The army embarked, landing at the port of Rutupiae (modern-day Richborough) on the coast of Kent in 43.

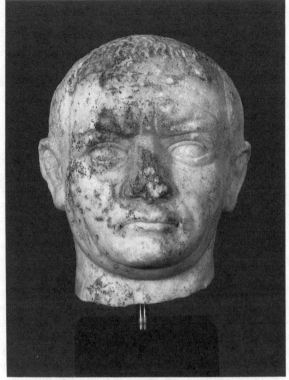

Head of Vespasian (Everard Studley Miller Bequest.
Courtesy National Gallery of Victoria, Melbourne)

According to Cassius Dio, shortly after arriving the Romans confronted the forces of one of the most prominent British leaders, Caratacus, and in a two-day battle emerged victorious, forcing Caratacus to flee. (There is, however, speculation that Caratacus may not have actually been present on this occasion.) Both Hosidius Geta and Vespasian were singled out for special praise after the battle. The legions then advanced north towards the River Thames, where Aulus Plautius met up with Claudius before continuing to march the seventy kilometres north to Camulodonum (modern-day Colchester). Claudius was present when his troops occupied Camulodonum, and proclaimed it the capital of the new Roman province of Brittania before returning to Rome. Camulodonum remained an important Roman administrative centre until the rise of Londinium (London) a few years later.

The continued success of Claudius's forces during this phase of the annexation of Britain and later was largely due to the failure of the British tribes to unite in their opposition to the invader. As a result, between 43 and 54 the legions of Rome whittled away at British resistance, gradually Romanising Britain.

In Rome, Claudius was hailed as a conqueror and awarded a triumph. He personally acknowledged his victory by changing his son's name to Britannicus.

By 47 the legions had pushed westward and controlled everything south-east of a line passing from near Isca Dumnoniorum (Exeter) to Lindum (Lincoln). At this stage the western boundary of Roman Britain was marked by a road, the Fosse Way.

Roman expansion in Britain continued over the next seven years, with expeditions against a number of British tribes such as the *Durotriges*, *Belgae*, *Silures* and *Deceangli*. One of Rome's most dogged opponents throughout the struggle was Caratacus. In 51 he was finally captured.

The British chieftains went round their men, encouraging and heartening them to be unafraid and optimistic, and offering other stimulants to battle. Caratacus, as he hastened to one point and another, stressed that this was the day, this the battle, which would either win back their freedom or enslave them for ever. He invoked their ancestors, who by routing Julius Caesar had valorously preserved their present descendants from Roman officials and taxes—and their wives and children from defilement. These exhortations were applauded. Then every man swore by his tribal oath that no enemy weapons would make them yield—and no wounds either.

This eagerness dismayed the Roman commanders disconcerned as he [sic] already was by the river-barrier, the fortifications supplementing it, the overhanging cliffs, and the ferocious crowds of defenders at every point. But our soldiers shouted for battle, clamouring that courage could overcome everything; and their colonels spoke to the same effect, to encourage them further.

After a reconnaissance to detect vulnerable and invulnerable points, Ostorius led his enthusiastic soldiers forward. They crossed the river without difficulty, and reached the rampart. But then, in an exchange of missiles, they came off worse in wounds and casualties. However, under a roof of locked shields, the Romans demolished the crude and clumsy stone embankment, and in the subsequent fight at close quarters the natives were driven to the hill-tops. Our troops pursued them closely. While light-armed auxiliaries attacked with javelins, the heavy regular infantry advanced in close formation. The British, unprotected by breastplates or helmets, were thrown into disorder. If they stood up to the auxiliaries they were cut down by the swords and spears of the regulars, and if they faced the latter they succumbed to the auxiliaries' broadswords and pikes. It was a great victory. Caratacus' wife and daughter were captured: his brother surrendered. He himself sought sanctuary with Cartimandua, queen of the Brigantes. But the defeated have no refuge. He was arrested, and handed over to the conquerors.

Tacitus, *Annals*, 12

What reasons given here inspired the Britons to fight well? What other reasons may have been significant to the Britons?

In your own words, describe the stages of the battle and list the types of weapons used.

What advantages/disadvantages did the two sides fight under?

Why was the capture of Caratacus significant for the Romans?

The British leader was taken to Rome where Claudius apparently treated him with the respect due an honourable foe, and spared his life. Tacitus recorded an interview which was supposed to have taken place between the two men, following which Caratacus was confined to Rome.

THE IMPLICATIONS FOR CLAUDIUS

Given Claudius's physical disabilities, he was an unlikely military leader. His success in Britain clearly demonstrated that the skill of a military commander was far more dependent upon intellect than it was on physical prowess. He was again able to apply the lessons of history and the theory of his study to the real world.

The fact that Claudius personally led the first Roman armies to land in Britain since Julius Caesar both satisfied Claudius's personal ambition and appears to have been instrumental in the popularity of his Principate. It was, therefore, a shrewd political move.

Other important spin-offs of the campaign were:

- it diverted public attention in Rome from the disastrous years of the Principate under Caligula (especially in the light of Caligula's abortive expedition that halted at the English Channel);
- it provided Rome with valuable raw materials such as metal and timber.

THE IMPORTANCE TO THE EMPIRE

Even though Claudius wanted to be hailed for adding new territories to the Empire, his greatest contribution was in the administrative area. Not only did he annex new territory, he was also responsible for the assimilation of provincials and new peoples into Rome. Expansion of the Empire had two important results. Firstly, it extended the Roman way of life to the provinces. An example of this is the urbanisation of Britain and other distant parts of the Empire. Secondly, the provinces beyond Italy were given status comparable with those nearer Rome, and Roman citizenship was extended to provincials. The corollary of this policy was that noblemen in provinces such as Gaul who had become Roman citizens were given the opportunity of senatorial office. According to Tacitus, it was not a popular move with the Senate:

The question aroused much discussion, and the opposing arguments were put to the emperor.

"Italy is not so decayed", said some, "that she cannot provide her own capital with a senate. In former times even people akin to us were content with a Roman senate of native Romans only; and the government of those days is a glorious memory. To this day, people cite the ancient Roman character for their models of courage and renown.

"Is it not enough that Venetian and Insubrian Gauls have forced their way into the senate? Do we have to import foreigners in hordes, like gangs of prisoners, and leave no careers for our own surviving aristocracy, or for impoverished senators from Latium? Every post will be absorbed by the rich men whose grandfathers and great-grandfathers commanded hostile tribes, assailed our armies in battle, besieged the divine Julius Caesar at Alesia. Those are recent memories. But are we to forget our men who, beside Rome's Capitoline citadel, were killed by the ancestors of these very Gauls. Let them, by all means, have the title of Roman citizens. But the senate's insignia, the glory of office, they must not cheapen."

These and similar arguments did not impress Claudius.

Tacitus, *Annals*, 11

What are the principal arguments against extending the office of senator to such provincials? How realistic were these arguments?

Claudius's reply according to Tacitus was:

The experience of my own ancestors, notably of my family's Sabine founder Clausus who was simultaneously made a Roman citizen and a patrician, encourage me to adopt the same national policy, by bringing excellence to Rome from whatever source.

ibid.

What is the basis, according to Claudius, for his decision?

Research

Narcissus was said to be the most influential of Claudius's civil servants. Prepare a brief biography of the man and his work.

FINAL YEARS

Claudius's infirmities became more apparent with his increasing age. This may well have contributed to his less diligent supervision of the Empire's administration and provided an opportunity for abuses of power by those close to him. Agrippina, his fourth wife, appears to have increased her influence during this period. It seems that she convinced Claudius to adopt her son Lucius Domitius Ahenobarbus in 50 as his own and name him successor. Claudius bestowed upon the boy his new and now famous name—Nero.

Agrippina began to display a calculation and ambition to rival that of Livia, Claudius's grandmother. It is generally accepted that Agrippina was responsible for Claudius's death. She is charged, according to the ancients, with poisoning her husband with a dish of mushrooms. There are two theories concerning her decision to act at this time.

Firstly, Agrippina may have been afraid that Claudius might change his decision favouring Nero as his successor and instead appoint Britannicus, his own son by Messalina. This would have robbed Agrippina of the power she sought. Secondly, had Claudius lived any longer, Nero may well have become old enough to rule without his mother's guidance. This would also have deprived Agrippina of an opportunity for power. She knew well the story of Tiberius's mother, Livia, whose influence was diminished when her son succeeded Augustus because Tiberius had both maturity and experience.

In much the same way that the archaeological evidence of coins bearing Agrippina's likeness on the reverse side indicated her influence when Claudius ruled, so when Nero became Emperor her image appears on the obverse (dominant) side. (See the coins on pages 209 and 210.)

When Claudius died in September 54 he was mourned, especially in the provinces, and proclaimed a god in Rome.

He not only had a remarkable knowledge of the problems of government, but he brought a new sense of responsibility to the throne and a strong conviction that the welfare of the people was dependent upon the policies of the *Princeps*. He stands out as a humane ruler. He did of course strengthen the State, enlarging its rights and defining them in favor of imperial centralization; but he was nevertheless conscious that among the duties of the State towards the individual there was that of protecting the weaker members of society, women, minors, slaves, and provincials. This was a constant preoccupation with him, whether he laid down policies as a ruler, or sat as a judge in the law courts, or acted in the ordinary course of administration . . .

His ability to win the affection of the common people deserves notice. When a false rumor was circulated that he had been murdered, the mob staged a riot. Since there is no indication that he purchased the popular favor by corrupt methods as did Gaius and Nero, we may perhaps assume that the man in the street looked upon him as a beneficient prince.

As Emperor he displayed prodigious industry. He would begin to work about midnight, and his days were packed full with business. He sat long with his counsellors, rarely missed a meeting of the Senate, presided from early morning to late evening at the tribunal, went from court to court and from bureau to bureau, checking the conduct of officials, and attended to innumerable details, even drafting his own speeches and official papers . . .

The charge of stupidity recurrent in the literary sources is traceable in large part to political bias. True, as a boy Claudius was thought to be wanting in judgment, and even his mother considered him a little fool. Strangely enough, he himself must have been trying to live up to this unenviable reputation if it be true that he feigned stupidity as a means of self-preservation. Here then was ample ground for the charge. It would be a mistake, however, to give Seneca and Tacitus full credence when they too accuse Claudius of stupidity, for their motivation was essentially political.

Scramuzza, *The Emperor Claudius*, 41–6

➤**Scramuzza claims that Claudius is vastly under-rated by the ancient sources. List the arguments he presents to support this view.**

➤**From your understanding of Claudius, list counter arguments.**

➤**Based on all that you have read, what is your evaluation of Claudius?**

CONCLUSION

How should the life and work of such a man be judged? At the outset we must acknowledge that there are gaps and contradictions in the evidence. These must be accepted and a judgement made within the limitations imposed by the information available to us. It would appear that Claudius was a good and capable ruler; he almost certainly was no fool, and his achievements and initiatives belie the charge of 'weakling'. In fact, his conduct of the affairs of state seems to follow the example of Augustus, whom he claimed as his model at the beginning of his Principate. The other claims of ancient writers, that he was bloodthirsty or a tyrant, are not substantiated by the facts. By modern standards, Claudius probably was bloodthirsty: he enjoyed the games and gladiatorial contests, and dealt ruthlessly with conspiracies. The blood-lust of an ancient Roman, however, cannot be fairly judged by modern standards. Claudius's behaviour in this area was typical of his time and far more humane than either Caligula or Nero.

The assessment of modern scholars also leaves room for debate. The arguments range from hailing Claudius as a genuinely great ruler to the assertion that, while he had a studious mind, it was the freedmen of his civil service who were the real source of power in Rome. The fairest possible judgement of Claudius probably lies between these two alternatives. The power of his office and his personal instigation of many reforms indicate that he was more than simply a tool or figurehead for his own civil service. Nevertheless, Claudius's apparent inattention to the activities of his civil service and the intrigues of his wives, stand as significant failings. It is upon these charges, most apparent in his declining years, that any claims to Claudius being a great leader falter.

LIST OF REFERENCES

ANCIENT SOURCES

Cassius Dio, *Dio's Roman History*, Vol. 7, Loeb Classical Library, 1968.
Tacitus, *The Annals of Imperial Rome*, Penguin, 1977
Suetonius, 'Claudius' in *The Twelve Caesars*, Penguin, 1975

SECONDARY SOURCES

Ball, Allan Perley, *The Satire of Seneca on The Apotheosis of Claudius*, Columbia University Press, New York, 1902
Graves, Robert, *I, Claudius*, Penguin, 1977
—— *Claudius the God*, Penguin, Harmondsworth, 1987
Scramuzza, V. M., *The Emperor Claudius*, Harvard University Press, Cambridge, Massachusetts, 1940

BIBLIOGRAPHY

SECONDARY SOURCES

Garzetti, A., *From Tiberius to the Antonines: A History of the Roman Empire AD 14 – 192*, Methuen, London, 1974
Kagan, D., *Problems in Ancient History Volume Two: The Roman World* Macmillan, New York, 1975
Salmon, E. T., *A History of the Roman World 30 BC to AD 138*, Methuen, London, 1985
Scullard, H. H., *From the Gracchi to Nero: A History of Rome 133 BC – AD 68*, Methuen, London, 1982

CHAPTER ELEVEN

AGRIPPINA THE YOUNGER EMPRESS OF ROME

JENNIFER LAWLESS

Let him kill me, so long as he reigns
—Tacitus

AD 15	Agrippina born in Germany
19	Her father, Germanicus, dies at Antioch
28	Agrippina married at age thirteen to Gnaeus Domitius Ahenobarbus Her aunt Julia (the Younger) dies in exile
29	Both her mother and eldest brother, Nero, arrested by Sejanus and banished
30	Agrippina's brother Drusus arrested
31	Her aunt, Livilla, executed for her part in husband Drusus' death Her brother Nero dies in prison
32	Agrippina's husband, Ahenobarbus, becomes consul
33	Her mother, Agrippina the Elder, and brother, Drusus, die in prison
37	Tiberius dies and Agrippina's brother Gaius (Caligula) becomes Emperor Agrippina gives birth to her first and only child, Lucius Domitius Ahenobarbus—later known as 'Nero'
38	Her sister Drusilla dies
39	In Germany, Gaius accuses Agrippina and sister Livilla of adultery and treason; they are exiled
40	Ahenobarbus dies
41	Gaius assassinated; Agrippina's uncle Claudius becomes Emperor
42?	Agrippina marries C. Sallustius Passienus Crispus
46?	Husband dies, leaving inheritance to Agrippina and Nero
48	Claudius's wife Messalina executed

49	Agrippina marries Claudius Nero engaged to Claudius's daughter Octavia
50	Nero formally adopted by Claudius Title 'Augusta' conferred on Agrippina
54	In October, Claudius dies; Nero becomes Emperor
55	Britannicus, son of Claudius is poisoned
56 – 59	Period of declining influence of Agrippina
59	Agrippina is murdered on orders of Nero

On 6 April AD 15 in Germany, a daughter was born to Germanicus (son of Drusus and adopted son of the Emperor Tiberius) and Agrippina the Elder (granddaughter of Augustus). She was named Julia Agrippina, after her grandparents, Agrippa and Julia. Agrippa had been the friend and confidante of Augustus; Julia was Augustus's daughter.

Agrippina the Younger became the most powerful and influential of the Julio-Claudian women. Her extraordinary family connections were unmatched by any female in Roman history: she was the great-granddaughter of an Emperor (Augustus); granddaughter by adoption of an Emperor (Tiberius); sister of an Emperor (Gaius Caligula); wife and niece of an Emperor (Claudius); and mother of an Emperor (Nero).

This chapter will examine the sources of Agrippina's power and influence and the reasons behind her efforts to secure and maintain for her family the position of 'first family of Rome'.

WOMEN IN JULIO-CLAUDIAN TIMES

Women of this period generally had more personal freedom than at any other time in Roman history. They could attend most social functions with their husbands, were often wealthy in their own right and sometimes administered their own properties. After Augustus, women with three children did not need male counter-signatures for legal contracts. Wives of provincial governors often accompanied their husbands overseas. However, women had no direct political power. They had to channel their energies, interests and talents into furthering the political causes of husbands, sons or lovers.

THE ROLE OF WOMEN

A woman's major role was to be a good daughter, wife and mother. Marriages were often arranged for women with the objective of uniting political factions or noble families. There were fewer females than males in the upper-classes (as infanticide of female babies was practised) so these women were able to marry and re-marry easily.

Motherhood was considered an esteemed occupation for women. Agrippina's grandmother Julia and her mother, Agrippina the Elder, were portrayed as examples of excellent women, having six and nine children

Bust of Agrippina (Uffizi, Florence.
Courtesy Mansell Collection)

respectively. It appears, however, that in Julio-Claudian times some women were rejecting this traditional role—a decline in birth rates amongst the upper classes so worried Augustus that he introduced laws to encourage larger families.

THE JULIO-CLAUDIAN WOMEN

Agrippina the Younger was one of a family of very strong and interesting women. The Julio-Claudian family included Livia, the wife of Augustus; Julia, his daughter; Agrippina the Elder, his granddaughter; and Octavia, his sister.

In general, the Julio-Claudian women were talented, highly individual, well-educated, confident and apparently attractive—probably similar to many other upper-class women of the time. However they received greater prominence and power through their membership of the 'first' political family of Rome—the descendants of Augustus. Because Augustus only produced one child, his daughter Julia, it was her descendants who had to supply the heirs-apparent to the Principate.

SOURCES ON WOMEN

It is difficult to piece together the lives of these women. In the sources available, they are rarely presented as 'rounded' characters in their own right. Roman history and literature was usually written by, and for, upper-class men. There were some female writers, but their works have not survived. One of the great tragedies for historians is the loss of Agrippina the Younger's 'memoirs'. What a wealth of information on the imperial family they might have provided!

Contemporary male writers were often highly critical of the Julio-Claudian women, dwelling on the qualities expected of a respectable Roman woman. They regarded independent and individual actions by women as unfeminine and morally suspect.

AGRIPPINA'S EARLY LIFE

Agrippina was the eldest of six children of Agrippina the Elder and Germanicus. The family was perhaps unusual among the imperial families, as it seems that Germanicus and Agrippina genuinely loved each other. Agrippina the Elder and her children accompanied Germanicus on his military campaigns in Germany and the East.

Germanicus's prestige and popularity with the army was also enjoyed by his children. In their early years they experienced army camps and witnessed the acclaim of the troops for their father. During Germanicus's triumph in Rome in AD 17 his children all rode with him in his chariot. The family was loved by the people of Rome.

From being perhaps the happiest and most beloved of the imperial families, they were to become the unluckiest and most ill-fated. In AD 14, Agrippina's grandmother Julia had been allowed to starve to death in exile by the new Emperor, Tiberius. This must surely have influenced Agrippina's attitude to Tiberius when she was old enough to realise what had happened; so too the events surrounding her father's death.

The family was much celebrated in the East and in AD 19 travelled to Egypt, where Germanicus was met with celebrations and goodwill. Such popularity would have irritated Tiberius, particularly as senators were not supposed to enter Egypt without his permission. Germanicus quarrelled with Tiberius's appointee to Syria, Piso, and relations between them became very difficult. Germanicus became ill and died at Antioch in October AD 19. Agrippina the Elder was convinced that her husband had been poisoned by Piso, suspecting Tiberius as well. The grief-stricken family returned to Rome with Germanicus's ashes. His burial in Augustus's Mausoleum in Rome was accompanied by wild scenes of anger and grief among the populace. Both Livia and Tiberius were absent from the proceedings, causing some observers to speculate on their involvement in Germanicus's death.

To gain a fuller appreciation of this period, read the account in Tacitus, *Annals*, 2.43, 53–5, 57–61, 69–84.

The next ten years or so must have been very difficult for the young Agrippina. Her mother and Tiberius constantly quarrelled, causing much unhappiness for the family. In AD 28, at thirteen years of age, Agrippina was married to Gnaeus Domitius Ahenobarbus, '. . . a man who was in every aspect of his life utterly detestable.' (Suetonius, *Nero*, 5) Ahenobarbus was the grandson of Augustus's sister Octavia. The family Domitii Ahenobarbi were of the old nobility, had provided consuls for over 200 years and were well known for both violence and cruelty.

In the same year, Agrippina's aunt Julia (Agrippina the Elder's sister) died in exile. In AD 29 both her mother and eldest brother, Nero, were harassed by Sejanus, the prefect of the Praetorian Guard who virtually ruled Rome during Tiberius's absence in Capri. Sejanus eventually arrested them and they were banished to the islands of Pandateria and Pontia respectively. Tiberius publicly denounced them, and in the following year his troops arrested Agrippina's brother Drusus. In AD 31, Livilla, Germanicus's sister (Agrippina's aunt), was executed for her role in the death of her husband, Drusus, who was Tiberius's son.

Agrippina's mother died in prison in AD 33 and two of her brothers also died about this time, leaving only Agrippina, her two sisters (Livilla and Drusilla) and their remaining brother, Gaius Caligula (who lived with Tiberius on the island of Capri).

Despite the upheaval in Agrippina's family, her husband, Ahenobarbus, became consul in AD 32. Agrippina somehow avoided the hostility directed at the rest of her family by Tiberius.

THE PRINCIPATE OF GAIUS CALIGULA

Tiberius died in March AD 37 and Agrippina's brother, Caligula, was hailed as Emperor. Nine months after Tiberius's death, Agrippina gave birth to her only child—a son, Lucius Domitius Ahenobarbus (later named Nero). It is unlikely that the birth of Nero nine months after the death of Tiberius was a coincidence; Agrippina had perhaps delayed conceiving until freed from the threat of Tiberius.

The beginning of Caligula's Principate was promising, and obviously more secure for Agrippina and her two sisters. Caligula immediately journeyed to the islands of Pandateria and Pontia and brought back the ashes of his mother and brother, burying them in Augustus's Mausoleum.

Agrippina and her sisters were showered with honours. They were made honorary Vestal Virgins, were able to watch circus games from the imperial seats, were used as figures on coins and their names were included in the annual vows for the Emperor's safety.

Late in AD 37, Caligula became ill. This illness apparently affected his mental state and marked the end of the short period of stability Agrippina had enjoyed since Tiberius's death.

During his illness, Caligula had made his favourite sister, Drusilla, and her husband, M. Aemilius Lepidus (a great-grandson of Augustus), his heirs. Rumours abounded in Rome that Lepidus would be his successor and that Caligula wished to marry Drusilla and had committed incest with Agrippina and Livilla.

In AD 38, Drusilla died. The following year Caligula accused his two remaining sisters, Agrippina and Livilla, of adultery and treason with Lepidus. He had Lepidus executed and forced Agrippina to return to Rome carrying Lepidus's ashes.

Why would Caligula have imposed such a punishment on Agrippina?

Research

Was there indeed a plot against Caligula?

Had Agrippina decided to support Lepidus in a bid for power and the Principate?

Caligula confiscated Agrippina's property and sent her into exile. Her husband died soon after and Nero was sent to live with his aunt, Domitia Lepida. Fortunately for Agrippina, Caligula was assassinated in Janury AD 41 and her uncle Claudius was hailed as Emperor. Claudius restored her property and allowed her to return to Rome.

THE ASCENDANCY OF AGRIPPINA

As a woman, Agrippina could not attain the emperorship herself. Her access to the position was through the men in her life. Her two alternatives were:

• to marry the Emperor;
• to help her son, Nero, to gain the Principate.

As events transpired she achieved both.

Nero's father, Ahenobarbus, had died in AD 40, leaving Agrippina a most eligible widow. Unfortunately for Agrippina, Claudius was married to Domitia Lepida's daughter, Valeria Messalina, and they produced a son in February 41 who was later to be known as Britannicus.

In her search for a new husband, it is possible that Agrippina first chose Servius Sulpicius Galba (the future Emperor of AD 69) who was both wealthy and influential, but she was not successful, as Suetonius notes:

Bust of Nero as a child (Alinari)

Nobody could interest him in a second match, not even Agrippina who, when her husband Domitius died, made such shameless advances to him—though he had not yet become a widower—that his mother-in-law gave her a public reprimand, going so far as to slap her in front of a whole bevy of married women.

Suetonius, *Galba*, 5

Agrippina eventually married C. Sallustius Passienus Crispus (heir to Augustus's friend Sallustius Crispus). He was enormously wealthy and when he died (sometime before AD 47) he left a great inheritance to Agrippina and Nero.

During this time, Agrippina had to behave very cautiously, as Messalina, the wife of Emperor Claudius, recognised that both Agrippina and Nero, the only surviving descendants of Germanicus, were very popular and posed a threat to her son Britannicus. However, Messalina was executed in AD 48 and Claudius became a widower. Agrippina once more saw her chance.

After living in fear and uncertainty during the Principates of Tiberius and Caligula, seeing her mother, father, brothers and sisters all die, it is hardly surprising that Agrippina desired security and power, and developed a reputation as ambitious and ruthless. If Agrippina had been a male, she would have succeeded Caligula as Emperor. She was very conscious of her family connections and her proximity to the basis of power in Rome.

THE MARRIAGE TO CLAUDIUS

Read the sources below and answer the following questions:

⟍Why did the marriage between Agrippina and Claudius take place?

⟍Who was to gain most from it—Agrippina or Claudius?

⟍Who supported Agrippina's bid to wed Claudius and why?

⟍What difficulties had to be overcome before they could wed?

• • • but it was Agrippina, daughter of his brother Germanicus, who hooked him. She had a niece's privilege of kissing and caressing Claudius, and exercised it with a noticeable effect on his passions . . . the wedding took place without delay . . .

Suetonius, *Claudius*, 26

❖ ❖ ❖

Pallas, proposing Agrippina, emphasized that the son whom she would bring with her was Germanicus's grandson, eminently deserving of imperial rank; let the emperor ally himself with a noble race and unite two branches of the Claudian house, rather than allow this lady of proved capacity for child-bearing, still young, to transfer the glorious name of the Caesars to another family.

Tacitus, *Annals*, 10.2

❖ ❖ ❖

After a little he married his niece Agrippina, the mother of Domitius, who was surnamed Nero. For she was beautiful and was in the habit of consulting him constantly; and she was much in his company unattended, seeing that he was her uncle, and in fact she was rather more familiar in her conduct toward him than became a niece.

Cassius Dio, *Roman History*, 61.31.5–6

❖ ❖ ❖

The freed men zealously aided in bringing about this marriage, since Agrippina had a son, Domitius, who was already nearing man's estate, and they wished to bring him up as Claudius's successor in the imperial office so that they might suffer no harm at the hands of Britannicus for having caused the death of his mother, Messalina.

ibid., 61.31.8

❖ ❖ ❖

• • • when the house next met, he persuaded a group of senators to propose that a union between him [Claudius] and her [Agrippina] should be compulsorily arranged, in the public interest; and that other uncles should likewise be free to marry their nieces, though this had hitherto counted as incest.

Suetonius, Claudius, 26

Having achieved this goal, Agrippina set about securing the position of successor for Nero. She began gradually to replace supporters of Britannicus in influential posts with her own supporters (e.g. Burrus as prefect of the Praetorians; Pallas as financial secretary). She was involved in the following events in Nero's life:

- Nero was engaged to Claudius's daughter Octavia in AD 49 and was formally adopted by Claudius the following year;
- he featured with Britannicus on some coins from the eastern and Danubian provinces;
- in AD 51 he assumed the *toga virilis* before the usual age, and took on the title 'Prince of Youth';
- financial donations were made to the troops and the public, and games were held for the populace in Nero's name.

Agrippina also worked towards increasing her own power. She was given her own Praetorian bodyguard; she was awarded the title 'Augusta' in AD 50; and she founded a colony of veterans where she had been born (modern-day Cologne) and named it 'Colonia Claudia Agrippinensis'. She also started to drive to the Capitol in the *carpentum* (carriage) which was usually reserved for priests and objects of worship—this was a privilege granted to her by the Senate. She also appeared on coins minted by Claudius.

. . . [all of this] increased the reverence felt for a woman who to this day remains unique as the daughter of a great commander and the sister, wife, and mother of emperors.

Tacitus, Annals, 12.42

Why did Claudius allow Agrippina to place Nero in such a prominent position?

Compare Nero and Britannicus on the family tree (see Table 11.1). Who had the greater 'legitimacy'?

Research

What was Britannicus doing in the meantime?

Historians cannot decide about the extent of Agrippina's influence on the reign of Claudius. Historian G. Ferrero comments:

. . . During the six years that Claudius lived after his marriage with Agrippina, scandalous tragedies became so rare that Tacitus, being deprived of his favourite materials, set down the story of these six years in a single book.

G. Ferrero, The Women of the Caesars, 284

Read book twelve of Tacitus. Do you agree with Ferrero's assessment of the years of Agrippina and Claudius's marriage?

TABLE 11.1 THE JULIO-CLAUDIAN FAMILY

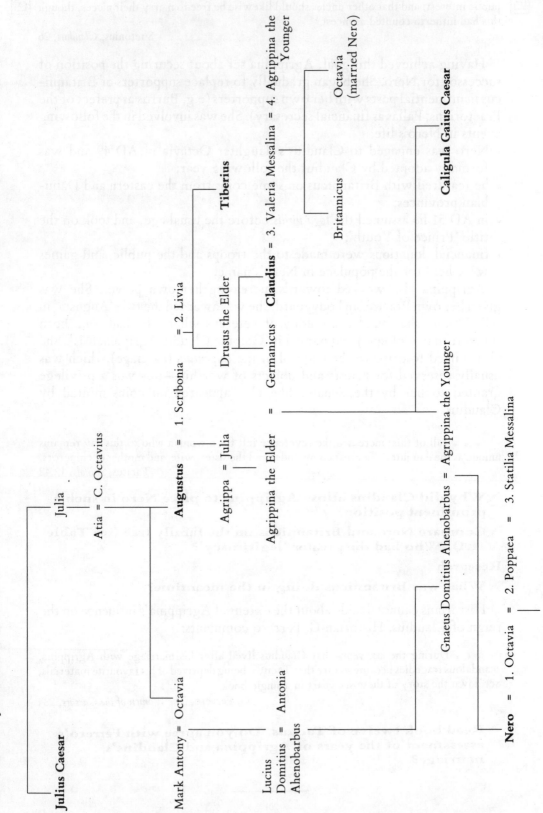

THE DEATH OF CLAUDIUS

Many historians, both ancient and modern, claim that Agrippina murdered Claudius by poisoning him.

Read the following sources and decide for yourself whether Claudius was killed by Agrippina; select your supporting evidence carefully and write out your judgement of the case.

Most people think that Claudius was poisoned: but when, and by whom, is disputed. Some say that the eunuch Halotus, his official taster, administered the drug while he was dining with the priests of Jupiter in the Citadel; others, that Agrippina did so herself at a family banquet, poisoning a dish of mushrooms, his favourite food.

Suetonius, *Nero*, 44

✻   ✻   ✻

. . . Claudius's death was not revealed until all arrangements had been completed to secure Nero's succession.

ibid., 45

✻   ✻   ✻

Agrippina had long decided on murder. Now she saw her opportunity. Her agents were ready. But she needed advice about poisons. A sudden, drastic effect would give her away. A gradual, wasting recipe might make Claudius, confronted with death, love his son again. What was needed was something subtle that would upset the emperor's faculties but produce a deferred fatal effect.

. . . Later, the whole story became known. Contemporary writers stated that the poison was sprinkled on a particularly succulent mushroom.

Tacitus, *Annals*, 12.66–7

✻   ✻   ✻

He [Claudius] would not endure her behaviour, but was preparing to put an end to her power, to cause his son to assume the *toga virilis*, and to declare him heir to the throne. Agrippina, learning of this, became alarmed and made haste to forestall anything of the sort by poisoning Claudius. . . she sent for a famous dealer in poisons, a woman named Locusta . . .

Cassius Dio, *Roman History*, 61.34.1–2

The preparations for Nero's accession seem to have been hurried. Would this have been the case if Claudius's murder had been planned? Was Agrippina fearing that Claudius was beginning to favour Britannicus? It is interesting to note a point raised by Suetonius in *Vespasian* (9):

He [Vespasian] started work on . . . a temple to Claudius the God on the Caelian Hill, begun by Agrippina but almost completely destroyed by Nero.

Would this have been the action of a murderer?

THE REIGN OF NERO

On 13 October AD 54, Nero presented himself to Rome as the next Emperor and was acclaimed as such by the army and, later, the Senate. He had the support of Burrus, the Praetorian prefect, and gave donations of 15 000 sesterces to each Praetorian guard.

Was the smooth transfer of power a result of Agrippina's planning?

Once Nero was Emperor, Agrippina wielded enormous power and influence herself. The sources differ in their estimates of the influence she had over Nero in the first few years, but it is clear that she and Nero's advisers, Seneca and Burrus, had great influence over the seventeen-year-old Emperor.

Read the following sources and answer these questions:

To what extent did Agrippina influence Nero in the early years of his reign?

Who gained from the actions described below?

He [Nero] also exalted the memory of his father Domitius, and turned over all his public and private affairs to Agrippina's management. On the day of his accession the password he gave to the colonel on duty was "the best of mothers"; and she and he often rode out together through the streets in her litter.

Suetonius, *Nero*, 9

✵ ✵ ✵

Nevertheless, publicly, Agrippina received honour after honour. When the escort-commander made the customary request for a password, Nero gave: "The best of mothers". The senate voted her two official attendants and the Priesthood of Claudius.

Tacitus, *Annals*, 13.2

✵ ✵ ✵

At first Agrippina managed for him all the business of the empire; and she and her son went forth together, often reclining in the same litter . . . She also received the various embassies and sent letters to peoples and governors and kings.

Cassius Dio, *Roman History*, 61.3.2

Agrippina gradually began to lose her influence for a number of reasons. Firstly, Seneca and Burrus, perhaps resenting such power in the hands of a woman and wanting more themselves, began to undermine her control by removing her main supporter, Pallas, the financial secretary. Their opposition to Agrippina culminated in a meeting with the Armenian ambassadors, where Agrippina tried to join Nero on the tribunal. Seneca and Burrus had Nero descend, greet his mother and continue negotiations from the floor:

. . . and thereafter they laboured to prevent any public business from being again committed to her hands.

Cassius Dio, *Roman History*, 61.3.3

The relationship between Agrippina and Nero began to decline. Agrippina threatened Nero that she would present Britannicus to the Praetorians as the legitimate heir to the emperorship—Agrippina had enormous influence with the army, so this was no idle threat. In AD 55, Nero had Britannicus poisoned.

When Agrippina made friendly moves towards Claudius's daughter Octavia and began to increase her patronage of senators and Praetorian officials, Nero removed her detachment of Praetorians, and her German bodyguard. He expelled Agrippina from his palace, sending her to live in his grandmother Antonia's house. In *Annals* (13) Tacitus explains that this was to prevent her from giving great receptions.

Conflict between Nero and Agrippina also arose over Nero's relationships with women. Seneca and Burrus encouraged Nero's love affairs, firstly with Acte, a freedwoman (she had no political influence and was thus no threat), and later with Poppaea Sabina. Agrippina opposed both of these unions, thus widening the gap between herself and Nero.

Agrippina began to acquire funds; Tacitus points out, '. . . she seemed to be looking round for a party, and a leader for it'. (ibid., 13.18) Had it been detected, this move would have indicated to Nero that she was looking for a 'puppet' general to help overthrow him.

Nero accused Agrippina of wanting to marry Rubellius Plautus, a descendant of Augustus, and to control the Empire and more. A match between Agrippina and such a man would have been particularly threatening to Nero. Agrippina was able to defend herself and Nero dropped the charge. Despite forcing Agrippina into retirement in Rome and cutting off all of her avenues of power, Nero continued to fear her and finally decided to have her killed.

Research

\\Is there any evidence that Agrippina was involved in political plots against her son?

\\Why did Nero go to the extreme of plotting to kill his mother?

THE DEATH OF AGRIPPINA

After making several attempts on Agrippina's life, Nero was finally successful in AD 59.

Read the detailed accounts of her death in Tacitus, *Annals* (14) and Suetonius, *Nero* (34), and answer the following questions:

\\Why was Nero so terrified when he learnt that his mother had escaped the boating accident?

\\What actions did he fear from her?

\\Considering her position and influence, do you think the people, the Senate or the army would have been likely to support Agrippina against Nero?

\\Had Agrippina expected to be killed by her own son? (Rumour had it that astrologers had warned her that Nero would become Emperor but would kill his mother. She apparently replied, 'Let him kill me, so long as he reigns!')

Nero was obviously afraid of the public reaction to her death. He sent reports to Rome from his estate at Baiae that she had tried to kill him and had then committed suicide. It is also interesting that he listed her many 'crimes'—mainly that, as a woman, she should not have desired power and involvement in imperial rule.

He [Nero] added older charges. "She had wanted to be co-ruler—to receive oaths of allegiance from the Guard, and to subject senate and public to the same humiliation. Disappointed of this, she had hated all of them—army, senate and people ..."

Tacitus, Annals, 14.11

The Senate, willing to appease their Emperor, offered up thanksgivings and declared Agrippina's birthday a black day for Rome.

Perhaps Agrippina had her revenge, as Suetonius notes:

● ● ● he [Nero] was never either then or thereafter able to free his conscience from the guilt of this crime. He often admitted that the Furies were pursuing him with whips and burning torches, and set Persian [magicians] at work to conjure up the ghost and make her stop haunting him.

Suetonius, Nero, 34

✴ ✴ ✴

AGRIPPINA'S RELATIONSHIP WITH NERO

❭The ancient sources present a variety of interpretations and opinions on the relationship between mother and son. Read the following source material and a selection of secondary source material, then make up your own mind about their relationship, based upon the available evidence.

❭A common accusation against noble Roman women with political influence was that of adultery or incest. How convincing are the following accusations against Agrippina?

The passion he felt for his mother, Agrippina, was notorious; but her enemies would not let him consummate it, fearing that, if he did, she would become even more powerful and ruthless than hitherto. So he found a new mistress who was said to be her spit and image; some say that he did, in fact, commit incest with Agrippina every time they rode in the same litter—the stains on his clothes when he emerged proved it.

Suetonius, Nero, 28

✴ ✴ ✴

Nearly everything, to be sure, that he and his mother said to each other or that they did each day was reported outside the palace, yet it did not all reach the public, and hence various conjectures were made and various stories circulated. For, in view of the depravity and lewdness of the pair, everything that could conceivably happen was noised abroad as having actually taken place, and reports possessing any credibility were believed as true.

Cassius Dio, Roman History, 61.8.5

✴ ✴ ✴

As if it were not notoriety enough for her that she had used her blandishments and immodest looks and kisses to seduce her uncle Claudius, she undertook to enslave even Nero in similar fashion. Whether this actually occurred, now, or whether it was invented to fit their character, I am not sure; but I state as a fact what is admitted by all, that Nero had a mistress resembling Agrippina of whom he was especially fond because of this very resemblance, and when he toyed with the girl herself or displayed her charms to others, he would say that he was wont to have intercourse with his mother.

ibid., 62.11.3–4

✦ ✦ ✦

According to one author, Cluvius Rufus, Agrippina's passion to retain power carried her so far that at midday, the time when food and drink were beginning to raise Nero's temperature, she several times appeared before her inebriated son all decked out and ready for incest. Their companions observed sensual kisses and evilly suggestive caresses.

. . . Another writer, Fabius Rusticus, agrees in attributing successful intervention to Acte's wiles, but states that the desires were not Agrippina's but Nero's. But the other authorities support the contrary version. So does the tradition. That may be because Agrippina really did intend this monstrosity. Or perhaps it is because no sexual novelty seemed incredible in such a woman. In her earliest years she had employed an illicit relationship with Marcus Aemilius Lepidus (V) as a means to power. Through the same ambition she had sunk to be Pallas' mistress. Then, married to her uncle, her training in abomination was complete.

Tacitus, *Annals*, 14.2

✦ ✦ ✦

WHY WAS AGRIPPINA SO POWERFUL?

One of the most important questions to ask about Agrippina is why she had so much power and influence, considering that Roman women had no direct involvement in politics. Agrippina held a unique position during her life and the basis for her power could be placed into the following categories:

• family connections;
• wealth;
• patronage;
• honours and position in society.

Read the sources below and try to explain more fully how each of the above aspects contributed to her overall power.

From this moment the country was transformed. Complete obedience was accorded to a woman—and not a woman like Messalina who toyed with national affairs to satisfy her appetites. This was a rigorous, almost masculine despotism. In public, Agrippina was austere and often arrogant. Her private life was chaste—unless power was to be gained. Her passion to acquire money was unbounded. She wanted it as a stepping-stone to supremacy.

Tacitus, *Annals*, 12.7

✦ ✦ ✦

As soon as Agrippina had come to live in the palace she gained complete control over Claudius. Indeed, she was very clever in making the most of her opportunities, and, partly by fear and partly by favours, she won the devotion of all those who were at all friendly toward him . . . She accomplished these ends partly by getting the freed men to persuade Claudius and partly by arranging beforehand that the Senate, the populace, and the soldiers should join together in shouting their approval of her demands on every occasion . . . She was amassing untold wealth for him [Nero], overlooking no possible source of revenue . . .

Cassius Dio, *Roman History*, 61.32.1–3

✦ ✦ ✦

Agrippina often attended the emperor in public, when he was transacting ordinary business or when he was giving an audience to ambassadors, though she sat upon a separate tribunal. This, too, was one of the most remarkable sights of the time.

ibid., 61.33.7

✦   ✦   ✦

Nevertheless, Agrippina did not yet venture to make her supreme attempt until she could remove the commanders of the Guard, Lusius Geta and Rufrius Crispinus, whom she regarded as loyal to the memory of Messalina and to the cause of Messalina's children. So Agrippina asserted to Claudius that the Guard was split by their rivalry and that unified control would mean stricter discipline. Thereupon the command was transferred to Sextus Afranius Burrus, who was a distinguished soldier but fully aware whose initiative was behind his appointment. Agrippina also enhanced her own status. She entered the Capitol in a ceremonial carriage. This distinction, traditionally reserved for priests and sacred emblems, increased the reverence felt for a woman who to this day remains unique as the daughter of a great commander and the sister, wife, and mother of emperors.

Tacitus, *Annals*, 12.42

✦   ✦   ✦

Moreover, the appropriate steps were taken to secure Nero's accession.

Tacitus, *Annals*, 12.68

✦   ✦   ✦

She became Octavia's supporter. Constantly meeting her own friends in secret Agrippina outdid even her natural greed in grasping funds from all quarters to back her designs. She was gracious to officers, and attentive to such able and high-ranking noblemen as survived. She seemed to be looking round for a Party, and a leader for it. Learning this, Nero withdrew the military bodyguard which she had been given as empress and retained as the emperor's mother, and also the German guardsmen by which, as an additional compliment, it had recently been strengthened. Furthermore, he terminated her great receptions by giving her a separate residence in the mansion formerly occupied by Antonia (II). When he visited her there, he would bring an escort of staff-officers, hurriedly embrace her, and leave.

Veneration of another person's power, if it is ill-supported, is the most precarious and transient thing in the world. Agrippina's house was immediately deserted.

ibid, 13.18

✦   ✦   ✦

"She may arm her slaves! She may whip up the army, or gain access to the senate or Assembly, and incriminate me for wrecking and wounding her and killing her friends! What can I do to save myself?"... Finally Seneca ventured so far as to turn to Burrus and ask if the troops should be ordered to kill her. He replied that the Guard were devoted to the whole imperial house and to Germanicus' memory; they would commit no violence against his offspring.

ibid., 14.7

✦   ✦   ✦

THE 'CRIMES' OF AGRIPPINA

Agrippina has been accused of causing the deaths of several people who supposedly stood in her way. The following is a list of her alleged victims.

Examine the evidence on *four* of the 'victims' listed in Table 11.2. Note any contradictions between the sources. What advantage was there for her to have each one killed? Is it possible to lay the blame elsewhere, for example on Nero?

TABLE 11.2   THE 'VICTIMS' OF AGRIPPINA

VICTIM	YEAR OF DEATH	SOURCE
Lollia Paulina	AD 49	Tacitus, *Annals*, 12.22
		Cassius Dio, *Dio's Roman History*, 61.32.3
Lucius Silanus	49	Suetonius, *Claudius*, 29
		Annals, 13.1
		Dio's Roman History, 61.31.8
Calpurnia	49	*Annals*, 12.22
		Dio's Roman History, 61.33.2
Sosibius		*Dio's Roman History*, 61.32.5
Statilius Taurus	53	*Annals*, 12.59
Claudius	54	*Annals*, 12.64ff
		Dio's Roman History, 61.34.1–4
		Suetonius, *Nero*, 44–5
Domitia Lepida	54	*Annals*, 12.64–5
Marcus Junius Silanus	54	*Annals*, 13.1ff
		Dio's Roman History, 61.6.4

ARCHAEOLOGICAL EVIDENCE

Apart from coins there is very little archaeological evidence for Agrippina. By studying the following coins, it is possible to trace Agrippina's career under three Emperors. Remember that imperial coinage presented official policies and messages to the Roman people.

\ **What does each coin represent?**

\ **What official policy is being stated?**

THE REIGN OF GAIUS

SESTERTIUS, AD 37 – 38, FROM ROME

Obverse: (Head of Gaius, laureate)
GAIUS CAESAR AUGUSTUS GERMANICUS, PONTIFEX MAXIMUS, WITH TRI-BUNICIAN POWER.

Reverse: (Gaius's three sisters, depicting Security, Concord and Fortune.) AGRIPPINA, DRUSILLA, JULIA, BY DECREE OF THE SENATE.

THE REIGN OF CLAUDIUS

AUREUS, AD 51 – 54, IMPERIAL ISSUE

Reverse: AGRIPPINA AUGUSTAE (bust of Agrippina, wearing crown of corn-ears).

THE REIGN OF NERO

AUREUS, AD 54 – 55, FROM ROME

Obverse: (Busts of Nero and Agrippina the Younger, facing each other, both bare-headed.)
AGRIPPINA AUGUSTA, WIFE OF THE DIVINE CLAUDIUS, MOTHER OF NERO CAESAR.
Reverse: BY DECREE of the SENATE (within an oak-wreath). TO NERO CLAUDIUS CAESAR AUGUSTUS GERMANICUS IMPERATOR, WITH TRIBUNI-CIAN POWER.

AUREUS, AD 54 – 55, FROM ROME

Obverse: (Busts of Nero and Agrippina, both bare-headed, Agrippina behind.) NERO CLAUDIUS CAESAR AUGUSTUS GERMANICUS, SON OF A GOD, IMPERATOR, WITH TRIBUNICIAN POWER, CONSUL.
Reverse: (Two figures seated in a chariot drawn by elephants.) BY DECREE OF THE SENATE, AGRIPPINA AUGUSTA, WIFE OF THE DIVINE CLAUDIUS, MOTHER OF NERO CAESAR.

(Coins reproduced by courtesy of the Trustees of the British Museum)

CONCLUSION

Most secondary sources treat Agrippina harshly. Your task at this point is to present a balanced, objective view. The following questions should assist you to make a judgement on Agrippina.

- **To what extent did Agrippina's family connections and the female role models she had been exposed to shape her visions for her own life?**
- **How much did she influence the reigns of Claudius and Nero?**
- **What do you see as Agrippina's strengths and weaknesses?**
- **To what extent did the tragedies of her early life shape her personality?**

If Agrippina's memoirs had survived, how might she have accounted for:
- **her marriage to Claudius?**
- **the death of Claudius?**
- **Nero's 'good years'?**

LIST OF REFERENCES

ANCIENT SOURCES

Cassius Dio, *Dio's Roman History*, Vol. 8, Loeb Classical Library, 1980

Suetonius, 'Claudius', 'Galba', 'Nero' and 'Vespasian' in *The Twelve Caesars*, Penguin, 1973

Tacitus, *The Annals of Imperial Rome*, Penguin, 1971

SECONDARY SOURCES

Ferrero, G., *The Women of the Caesars*, The Century Company, New York, 1911.

Sutherland, C. H. V., *The Roman Imperial Coinage*, Vol. 1, Spink & Son Ltd, London, 1984

BIBLIOGRAPHY

SECONDARY SOURCES

Balsdon, J. P. V. D., *Roman Women: Their History and Habits*, The Bodley Head, London, 1977

Griffin, M. T., *Nero, The End of a Dynasty*, B. T. Batsford Ltd, London, 1984

Pomeroy, S. B., *Goddesses, Whores, Wives and Slaves*, Shocken Books, N. Y., 1976

Rawson, B., *The Position of Women in Roman History*, History Teachers Association of NSW

CHAPTER TWELVE

NERO
THE SINGING EMPEROR

NIGEL IRVINE

How ugly and vulgar my life has become
—Nero

AD 37	Lucius Domitius Ahenobarbus (Nero) born at Antium during the reign of the Emperor Gaius Caligula
39	Agrippina is exiled; Nero lives with his aunt Domitia Lepida
40	Death of Gnaeus Domitius Ahenobarbus from dropsy
41	Murder of Gaius Caligula; Claudius proclaimed Emperor; Agrippina recalled from exile
43	Roman invasion of southern Britain
48	Emperor Claudius's wife, Messalina, executed for treason
49	Claudius marries Agrippina Seneca is recalled from exile to tutor Nero Octavia, the Emperor's daughter, is engaged to marry Nero
50	Claudius adopts Nero
51	Nero assumes the *toga virilis*, the mark of adulthood
53	Octavia and Nero marry
54	Death of the Emperor Claudius Nero is proclaimed Emperor Nero's romance with Acte; he becomes estranged from his mother, Agrippina
55	Nero has Britannicus murdered Agrippina loses power and is forced to leave Rome Appointment of Corbulo in the East
58	War between Rome and Parthia over Armenia
59	Murder of Agrippina Nero's youth games—*Juvenalia*—introduced; Nero performs on stage

60	The Neronian Games
60 – 61	The revolt of Queen Boudicca (Boadicea) of the *Iceni*
62	Tigellinus becomes commander of the Praetorian Guard with Faenius Rufus Nero divorces Octavia and marries Poppaea Sabina
63	Birth of Nero's daughter to Poppaea Sabina; named Claudia, the child dies in less than six months
64	The Great Fire of Rome; Nero's famous *Domus Aurea* (Golden House) commenced; persecution of the Christians
65	Open opposition to Nero The conspiracy of Piso revealed; Seneca ordered to commit suicide because of alleged involvement Poppaea Sabina accidentally killed by Nero
66	Nero marries Statilia Messalina Nero makes his long awaited visit to Greece
67	Nero performs in the Greek Games at Corinth and declares the liberation of the Greeks from Rome Trouble in Gaul and Spain; riots in Rome Nero returns to Rome
68	Julius Vindex, Governor of Lugdunensis in Gaul, revolts Galba proclaims himself for the Senate and the people of Rome, supported by Otho Vindex defeated at Vesontio and commits suicide Nero's northern armies defect to Galba; the Senate and Praetorian Guards do likewise Nero attempts to flee to Egypt but only gets to the house of his freedman, Phaon, where he commits suicide Acte gives Nero an expensive funeral and his ashes are taken to the Domitian family plot

In AD 54, Agrippina was thirty-nine years old. Her life so far had had one purpose: to secure for her son, Nero, the position of Emperor. She had been Claudius's co-regent; having had him poisoned, she became the real power behind the throne. When in October 54 Nero was proclaimed Emperor, he described Agrippina as *'optima mater'* (the best of mothers).

In his first oration, Nero spoke of the long history of the imperial family, his famous ancestors and the consulships and triumphs they had won. He pointed out that during Claudius's reign, Rome had sustained no losses to its Empire. The new Emperor made a favourable impression; the Senate voted him the title *'Pater Patriae'* (father of his country) as they had done for Augustus in his thirteenth consulship. Nero, who was only seventeen, declined this honour, remarking that he was far too young for it. This speech had, presumably, been written by his tutor, Seneca, who knew only too well what Rome expected of an Emperor. Nero was an unusual youth who did not really fit this mould; he painted, sculpted, wrote poetry, took singing lessons and harboured secret desires to race his chariot team in the Hippodrome.

Nero began his reign with the solemn promise that he was no man's enemy, for he was mounting the throne free from the desire for vengeance. The abuses of the past would be forgotten: favouritism, nepotism, corruption and lobbying for appointments would be abolished. The Senate would be given every freedom, the courts would be reformed and peace would prevail in the Empire. Nero promised these things to the Senate and people of Rome in the name of the 'Divine Augustus'.

THE DEATH OF BRITANNICUS

Soon after Nero became Emperor, his relationship with his mother began to decline. Agrippina strongly opposed his affair with Acte, a freedwoman concubine, and reacted strongly to rumours that they might marry. She threatened to back the thirteen-year-old Britannicus as rightful heir to the throne. She also began to show some interest in Nero's wife, Octavia, who was Claudius's daughter.

The historian E. T. Salmon describes Agrippina's renewed interest in her stepchildren as her 'kiss of death'. Nero realised that Britannicus was a threat to him and decided to have him killed. It is likely this decision was made independently of his advisers, Seneca and Burrus; while they encouraged him to be independent of Agrippina it is unlikely that they would have gone to the extent of encouraging him to murder Britannicus.

Once he had decided to kill Britannicus, Nero arranged for a renowned poisoner, Locusta, to produce an appropriate poison. Her first attempt produced only a mild laxative effect. Suetonius says that Nero summoned her and beat her until she promised the fastest-working concoction possible. (*Nero*, 33) Nero supplied Locusta with research animals, and eventually she produced a brew which killed a pig instantaneously. When administered to Britannicus in the guise of water to cool a hot drink, its effect was immediate.

Nero's reign was merely twelve months old and was already tainted by bloodshed. In *Annals* (13.17) Tacitus claims that several days before the murder, Nero had visited his stepbrother and committed homosexual acts upon him, taking full advantage of the boy's innocence. Tacitus concludes, 'Such was this hurried murder of the last of the Claudians, physically defiled, then poisoned...'

THE AUGUSTAN MODEL

In an attempt to demonstrate his virtuous intentions, Nero had promised to model his rule on Augustan principles. Rome did not fare too badly during

Nero's first year. He distributed vast sums of money and his largess to the proletariat of Rome included birds of every variety, coupons for grain, gold, silver, precious stones, pearls, articles of clothing, slaves and even breeding cattle. He also gave away ships, real estate and apartment blocks. He presented noblemen and senators who owned no property with a year's income.

On the advice of Burrus, Nero made many improvements to the judicial system and its administration. He made a genuine attempt to cultivate the Senate; he greeted Roman noblemen by name and tried to remember them all. Whenever the Senate wished to offer him honours, he would accept them only if he deserved them. When dispensing justice, Nero also showed his more humane side by a demonstration of his abhorrence at having to sign death warrants.

In keeping with his Augustan model, Nero introduced a new style of architecture to Rome. Porches had to be built on to the front of houses so that they could be used as fire fighting platforms. These improvements were built at Nero's own expense. As well, he attempted to limit the extravagances of wealthy Roman society. Public feasts were to consist of a fixed number of courses and inns were restricted to selling only cold snacks, not cooked meals.

Nero was a patron of the theatre and organised a large variety of entertainments, including the youth games (the *juvenalia*), circuses, theatre performances, pantomimes and gladiatorial contests. He encouraged the arts, holding competitions and awarding prizes for poetry and Latin rhetoric. (He took one of these prizes himself for his poetry, but declined a victor's wreath for his lyre-playing.) Some of his entertainments were similar to those held by his great-grandfather: Augustus had staged a naval battle on the Tiber in which 3000 men took part; Nero held a mock naval battle on an artificial lake.

From AD 54 – 59, Nero ruled with wisdom and moderation. Michael Grant, in the introduction to his book *Nero*, believes that Nero's foreign policy was a sensible and sound one. He also states that Nero, who had a distaste for war, averted disaster with Parthia and despite two rebellions (in Britain and Israel) governed the Empire well.

THE SINGING EMPEROR

Immediately after his accession, Nero engaged Terpnus the lyre-player as his court musician and soon began to study singing and lyre-playing. Suetonius claims that Nero was so conscientious about following his teacher's instructions that in order to strengthen his voice he would lie on his back with a slab on his chest, use enemas and emetics to reduce his weight and carefully watch what foods he could eat.

At first Nero restricted himself to private performances but eventually succumbed to the attraction of the stage. His voice, although feeble and

Bust of Nero (Uffizi, Florence. Courtesy Mansell Collection)

husky, had improved enough for Nero to consider a public performance. According to Suetonius, his first was in the Greek town of Naples (perhaps the possibility of a hostile reception in Rome influenced this decision). Despite an earthquake which shook the theatre, Nero sang his piece through to the end. He was so pleased with his first performance that he performed in Naples for several consecutive days.

With his first public performance considered a success, Nero made plans to perform in Rome at the second Neronian Games in AD 65, a grand contest which included music, singing, poetic composition, rhetoric, field sports and chariot racing. His performance of the opera *Niobe* lasted about four hours, so long that the other competitors were unable to perform!

Nero also began to take part in tragedies, complete with costume and mask (the masks were fashioned on his own features or those of his current mistresses). Then he turned to equestrian sports. Like his father, Nero had always been interested in chariot racing. At first he was content to play with model horses on a table; then he began to visit all the races held in Rome. Suetonius tells us that Nero soon wanted to be a charioteer; he practised in the imperial gardens in front of slaves and eventually appeared in the Circus Maximus as a charioteer. During his visit to Greece in AD 67, Nero raced on the famous track at Olympia.

THE PENULTIMATE CRIME—MATRICIDE

The relationship between Agrippina and Nero continued to decline. Nero wished to free himself from his role of 'puppet-king', if only to indulge his artistic and sensual desires. Neither Seneca nor Burrus helped matters, for they also resented Agrippina's power. In an attempt to deprive Agrippina of her power, they directed their attention to the freedman, Pallas, who was Agrippina's strongest supporter in court; he was deprived of his position and forced into retirement. Phaon, who replaced Pallas in AD 55, proved to be more amenable.

Agrippina, who had been banished from the palace, was not prepared to live quietly in the countryside. Apparently, after a discrete period of time, she attempted to win back Nero's affections by seduction. The prospect of a reconciliation alarmed those close to the Emperor. Seneca sent Acte to inform Nero that the army would not tolerate an Emperor who was sacrilegious, and that Agrippina had made their indiscretions common knowledge. Nero, once again, felt threatened by a close relative. It is quite possible that both Nero and Agrippina decided to kill one another at this time. Each, it seems, was playing a dangerous game of cat and mouse with the other, and the one who took the initiative would be the winner.

Nero's murder of Britannicus had been a relatively simple crime to organise; Agrippina, however, would not be so easy. Poisoning seemed out of the question, for she took precautions to guard herself by downing copious amounts of antidotes. If Nero was to be successful in killing Agrippina he needed an elaborate plan that could not be betrayed through a breach of security, but most of all the murder should look to be accidental.

Nero's former tutor Anicetus, a Greek admiral, came to Nero's rescue. Anicetus, who commanded the fleet stationed at Misenum, convinced Nero that it would be an easy task to create a prefabricated ship that would fall apart on cue. If the Emperor's mother drowned at sea it could hardly be attributed to Nero, as such accidents were common. Anicetus's collapsible ship was made ready for the Festival of Minerva in March, when Nero would be at Baiae for the holiday. Under the pretence of a reconciliation, he invited Agrippina to join his party.

Nero made quite a fuss over Agrippina and was so friendly and open towards her that Agrippina was confident their differences were behind them. However, she had not long been aboard the ship which was to take her home when the order was given to collapse the ship. The roof of Agrippina's cabin, which had been weighed down with lead, collapsed inwards. Miraculously, Agrippina escaped injury. There was a good deal of confusion on board, since only a small proportion of the crew were privy to the plot. While some did their best to kill the Emperor's mother, others were intent on her salvation. Agrippina was eventually rescued by a group of fishermen and taken back to their village.

Nero, meanwhile, waited for news of his mother's death. Towards dawn, Agrippina's freedman arrived and begged an audience with the Emperor. To his surprise, Nero was told that his mother had escaped and was resting at home. Nero had Agrippina's freedman arrested and charged with the attempted assassination of the Emperor: under torture the freedman confessed that Agrippina had sent him to kill her son.

Nero ordered Burrus to send a squad of the Praetorian Guard to kill Agrippina. Burrus, however, pointed out to the Emperor that this was not in his best interests since the Praetorian Guard, being mostly German, were devoted to the memory of Germanicus, and an attack on his daughter might cause deep resentment within their ranks. The argument was not lost on Nero, for he knew just how important the Praetorian Guard was in the creation of Emperors. Instead, a detachment of marines was sent to Agrippina's villa to kill her; she died from a number of wounds. Nero visited his mother's corpse and, with a cup of wine in hand, discussed the good and bad points of her body. She was cremated without ceremony and her ashes buried in an unmarked grave. Agrippina had been warned twenty-two years earlier that her son would be responsible for her death, to which she is said to have replied 'Let him kill me—provided he becomes Emperor'. (Tacitus, *Annals*, 14.7)

THE DIVORCE OF OCTAVIA

It was four years after Agrippina's death before Nero made any attempt to divorce Octavia. The daughter of the 'Divine Claudius' was still immensely popular with the people and any attempt to replace her might not be tolerated. Certainly, Seneca and Burrus would not have advised him to do so. By AD 62, however, Seneca had retired to private life and Burrus had died. The Praetorian prefect Tigellinus would not try to prevent Nero divorcing Octavia. Tigellinus had created an atmosphere of fear in Rome. He presided over the intelligence services and was more than willing to provide evidence to use as grounds for divorce.

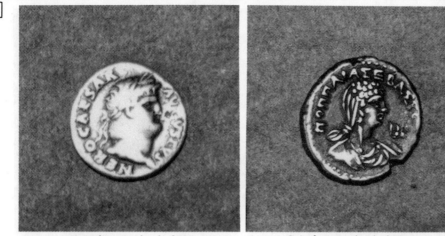

Coin depicting head of Nero
(Macquarie University, NSW)

Coin depicting head of Poppaea
(Macquarie University, NSW)

Nero's first attempt to divorce his wife was on the grounds that she was barren. When this attempt failed, he accused her of committing adultery with one of her Alexandrian slaves. Octavia's household servants were interviewed and some tortured to obtain confessions, but none would bear false witness against their mistress. Tigellinus must have obtained some evidence, however, as Nero began his divorce proceedings against Octavia. He forced her out of the palace into a suburban villa, then had her transferred to a country villa and placed under house-arrest. The Roman people, however, were unhappy about the removal of their princess and their demonstrations were instrumental in having Octavia returned. This too proved an embarrassment, as once the rumour circulated that Octavia had returned, joyous rioting broke out in the streets and could only be quelled by force. If Nero was to divorce Octavia, he needed stronger evidence.

The charge of high treason (*maiestas*) was the weapon successfully used against Octavia. Nero's former tutor and minion Anicetus claimed that he and Octavia had been lovers and that she had seduced him because of his position in the fleet. Her seduction, it was claimed, was to foster revolution and to endanger the Empire. As a result of Anicetus's perjury, the Senate exiled Octavia to the island of Pandateria and a few days after her arrival she was murdered by her guards. Her head was sent back to Rome as a wedding gift for Poppaea Sabina, Nero's lover and new wife.

THE REVOLT OF BOUDICCA IN BRITAIN

Although under Nero policies towards the Empire were usually sound and just, trouble developed in the province of Britain. Nero had, at the beginning of his reign, considered a total withdrawal from the island but decided against this. However, trouble developed with a Celtic tribe called the *Iceni* who, during the reign of their king Antedios, had been one of the

Romanticised statue of Boudicca and her daughters (City Hall, Cardiff, UK)

first British tribes to form an alliance with Rome. The *Iceni* held land in what is now Suffolk, Norfolk and parts of Cambridgeshire, and were known and respected for their breeding of horses. It seems that their relationship with Rome was quite good. When King Antedios died, his successor, King Prasutagus, continued to honour their original treaty with Rome.

When Prasutagus died in AD 60, Rome decided to annex the *Iceni's* kingdom, and plundered it. Prasutagus's widow, Boudicca, was ill-treated and her daughters raped. The resulting rebellion soon spread to include a neighbouring tribe, the *Trinovantes*, who had also been on friendly terms with Rome.

Cassius Dio, writing over a century after the rebellion, described Boudicca as a woman:

In stature she was very tall, in appearance most terrifying, in the glance of her eye most fierce, and her voice was harsh; a great mass of the tawniest hair fell to her hips; around her neck was a large golden necklace; and she wore a tunic of divers colours over which a thick mantle was fastened with a brooch. This was her invariable attire. She now grasped a spear to aid her in terrifying all beholders...

Cassius Dio, *Roman History*, 62.2.4

Under Boudicca's leadership the *Iceni* and *Trinovantes* swept south. Colchester, a Romanised town occupied mainly by Roman veterans and their families, was the first to fall to the rebels. Although surrounded by walls, the town's defences had been long neglected. The last defenders were forced to take refuge in the partially completed temple of the 'Divine Claudius' before it too was burnt and those inside massacred. A relief force hurried to the town but was caught in open country—only the commander and a few of the cavalry escaped.

St Albans and London were both overrun and plundered by the rebels. It is estimated that they massacred nearly 70 000 people in the three towns, some of whom were tortured and mutilated. News of the rebellion brought the military governor, Suetonius Paulinus, back from his campaign against the Druids in Wales.

Boudicca's force arrived at the Watling Street battlefield accompanied by a large number of non-combatants and their wagons. They formed an encampment by arranging their wagons into an arc at the rear of their army. When the Celts attacked Paulinus's legions, they met a well disciplined opposition which forced them back towards their campsite. The arc of wagons and the non-combatants acted as a trap; unable to retreat or advance. Boudicca's force was destroyed by the Roman cavalry.

With her rebellion in defeat, Boudicca ended her own life. The Romans shipped over reinforcements from Gaul and levied heavy retribution on the tribes. Eventually a new governor replaced Paulinus and a more moderate attitude was adopted. Britain settled down to a period of peace and Nero was able to withdraw one of his legions for service in the East.

NERO AND THE OTHER PROVINCES

Nero showed little interest in matters of a provincial nature throughout his reign, but a situation arose in Armenia in AD 58 which required the attention of the new Emperor.

In *Annals* (13.34) Tacitus tells us 'a war between Parthia and Rome about the possession of Armenia, which, feebly begun, had hitherto dragged on, was vigorously resumed.' The Parthian King, Vologeses, had given Armenia to his brother, Tiridates. Rome could not tolerate such a situation, for although Armenia was not part of the Roman Empire it had to be ruled by someone friendly to Rome because it bordered Roman provinces. Parthia had always been a problem for Rome, and Armenia was an important buffer zone.

Nero appointed Domitius Corbulo to secure Armenia. Corbulo was a well-respected general who was very popular among Romans and provincial nationals alike. His 'appearance was impressive, and so was his oratory—superficial advantages matching his experience and ability'. (Tacitus, *Annals*, 13.8)

A further indication of the professionalism and greatness of Corbulo is given to us by Tacitus who describes how he had to pull his soldiers into line:

Corbulo found his own men's slackness a worse trouble than enemy treachery. His troops had come from Syria. Demoralized by years of peace, they took badly to service conditions. The army actually contained old soldiers who had never been on guard or watch, who found ramparts and ditches strange novelties, and who owned neither helmet nor breastplate—flashy money-makers who had soldiered in towns. Corbulo discharged men who were too old or too weak, and filled their places with Galatian and Cappadocian recruits, augmented by a brigade from Germany with auxiliary infantry and cavalry. The whole army was kept under canvas through a winter so severe that ice had to be removed and the ground excavated before tents could be pitched. Frostbite caused many losses of limbs. Sentries were frozen to death. A soldier was seen carrying a bundle of firewood with hands so frozen that they fell off, fastened to their load.

Corbulo himself, thinly dressed and bare-headed, moved among his men at work and on the march, encouraging the sick and praising efficiency—an example to all. But the harsh climate and service produced many shirkers and deserters. Corbulo's remedy was severity. In other armies, first and second offences were excused: Corbulo executed deserters immediately.

Tacitus, *Annals*, 13.35

Corbulo soon realised that he had to show Tiridates the strength of the Roman army. When an attempted meeting between these two failed to eventuate, Corbulo captured Artaxata, the Armenian capital; then the city of Tigranocerta surrendered.

Tiridates had fled from Armenia and in his absence Corbulo placed Tigranes, a Romanised Cappadocian noble selected by Nero, upon the Armenian throne. Corbulo left for his new appointment as Governor of Syria, leaving Roman troops to support Tigranes.

Peace did not last long; Tigranes made unprovoked moves against Armenia's neighbours. Corbulo, fearing the worst if he left his province for any length of time, requested that Nero appoint a special commander for Armenia. This was done. However the man appointed, Caesennius Paetus, proved to be totally incompetent, resulting in Armenia falling back into the hands of the Parthians and the disgrace of the Roman army. Nero had to chose between a 'dangerous war or a disgraceful peace'. (Tacitus, *Annals*, 15.25) Corbulo was nominated immediately to carry out the war, and all of Rome's allies in the region were instructed to obey his commands. However, very little blood was shed. The final settlement was negotiated between Corbulo and Tiridates:

- Rome would recognise Tiridates as the King of Armenia;
- Tiridates would go to Rome to accept the diadem (the symbol of royal power) from the Emperor.

THE EMPEROR'S PERSONAL LIFE

With his passion for singing, dancing and chariot-racing already commonly known, Nero's personal life became the focus of much of Rome's gossip. All of the previous Emperors had faced some rumours about their personal lives, but rumours about Nero were so persistent that some of them must have been true. Stories of the Emperor's unusual sexual practices became common knowledge. These practices included his mock marriage to the freedman Doryphorous; his attraction to his eunuch Sporus, whom he dressed as his bride and treated in public as his wife; and the parties he held in the Imperial Palace where Nero crawled around on the floor, dressed only in the skin of some wild beast, performing indecent acts upon unwilling victims. Such tales did little for the Emperor's reputation, not only with the aristocracy but also the people in general. To conservative Romans, it was all a little too 'Greek'.

THE GREAT FIRE

The public's perception of Nero deteriorated further following the 'Great Fire' of AD 64. Rome had always been prone to fires. The design of the city, the crowded conditions of the poorer sections of the town and the hot summers made fire a common catastrophe in ancient times.

The circumstances surrounding the fire's origin and the measures taken to contain it are sketchy. Apparently the fire started in or near the Circus Maximus among the stores which sold flammable goods. Fanned by the wind, it quickly spread to the wealthier suburbs where it destroyed temples and villas. The fire spread unabated into the woodlands outside the city. Had it not been for a change of wind direction, which brought it back to the city, the fire would probably have burnt itself out. Once in the older, poorer parts of the city there was little which could stop it. The streets, narrow and winding, were choked with people attempting to escape. The general confusion and the extremely combustible nature of the buildings made fire-fighting difficult.

Also, lawless gangs, presumably intent on plunder, threatened anyone who attempted to fight the fire. These gangs apparently claimed that they were acting under orders to set alight some properties which had not been touched by the fire. Suetonius firmly places the blame on Nero, claiming that these gangs were positively identified as his agents and were sent out to burn down properties which he had coveted. Nero had also ordered that a siege engine be deployed to knock down several stone buildings which stood near his palace, presumably so he could claim this land.

These claims may well be true, although it is possible that the gangs had been instructed to burn down properties in the path of the fire to create a 'backburn'; as for the siege engine, its use as an instrument to create a fire-break seems infinitely wise. While it seems unlikely that Nero was responsible for the fire, he quite possibly referred to it as a good thing, and his plan for a grand new palace would have placed him under suspicion. Nor would it be unusual for such a disaster to be seen as a dramatic background in which an artist could take up his lyre and compose an epic sonnet about the 'Fall of Troy', which is what Nero did. To Nero, the fire was an inspiration given to an artist by the gods. To the ordinary people who had lost their entire worldly goods, it was neither poetic nor romantic.

Rumours that Nero had started the fire quickly gained hold and the fact that he was not even in Rome at the time, but in Antium, did not seem to matter. He had actually rushed back to the city when he was informed of the disaster, and helped the homeless by opening the temples, the Campus Martius and his own gardens to them so that they had a place to camp. Emergency supplies of food were shipped to the city from Ostia and the neighbouring towns. Steps were taken to stop the black market in grain by keeping the price artificially low. A relief fund was set up to which the Emperor gave generously from his own purse. Stricter fire-fighting codes were drawn up and the city was redesigned to avoid such a disaster in the future.

Despite all of these good deeds, the rumours of Nero's involvement in the fire grew stronger, and became so alarming that he decided to divert the public's resentment elsewhere. Nero's decision to blame the Christians for the fire has been greatly responsible for his infamy. Christianity was a relatively new religion at the time of Nero, and there was still a good deal of confusion in the minds of most Romans as to who the Christians were. Both Tacitus and Suetonius, writing half a century after Nero, still shared this confusion. To most Romans, the Christians were Jews and there was enough anti-Semitic feeling in Rome to make their persecution acceptable.

It was not a coincidence that Nero chose the Christians to persecute rather than the Jews as a broader group. Since childhood he had cultivated an interest in eastern religions and any attack on Jews in Rome might well have had repercussions in the East. Also, it would have been out of character with his usually conciliatory foreign policy. The Christians, then, made an excellent scapegoat; they were more than willing to be martyrs.

The Romans' view of Christianity was of a religion popular with slaves, which preached of an apocalyptic end to the world in order to prepare for a second coming of their saviour. The Romans associated the doctrine of the body of Christ with strange acts of cannibalism. There was a great deal of confusion about what Christianity actually meant. To persecute such 'fanatics' made very good sense to the Romans; Suetonius thought it to be one of Nero's better acts and lists it as one of his 'good works'. Tacitus also felt that the Christians deserved their punishment, not so much for the acts of arson they had supposedly caused but because of what he perceived as their hatred of the human race. Tacitus makes his reader almost feel sympathy for Nero since, for once in the Emperor's life, he had identified a suitable victim to focus national hostility against, rather than himself. However, his zealous persecution of the Christians turned public opinion towards sympathy for his victims. Soon, however, Nero would have more serious problems from within the Roman aristocracy to worry about.

THE CONSPIRACY OF PISO

The Roman aristocracy was becoming fed up with its 'singing Emperor'. Nero's personal life had become scandalous. In his quest for novel amusements he began to neglect totally the public interest. Also, his promotion of freedmen caused great resentment among the Senate. The appointment of Ofonius Tigellinus as Praetorian prefect made matters worse, as his spies and informants created an atmosphere of mistrust and suspicion.

In AD 65 a plot developed within the ranks of the aristocracy to kill the Emperor and replace him with one of their own choosing. The exact circumstances surrounding the plot are unclear; who exactly was involved remains somewhat of a mystery although the other Praetorian prefect, Faenius Rufus, took an active role. The aims of the conspirators also seemed somewhat confused, their choices ranging from a restoration of the Republic to the appointment of Seneca as a Philosopher Emperor. The conspirators decided on C. Calpurnius Piso as the heir to Nero. Piso was an unusual choice, as in some ways he was similar to Nero, enjoying both singing and acting.

Research

◢**Copy Table 12.1 into your notebook and fill in the missing information.**

◢**Why is this 'conspiracy' unusual?**

◢**What does it tell us about the popularity of Nero?**

◢**Do you think it would have achieved anything, had Nero been assassinated?**

◢**Why did it fail?**

The plot never eventuated; it was betrayed by a slave who was instructed to sharpen one of the murder weapons.

So at daybreak Milichus [freedman employed by Scaevinus, one of the conspirators] left for the Servilian Gardens. At first he was kept out. Finally, however, after insisting on

Table 12.1   The Conspiracy of Piso 65 BC

CONSPIRATORS	POSITION	COMMENTS
Subrius Flavus	Tribune of the Praetorians	
Sulpicius	Centurion	
Marcus Annaeus Lucanus	Poet	Personally hated Nero
Plautius Lateranus		Extremely rich, old Roman family; saw Nero as a hideous tyrant who was a disgrace to Rome
Flavius Scaevinus	Senator	Supposedly some sort of 'social degenerate'
Afranius Quintenus	Senator	Nero had satirised his effeminate appearance
Gaius Calpurnius Piso		Popular figure, handsome, an advocate. A poor choice as potential successor to Nero.
Faenius Rufus	Praetorian Prefect	
Other conspirators included many equestrians and soldiers; two more tribunes of Praetorian Guard; two more centurions; Faenius Rufus; and possibly Seneca.		

the dreadful gravity of his news, he was taken by the doorkeepers to Nero's freed slave Epaphroditus—who conducted him to Nero. Milichus then revealed the resolute determination of the senators, the danger to Nero's life, and everything else he had heard or guessed. Exhibiting the dagger destined for Nero's murder, Milichus urged that the accused man be fetched.

Tacitus, *Annals*, 15.55

Alarmed by the plot, Nero took a savage revenge. Arrests quickly followed and nineteen senators were executed for their alleged involvement, Piso, Rufus, Seneca and the poet Lucan being among the first.

As well as the executions, a number of prominent Romans were forced into exile. Tigellinus, the commander of the Praetorian Guard, managed to play on Nero's paranoid fears, using the plot to increase his hold over the weakened Emperor and to pervert the government into an irresponsible despotism similar to that of Caligula's.

JOURNEY TO THE EAST

Near the end of AD 66, Nero felt sufficiently confident in the security of his administration to leave Rome for his long awaited visit to Greece. Rather than appoint a prefect for the city, he left one of his freedmen, Helius, in charge, a decision which caused deep resentment within the Senate's ranks. Nero, however, had long since lost interest in the Senate's affairs and, indeed, with those of the state. He was preoccupied with his visit to what he considered his cultural and artistic homeland.

It seems that Nero had deluded himself into believing that he was divine. Already the Senate had deified Poppaea (whom Nero had accidentally killed in a fit of pique), and Nero's coins began to show his image wearing a radiant crown which had, in the past, usually been reserved for those who had already been deified. Like his uncle (Caligula) before him, Nero wanted to journey to the East where god-like kings were tolerated.

Included within the imperial party was Tigellinus, Nero's Praetorian prefect; the Emperor's latest wife, Statilia Messalina; and the pretty eunuch, Sporus. The Greeks were delighted by their Emperor's visit. They postponed the Olympic Games to coincide with Nero's visit, and scheduled events so he could appear in them all. He appeared as a herald, a lyre-player and a tragic actor, the last two categories having been especially adopted into the games for Nero's benefit. The Emperor was awarded 1808 first prizes while in Greece, many of which he received without actually entering the competition.

In November AD 67, Nero was called back to Rome. On his departure from Greece, Nero showed his appreciation by rewarding the whole province with an exemption from taxation. Other rulers, he claimed, may grant a city its freedom but Nero gave it to the whole country. The Senate had to be satisfied with the new province of Sardinia to make up for any loss of revenue. Although on the surface the Emperor looked to be over-generous, it should be remembered that he took the opportunity during his visit to plunder any wealthy city-state that took his fancy.

Nero returned from his sojourn to the East even more self-obsessed and despotic. Dressed in purple robes and a Greek cloak embroidered with golden stars, Nero rode through the streets on Augustus's triumphal chariot. No more, he announced, would he speak to his troops—any future communications must be in writing, for the Emperor was not about to waste his voice on common soldiers. Nero would live to regret that he had not cultivated his soldiers' society.

THE FALL OF NERO

Nero's premature return from Greece in AD 67 was precipitated by problems in Rome. The grain supply had been interrupted and the people blamed Nero's agent, Helius, a freedman. Nero's patronage of freedmen had long been a contentious issue among the people.

Nero had only just made his spectacular entrance to Rome when a serious revolt occurred in Gaul. The leader of the Gallic revolt was a Romanised Gaul, C. Julius Vindex, who proclaimed as his battle cry 'freedom from tyranny'. Whether Vindex aimed at usurping Nero's position or merely winning provincial freedom seems uncertain. However, his revolt was seriously flawed from its very conception and consequently short-lived.

Although Vindex appeared to be a charismatic leader, not all Gallic towns joined his revolt. Most of the provincial armies remained loyal to their oaths of allegiance. Vindex's hopes were crushed when the Governor of Upper Germany defeated him at Vesontio. With his army in ruins, Vindex did the most honourable thing—committed suicide.

Nero was quite nonchalant about the revolt. He was concerned only by Vindex's accusation that he was a poor singer and a sad lyre-player. Nero's overconfidence, it seems, arose from a visit to the Delphic Oracle; he was informed that he had nothing to worry about except the 'seventy-third year'. This he took to mean his own seventy-third year, so looked forward to a run of unbroken luck.

The seeds of revolt are often fertile. Not long after Vindex's declaration for freedom, he was joined by the Governor of Spain, Ser. Sulpicius Galba. It seems that Galba suspected Nero was plotting his death, so when he received the support of the neighbouring Governor of Lusitania, M. Otho (Nero's old friend), Galba declared himself the legate of the Senate of Rome and announced his intention to overthrow Nero.

At this stage the revolt was only localised. Galba had only one legion and provincial armies had shown their willingness to remain loyal to Rome. The Senate, possibly suspicious of Galba's proclaimed republican sympathy, decided it was expedient to support the Emperor in Rome rather than opt for one in Spain. As well as this moral support, Nero had all of the resources of the East at his disposal, but he procrastinated and allowed his advantage to slip away.

When Tigellinus, recognising the hopelessness of the situation, struck a bargain to save his own life and defected to Galba, all was lost for Nero. Galba, through his agents in Rome, promised the Praetorian Guard 30 000 sesterces per man to desert, a deal they willingly accepted. The Senate, not slow to realise which way the wind was blowing, settled for the Emperor in Spain rather than the coward in the Imperial Palace. Galba had won.

POOR NERO DIES A COWARD'S DEATH

On the night of 8 June AD 68, Nero was awoken by noise in the palace. With no Praetorians on duty, Nero was panic stricken. He fled the palace with some servants and headed towards the suburban villa of his freedman, Phaon. There they hid, Nero sobbing and bemoaning his fate. It was impossible to move him and in between tears he would wail 'Dead! And so great an artist!'

Later a message arrived from Phaon informing Nero that the Senate had condemned him in his absence to be put to death. With the sounds of approaching horses, Nero ordered his scribe to help him finish it all. Together they managed to stab Nero in the throat and he died just after the arrival of the arresting officer.